THE POETICAL PURSUIT OF FOOD

THE POETICAL PURSUIT OF FOOD

JAPANESE RECIPES FOR AMERICAN COOKS

BY SONOKO·KONDO
WITH LOU STOUMEN

ILLUSTRATED BY ETIENNE DELESSERT
DESIGNED BY RITA MARSHALL

CLARKSON N. POTTER, INC./PUBLISHERS
DISTRIBUTED BY CROWN PUBLISHERS, INC., NEW YORK

Published by Clarkson N. Potter, Inc., 225 Park Avenue South,
New York, New York 10003, and represented in Canada by
the Canadian MANDA Group

CLARKSON N. POTTER, POTTER, and colophon are trademarks of
Clarkson N. Potter, Inc.

Manufactured in the United States of America

Library of Congress Cataloging-in-Publication Data
Kondo, Sonoko.
    The poetical pursuit of food.

    Includes index.
    1. Cookery, Japanese.   I. Stoumen, Louis Clyde.
II. Title.
TX724.5.J3K6624   1986   641.5952   85-25688
ISBN 0-517-55653-7

10 9 8 7 6 5 4 3 2 1

First Edition

My special warm thanks are due to Lou Stoumen, who labored skillfully with me for three years throughout the conception, making, and tasting of this book.

And to two great cooks—my grandmother, Hatsuki Ishikawa of Kamakura, and my mother, Akiko Kondo of New York, San Francisco, Mexico, and Tokyo—this book is dedicated with gratitude and tender thoughts.

CONTENTS

CHAPTER 1
GROWING UP IN A JAPANESE KITCHEN

WHEN I WAS FOUR YEARS OLD I went to Japan with my family to live at Grandmother's house in Kamakura, an ancient city near Tokyo. Though an American child born in New York City, I have a Japanese face and Japanese parents.

In Japan I discovered the poetical pursuit of food. This started when I grew out of playing with my collection of American Kewpie dolls and became Grandmother's helper.

There were wonders to explore in Kamakura—its forests and mountains, its famous forty-foot-high Buddha, its very old Zen temples and Shinto shrines. White cranes flew down from the north. The local fishermen drew in their nets full of fish at dawn. In spring, the plum trees blossomed in Grandmother's yard and soon grew fruits. Grandmother prepared plum pudding and dried plums. In summer, purple eggplants and orange pumpkins added rainbows to Grandmother's back hillside. In fall, the persimmon leaves turned red; we used them to wrap sushi. In winter, it gave me pleasure to play in the snow while Grandmother broiled rice patties.

I loved Grandmother's home, and particularly her kitchen. My favorite people visited through the kitchen entrance. There was the tofu man with his soft fresh tofu, who would announce his coming with a polite toot of his horn. The neighbor farmer bringing his delicacy of fermented soybeans. The jolly butcher with chicken and meat, and his specialty, potato croquettes. Also the fisherman, who always remembered to bring fish bones and fish heads for my kittens along with his catch of the day. The knife sharpener, with his assortment of sharpening tools, rode a rusty bike that sang *kheen kheen kheen* as he peddled. There was the sushi deliveryman. And there was the citified sake merchant, who liked to pretend he was more important than all the others, as perhaps he was.

"What would you like today, Ishikawa-san?" they would ask Grandmother. She would always reply with her favorite question: "What is in season?" To Grandmother there was more than just spring or fall. There was early spring, middle spring, and late spring, and so on. Her choice of foods depended on what was freshly available in the market, in her garden, or wild in the hills and woods. I learned that the poetical pursuit of food was largely a matter of the taste of seasons.

Grandmother, who was of samurai warrior lineage, enjoyed the discipline of being an artistic cook. In the kitchen her hands, eyes, facial expressions, and body movements took on a special lightness and precision. I learned through admiration and imitation. Soon I took an active apprentice's role in making meals.

In early spring I would go to the forest with her to hunt for young bamboo shoots. Because the shoots begin to harden after the tenth day, it is important to know when the tender young ones are maturing. Grandmother knew when. I eventually learned.

"We'll make bamboo miso soup with these shoots," she would say. To make this soup Grandmother used only the tips and outer leaves of the bamboo shoots called "princess's skin." Wakame seaweed went into the soup for color and additional flavor. Grandmother served the soup in a ritualistic way. From behind the sliding screen of a closet she would bring out a wooden box in which were kept beautiful spring lacquerware bowls. They were wiped out carefully with a fresh cotton cloth, used only for the occasion of spring soup.

The bowls had inlaid mother-of-pearl plum blossoms, which added beauty (and perhaps flavor?) to the soup. "Drink it all, for it will bring you life like the young bamboo," Grandmother would insist. To children, bamboo tastes bitter. But I believed in everything Grandmother told me and would drink it all. When the spring was over, she would carefully wash the bowls and put them in their boxes, where they would remain until next spring.

Our family was not unique in enjoying meals in such seasonal ways. I learned that all Japanese people indulge in this poetical pursuit of food. The tastes of the seasons are savored in simple farm homes as well as in city apartments, and in excellent restaurants everywhere. Even railway travelers can buy attractive inexpensive box lunches freshly prepared at the train stops by local entrepreneurs, with bright crisp vegetables, seasonal fruits, fresh or smoked fish, rice, and little flasks of hot green tea.

During my junior year in high school I returned to the United States with my family. (My father worked for Japan Airlines, which is why we moved so much.) One of the first things I observed was that when grocery shopping in the United States there was no need to go separately to a butcher, a greengrocer, and a fish market. Everything was to be had, for Americans, in supermarkets.

At first I was nostalgic for Japan. People seemed more casual and informal, which I liked, but the food was very strange. I was amused by the bigness of American cucumbers and eggplants, but found their taste rather bland. The apples had thick skins, were waxed (ugh!), and lacked flavor. If I went to a party, people served food in decorative paper dishes and cups that they later threw away. Most dinners were called casseroles and were served in huge dishes rather than many small dishes, as Japanese dinners are. A huge bowl of fresh salad greens with a pink dressing called "Thousand Island" was popular among my friends. I liked the name but not the flavor. Hamburgers were too greasy for me, but I could eat *two* hot dogs with lots of onions and mustard. Oranges, honeydew melons, and raspberries became my favorite fruits.

Instead of yearning for Japan, I became fascinated by American culture. American holidays were added to my list of special Japanese occasions. My mother was mistress of the kitchen now, and I was her apprentice. I helped her make family feasts on Japanese New Year, sushi on Girl's Day, ohagi (rice-stuffed azuki bean balls) for the day of the ancestors and other Japanese holidays. But we also baked turkey and stuffing for Thanksgiving, apple pies and special butter cookies for Christmas, and a glorious clove-studded ham for Easter. At no additional expense, our kitchen soon accommodated both cuisines. Japanese cooking in America, I learned quickly, does not require exotic or hard-to-get ingredients. In fact, because somewhat less meat is used, Japanese cuisine may actually be less expensive to prepare than the standard American menu.

The preparation of Japanese foods does require some understanding of useful tools, spices, and ways, and an especially sharp eye for freshness in vegetables, fruits, fish, and meats. Freshness is key to Japanese cooking. A young honest string bean, a brilliant red slice of watermelon, an egg with a pretty yellow yolk, a firm, really fresh fish, a spirited intuitive cook—these add up to good eating and good health.

Recently, I was on the Côte d'Azur with Grandmother, Mother, and Sakae, my eight-month-old baby. My childhood memories of the sea at Kamakura all came back. As we all got to know the town better, Grandmother and Mother began to cook, replicating the seafood meals I used to love so much. Just like old times, we were able to buy fish directly from the fisherman. The stores were only the size of a small table, to which the fishermen transferred the catch of the day from their huge baskets. It was thrilling to see what came out of their baskets each morning. Flounders were in abundance, as were mackerels, squid, tuna, bonitos, octopus, shrimp, clams, crabs, mussels, perch, sea bass, and sculpin, to name a few. Most of these fish were so fresh they hopped off the table, often landing in Sakae's carriage. Grandmother gave all the fish an AAA grading for their freshness. "Let's make sashimi!" was her immediate thought after she took a glance at the fish. Mother was prepared. She had brought a knife, a miniature cutting board, wasabi paste, and soy sauce from Japan. She always traveled with such things, prepared for the unexpected. Grandmother, on the other hand, had brought a small travel electric cooking pot, in which we were able to cook rice, asparagus (the white asparagus with blushing tips were in season), green beans, small potatoes, sweet carrots, and fish bones to make soup. The meals they came up with, including the sashimi dinners, were so innovative that we were proud how little in the way of tools we needed to prepare such feasts.

It has been my intention in writing this book to share with you those season-to-season days in Grandmother's kitchen, and to make use of recipes and lessons taught by my mother in her kitchens in Tokyo, New York, San Francisco, Mexico City, and Los Angeles. Grandmother and Mother both continued to send me recipes (I can *smell* their letters). I have also ventured to add recipes and food discoveries from my own Japanese-American kitchen in Los Angeles.

It is my hope that this book can be a useful guide to good health and culinary accomplishment. It's no accident that the rates of heart disease, cancer, and obesity in Japan are extraordinarily low.

So join me, please, in pleasure over the crunch of a crisp daikon radish, the cool pure taste of fresh tuna sashimi, the warm steam rising from a delicious bowl of miso soup, the healthy aroma of vegetable and seafood hot pot simmering at the table, the adventures of making azuki bean paste desserts, and the special joy, spiritual and aesthetic as well as tasteful, of the traditional tea ceremony. Begin your poetical pursuit of food and become a kitchen poet!

Sonoko Kondo

近藤園子

CHAPTER 2

THEORY OF THE JAPANESE MEAL AS APPLIED TO YOUR OWN KITCHEN

THE KEYS TO JAPANESE COOKING ARE FOUR: freshness, beauty, simplicity, and health. To which might be added, ease and quickness of preparation, economy (because not much meat is used), seasonality (foods of the season for winter, spring, summer, and fall), and a special kind of artistic fun for the creative cook.

Like all national cuisines, Japanese kitchen work is the product of national history, physical resources, and tradition. Japan consists of four main islands and perhaps a hundred small ones. The country's primary environmental factor is the sea. Hence, the emphasis in its cuisine is on marine foods—nutritious seaweed, crabs, squid, octopus, shrimp, eel, clams, oysters, and a marvelous variety of fish.

Though Japan's land area is only three quarters that of California, its population is about half that of the United States. That's crowded, as a visit to Tokyo or even the Japanese countryside will show. There is little space to grow such expensive crops as wheat, corn, and soybeans, and little pasturage to raise beef (an uneconomic food in any case, since cattle must be fed several times their weight in grains). A bit of wheat is grown, and some prized high-grade cattle, but almost all arable land is devoted to growing rice, a great variety of vegetables, and much fine fruit. It is perhaps characteristic of the Japanese that they also do find land for the extensive growing of flowers.

Japanese cuisine is not just one kind or style of food. Like the cuisines of China, the United States, Soviet Russia, and Italy—all countries with long distances from their northern areas to their southern extremities—Japanese foods vary according to the region. In cold northern Hokkaido, the farmers, fishermen, and miners favor salmon, lamb (which they raise), and potatoes, hearty food for an inclement climate. Farther south and west, the ancient city of Kyoto features delicate nabes (one-pot meals) and a special Kaiseki cuisine that derives from Zen Buddhist philosophy and is vegetarian (except for fish) and beautifully arranged and served. Still farther south in Hiroshima, which is on the inland sea, the menu features oysters and other seafood, plus the specialty of vegetables and seafood pancakes.

On the southernmost main island of Kyushu, favorites are seafood and nabes, and the special delicacy is wild pig. Far out and southerly in the Pacific, the cuisine of the people of semitropical Okinawa features pork. An Okinawan menu often begins and ends with pork.

Metropolitan Tokyo of course has everything available—foods from all the provinces of Japan as well as its own cosmopolitan cuisine, which reflects the influence of the many imported delicacies available there.

The recipes included in this book represent a seasonal variety of dishes from each of these regions. Except for a few dishes, Japanese meals can be prepared quickly, easily, and economically in your own kitchen. There is no long simmering of stews, no compounding of complex sauces, no tricky baking or roasting. In addition to the kitchen tools you already have, you will probably need to buy only chopsticks, a small wooden paddle for mixing, and perhaps a small mortar and pestle for grinding sesame seeds. A few inexpensive Japanese bowls and side dishes (nice blue and white ones?) for both preparation and serving would add authenticity and eye appeal to your productions. (See page 20 for a list of kitchen tools needed for Japanese cooking.)

In general, the following theory and practice of Japanese cuisine apply. Keep these principles and tips in mind when planning, shopping for, and preparing a Japanese meal.

TEN COMMANDMENTS OF JAPANESE CUISINE

1. Use broth as your basic "sauce." Japanese cooking is mostly oil-free, with no cream, cheese, or oily sauces and dressings. Use broths made from fish, mushrooms, and seaweed in flavoring foods. Another type of sauce commonly used in Japanese cuisine is "teriyaki sauce," made of soy sauce, a little sake, and sugar (or honey, if you prefer). This sauce is thicker than broth, but much lighter than flour-based Western sauces. Chicken and meat broths are not traditionally used, but in modern big-city Japan (and in your American kitchen) they are acceptable.

2. Dairy foods have no role in Japanese cooking. That means no milk, cream, or cheese. This accounts, in large part, for the rarity of cholesterol disease in Japan. But you may use small amounts of butter as modern Japanese do occasionally.

3. Concentrate on these basic kitchen preparations: sliced raw, boiling, broiling, steaming, braising, and deep frying. They are quick, healthful, and already familiar to you. Though much of Japan's culture derives historically from China, the wok was not used until recently; Japanese cooking is done in pots and on grills. But if you have a wok, do make use of it in sautéing and deep frying Japanese foods. Japanese did not fry foods until the Portuguese arrived in the sixteenth century. They introduced Christianity, medicines, guns, and deep-fried fritters. These were modified by the Japanese to what today is called tempura (deep-fried vegetables, fish, and shrimp). Some Japanese found such foods too heavy and discovered that serving grated daikon radish with tempura acted as a natural digestive agent; adopt this tasty and traditional practice. Japanese braising involves sautéing foods lightly in oil and then simmering them in broth or stock, so the foods are never greasy.

4. Use spices, herbs, and pungent vegetables sparingly. Compared to Indian or Szechuan foods, Japanese dishes are very lightly seasoned, and herbs and spices are often used for their medicinal properties. What's emphasized is the natural seasonal taste of fresh vegetables, seafood, and fruits. These original and sometimes subtle flavors must not be diminished. Use spices and strong flavorings such as mustard seeds, ginger, red pepper, sesame seeds, and green horseradish sparingly, for their healthful properties and to accent flavor. Two important exceptions are ginger ice cream, an idea imported from America, which has a pronounced ginger flavor, and sushi and sashimi, the unique deliciousness of which requires that each mouthful be dipped in soy sauce mixed to taste with pungent green horseradish.

5. Include some type of seafood in your menu every day. Seafood is the most traditional and popular main course. A typical meal, whether breakfast, lunch, or dinner, is based on food from the sea. Tiny shrimp are used in salads. Dried sardines are a principal ingredient of many broths. Dried squid is a favorite snack. Tuna fillets are popular for sashimi. A whole fresh red snapper might be the Japanese family's Thanksgiving turkey. Japanese often plan their menus around seafood and a bowl of rice; other dishes are served to enhance and balance these two main foods (one reason why many Japanese appetizers use small amounts of meat and chicken). The high consumption of seafood is another reason for the rarity of cholesterol disease in Japan.

6. Serve meat in moderation. Buddhist tradition prohibits the eating of animals with four feet. Land is too scarce in Japan to graze cattle. Birds, the rooster in particular, were not commonly eaten as they had the sacred role of telling time. Not until the nineteenth century did meat and chicken begin to appear on the dining tables of a few Western-minded upper-class families. Today, young Japanese eat more meat than their parents. While chicken (quick-broiled teri-yaki) and pork are very popular and reasonably priced, beefsteak is reserved for special occasions, perhaps once or twice a year. Imported American and Australian steaks are very expensive. Even more expensive is Japanese beef from Kobe, a famous delicacy produced by feeding beer to the cattle and patiently massaging their bodies by hand to disperse and marbelize the fat. Enjoy meals with meat, but in moderation.

   7. **Create contrasts in your presentations**. Flavor, color, and kitchen swordplay are very important. There are many different styles of cutting, slicing, and arranging, each with both practical and artistic purposes. Since chopsticks are the basic tools for eating, the foods when served should not require cutting with a knife; they must be uniformly bite-size morsels. Irregularity of size can make them clumsy to eat, less attractive, and less flavorful. The Japanese say that a person with a dull or rusty knife can never be a good cook. Knives must be washed after each use, wiped completely dry with a clean cloth, and sharpened when needed. Foods are combined and arranged on their separate plates, very much like flower arrangements. Each dish should be a beautiful small landscape. The cutting and slicing techniques below will help vegetables keep their shapes during cooking and make your dishes look more beautiful. The flower cut takes a simple slice of carrot and transforms it into a beautiful plum blossom; it takes some time and practice, but will

Wave cut

Decorative citrus rind

Flower cut

Matchstick cut   Bevel cut   Snake eye

Random cut   Fan cut   Peaked cut

bring a lovely message of spring to your table. Put the food processor aside and hone your knife as sharp as possible.

In color choice you must become a kitchen artist. If you begin the arrangement with something *white* (like daikon radish or tofu), a morsel of *red* color will enhance it (common red and orange foods are shrimp, carrots, pickled ginger, red pepper, and tomato). A few crisp pea pods will give you an intense *green*. Other common greens are gently washed and wiped leaves such as lemon, bamboo, apple, mint, parsley, camellia, maple, shiso, etc., and shoots, such as daikon radish shoots (kaiware). Use egg yolk for a strong *yellow* (also edible chrysanthemum flower, lemon rind, and squash). *Brown* colors (like shiitake mushrooms, burdock, or deep-fried tofu) can be arranged on the side of the dish, while red, green, and yellow foods are arranged toward the center. No meals should be all white (rice and white fish) or all green. Spot your colors around.

Use combination *sweet* flavor (such as braised vegetables sweetened with sake, mirin, and sugar); *sour* (a salad with a piquant vinaigrette dressing); *salty* (pickled foods); *bitter* (ginkgo nuts, fern, bamboo shoots); and *hot* (green horseradish, Japanese chili pepper). Bland (tofu) and rich (teriyaki) flavors can also give variety to meals. Also, when serving a grilled dish, such as grilled salmon, which is on the dry side, serve it with a moist condiment, such as grated daikon radish or ohitashi, a vegetable such as asparagus, spinach, dandelion, bean sprouts, etc. that has been blanched briefly in hot water, drained, and chilled to be served like a salad with soy sauce.

8. Shop creatively and choose the freshest and most nutritious foods. Because Japanese foods are largely sauceless, spiceless, and oil-free, the ingredients themselves must be beautiful, flavorful, and fresh. This usually means foods in season. Fresh spinach leaves must have no bruises. Shrimp fresh from the market don't need the disguise of a soupy sauce. Make a fetish of freshness. Buy avocados, apricots, cherries, the fisherman's morning catch!

These days it's hard to find foods fresh from the ocean or just picked by the farmer. Some frozen and dried foods have to be accepted. But do grow your own tomatoes, beans, cucumbers, sprouts, and eggplants if you have garden space. Don't hesitate to improvise with non-Japanese foods like okra, squash, kiwi fruit (but not scrapple!). Avoid bottled or canned foods if you can—they're mostly heat-processed, lacking in vitamins, and have added chemicals that won't do their taste or your health much good. Visit small ethnic shops that often have fresh specialties of high quality (Korean, Chinese, German, Italian, African, Arabic, Hungarian as well as Japanese). Become a food detective.

9. Serve a variety of dishes in small portions. Western eaters new to Japanese cuisine often inspect with some dismay their first Japanese meal. It all *looks* beautiful, they will admit. But, they ask, will these little bits of food satisfy my hunger?

The answer, they will soon find out, is a tasty *yes*. Japanese portions are indeed small. But they are eaten in combination with several other dishes. That's how Japanese meals are structured. The advantages of this tradition are many. A combination of dishes makes possible entertainment of the tongue by many colors, textures, flavors, and aromas. Small portions mean minimum waste of food in leftovers. Finally, nutritionists and doctors of both East and West agree that a healthy diet should include a great variety of nutrients, including enzymes, minerals, and all the vitamins. The best way to achieve this healthful balance is to serve a great variety of dishes.

10. Health and pleasure are the ultimate culinary goals. Eating a variety of fresh foods in their seasons is the Japanese way to table satisfaction and health. So is eating in moderation (few Japanese are fat and heart trouble is rare). Once you've prepared a few Japanese meals, the creative kitchen work and the deliciousness of the food will likely modify decisions and techniques in your regular American cooking. You're just liable to cut down on expensive butter, beef, and rich desserts. You'll discover that fresh vegetables, fish, and fruits are even more delicious than you thought. Your holiday roast will look prettier on its platter. And you'll find you have happier, leaner eaters who will live nearly forever.

STAPLE FOODS YOU WILL NEED

Most of the foods you prepare and serve—vegetables, meat, fish, fruits, etc.—will be fresh. That's the cornerstone of all Japanese cooking. (Check the Glossary, page 272, for more detailed explanations of the foods listed below and other common Japanese ingredients.) You will need to keep in regular supply, however, the following basic foods and seasonings:

SOY SAUCE: This ubiquitous seasoning is made from fermented soybeans, water, wheat, and salt. For Japanese cooking you will need regular *and* mild soy sauce. Mild soy sauce is not less salty than regular soy sauce; it is simply lighter in color and used to tint deli-cate broths and tofu dishes. Chinese soy sauce is flavored differently from the Japanese type, so its use is not recommended in Japanese cooking. Low-sodium soy sauce is also available; it is inferior in taste to regular soy sauce, but useful for cooks who want to cut down on salt.

RICE VINEGAR: Available in most Oriental and American supermar-kets, rice vinegar is milder than cider or distilled vinegar. I do not recommend seasoned vinegar, because it may contain MSG, too much sugar, and flavorings that may be incompatible with my reci-pes.

SAKE: This smooth rice wine is used sparingly in the preparation of many Japanese dishes. Cooking sake is available, but regular drinking sake is as good or better. Just a dash of sake tenderizes and flavors foods and adds a rich flavor to broths.

MIRIN: This rice wine sweetens and firms food. Use it sparingly to glaze foods, such as teriyaki dishes.

OILS (abura): Butter is seldom used in Japanese cooking. Instead, put in a supply of vegetable oils. They are light, easy to use, less expensive, and much better for the health. Soy, corn, peanut, saf-flower, and sesame oils are all recommended. Sesame seed oil has a nutty taste that is wonderful in salads and braised food. Olive oil is never used (its flavor drowns natural taste). Choose the one(s) you like best on the basis of taste and aroma.

DASHI CONCENTRATES: This basic broth is one of the quintessen-tial Japanese flavorings. Although it is fairly simple and quick to prepare from scratch (see page 50), concentrates are useful to have on hand if only a small amount is needed, or when you are pressed for time.

BONITO FLAKES, DRIED: A basic ingredient for making broth, shavings from dried bonito fish are also used for sprinkling over boiled, broiled, and fresh vegetables, such as cooked spinach, green beans, or tofu.

KONBU SEAWEED: Konbu is the king of all seaweeds, used for making dashi broth.

NORI SEAWEED: Nori is a thin black sheet made of tangle seaweed. Nori is most commonly used to wrap sushi, but is delicious sprinkled over rice and noodles, too.

SESAME SEED PASTE (atari-goma): This sesame paste is becoming quite popular in the West. Most Americans may be more familiar with the Middle Eastern version called tahini paste. If you cannot find atari-goma, the latter will do. Used in making salad dressings and dips.

MISO: This is a seasoned paste made of fermented soybeans and is used to season soups, seafood, meat, and vegetables. There are white and red miso pastes, each with its own distinctive flavor. Both are salty, so use sparingly.

SHIITAKE MUSHROOMS: I use these fragrant mushrooms in salads, soups, braised dishes, etc., every day, but they are quite expensive. Californians are starting to grow these mushrooms, so maybe the price will drop soon. They are available both fresh and dried.

FLOUR: Japanese flours made of rice (joshinko and mochiko) are used primarily for desserts. Soy flour (kinako) is also used for desserts and has a distinctive fragrance.

STARCH: There are two types: katakuriko and kuzu. Both are used as thickeners like cornstarch, and coat foods for braising or deep frying. If potato or kuzu starch is not available, substitute cornstarch.

RICE: The short-grain variety is used exclusively in Japanese cooking. Its stickier consistency makes it easy to pick up with chopsticks.

GINGER: This bumpy root is available fresh in most markets. Never use the powdered form—its taste can't compare. The root is usually peeled and grated or minced. The juice obtained while grating can be used also.

WASABI PASTE: A potent condiment essential to sushi and sashimi, powdered wasabi should be mixed with equal amounts of water to make paste. Careful, not too much!

JAPANESE CHILI PEPPER, DRIED (togarashi): Hot peppers not unlike Mexican peppers, used sparingly in preparing braised foods.

SANSHO PEPPER: Much milder than Western black pepper. Use whenever pepper is called for in a recipe.

SESAME SEEDS: White and black sesame seeds, hulled, raw or roasted, are extensively used in Japanese cooking, sprinkled on salads, rice, and meat dishes. Both types are used interchangeably.

STAPLE TOOLS FOR YOUR KITCHEN

You probably already have in your kitchen most of the utensils and tools needed to prepare Japanese cuisine—knives, pots and pans, colander, bowls, skewers, steamer, tableware.

You will also want chopsticks, both for eating and cooking. I suggest you buy a dozen pairs of the disposable wooden type. They are inexpensive and easy to master.

Here is a rundown of what I have in my kitchen and find useful in preparing Japanese meals:

BOWLS: Small, medium, and large bowls to mix sauces and batter.

CUTTING BOARD: Wooden or plastic cutting boards. Always rinse under hot water after each use and wipe with a dry cloth. From time to time dry the board in the sun. Steamed fish cakes come packaged on a small piece of wood that makes an ideal mini–chopping board for chopping ginger and garlic.

COLANDER: Enameled, stainless-steel, and bamboo colanders are essential for draining vegetables and noodles, rinsing greens, etc.

WOODEN SPOON: These are always preferable to stainless-steel and aluminum paddles and spoons, which can scratch delicate lacquerware. Japanese shamoji paddles made of bamboo are handy for scooping rice and mixing foods.

RICE TUB: These big, shallow tubs accommodate rice preparations such as vinegared rice for sushi. Plastic, wood, and lacquer ones are available in Oriental cookware stores.

VEGETABLE SLICER: Japanese vegetable choppers are practical for slicing and shredding hard vegetables like carrot and daikon radish. It takes up little room and does not require electricity, unlike a food processor. It's wonderful for making sushi and sashimi garnishes. Available in Japanese food and cookware stores.

GRATER: An essential tool in Japanese cooking. Grated daikon radish and ginger appear daily in the Japanese menu as a garnish for many dishes. Most have a detachable container under the grater to catch liquids. They are sold in Japanese food and cookware stores.

STRAINER: A fine strainer is necessary for making custards, straining broths, and crumbling tofu for sauces.

MORTAR AND PESTLE (suri-bachi and suri-goki): The ridged interior of a Japanese mortar and pestle works efficiently to grind sesame seeds to make sesame paste. Also used to mix miso paste and nuts, and make tofu dressing and sauces.

BAMBOO MAT (sudare): For rolling sushi and shaping egg omelettes and vegetables such as spinach. Its loose-woven texture drains water well.

CHOPSTICKS: There are lacquered, wooden, bamboo, and plastic chopsticks. Japanese-style chopsticks are narrow and have pointed ends. The wooden ones are easiest to handle; lacquer chopsticks can be quite slippery and tricky. Long ones are available for cooking.

SKEWERS: Useful for chicken yakitori and other skewered dishes. Bamboo and metallic ones are available. Bamboo types burn easily,

Chopsticks   Grater   Mortar and pestle

Rice tub   Bamboo mat   Custard cups

Shamoji paddle   Strainer   Dropped lid

so they are not recommended for use over a hot grill. Toothpicks are useful for holding vegetables and tofu pouches together.

STEAMER: Both Japanese and Chinese steamers are large and accommodate large plates of vegetables, meat, etc. You can put a whole fish in the steamer. Always bring water to a rapid boil before putting any foods inside.

INDOOR GRILL: Japanese cooking involves many grilled dishes. This gas- or electric-powered tabletop unit makes a lot of smoke, so if you don't have good ventilation, I do not recommend it. Your broiler will do the job.

METAL MOLD (nagashi-bako): Used for making egg custards, these come in various sizes. They have an inner tray that lifts up, making it easy to slide custards out in clean squares.

JAPANESE SCRUB BRUSH (tawashi): This brown scrubby tool is made of hemp palm. It is useful for washing dirt off burdock root and potatoes, and sand off clams. You may want a second one for washing dishes.

DROPPED LIDS (oto-shi-buta): Made of wood, these lids drop inside the pot and come in direct contact with the food. The lid is designed to keep food from bouncing and falling apart while cooking, and also to retain moisture as well as flavor. If you cannot obtain one, use a lid that is slightly smaller than your pot. Whenever simmering is called for, drop the lid inside the pot.

UTENSILS FOR YOUR TABLE

Collecting Japanese pottery can become a lifetime obsession. I happen to have that obsession, which means I never have enough space for my pottery because I always want to add to my collection. There are some unique utensils that have no Western counterpart. Others, such as plates and bowls and large platters, are more familiar. Be flexible about using what you have in your cabinets. You can do without custard cups if you have mousse cups. You can use a twig or a seashell to make a chopstick rest. And don't be afraid to add a few pieces at a time to your collection. The Japanese do not buy one pattern or one set of dishes that look the same. They like variety. Pottery and china from different regions are appreciated. Antiques and collectibles often appear on special occasions, and one can expect the host to talk about the dishes. Seasons are also considered. Glass is a summer ware, to bring coolness. Dishes with tulips would be for spring; bowls with a chrysanthemum would be for fall.

CHOPSTICKS: See "Staple Tools for Your Kitchen."

SPOONS: Porcelain spoons are often used for scooping up broth and condiments.

CONDIMENT DISH: Very small porcelain dishes are used to serve soy sauce, wasabi, pickles, and nibbles. They come in a variety of colors and shapes.

NOODLE BASKET: A flat, rectangular or round dish woven of bamboo or wicker designed to hold noodles or, lined with a napkin, tempura.

BOWLS FOR SIMMERED AND STEAMED FOODS: These shallow, medium-size bowls have lids to keep the food warm.

DISHES FOR FRIED AND BROILED FOODS: Smaller than Western dinner plates and often more decorative, these may be square, rectangular, or fan-shaped as well as round.

SOUP BOWLS: Small, deep lidded bowls are best, preferably in a dark color to contrast nicely with the soup.

RICE BOWLS: They come with or without lids. Wood, lacquerware, china, pottery, and plastic types are available.

DONBURI BOWLS: Oversize, deep bowls ideal for noodles in broth, soups, and rice dishes. Some come with lids.

DIPPING SAUCE CUP: These are nice for tempura and noodles, but not essential. Small, deep soup or salad bowls will do.

CHOPSTICK RESTS: Small porcelain, glass, pottery, or wooden ornamental objects on which to rest chopsticks between courses.

TEA CUPS: Porcelain and pottery types are common. Tea cups sold in a pair are called me-oto-chawan and are for husband and wife.

TEAPOT: Cast-iron, porcelain, and pottery types are all commonly used.

SOY SAUCE BOTTLE: Useful for soy sauce.

CUSTARD CUPS (chawan-mushi-no-ocha-wan): Porcelain and pottery cups that come with lids. Though not used while steaming the custard, the lids help retain heat and keep the custard warm once they're removed from the steamer.

EGGPLANT WITH CHERRY BLOSSOM SAUCE

ASPARAGUS WITH BONITO FLAKES (OHI-TASHI)

VINEGARED CRAB

BLUSHING PINE NUTS

OKRA AND AVOCADO COCKTAIL

OYSTERS WITH GRATED DAIKON RADISH

C H A P T E R 3

APPETIZERS

MATSUTAKE MUSHROOM AND SHRIMP SURPRISE

SPRING RAIN SHRIMP

SQUID WITH GINGER

CHILLED EGGPLANT WITH GINGER SAUCE

SHIITAKE MUSHROOM MOUNTAINS

GRILLED TOFU WITH MISO (DENGAKU)

ICICLE RADISH WITH LEMON SAUCE

ROE ROE ROE YOUR BOAT

SESAME TOFU

CARROTS WITH WALNUT SAUCE

SHRIMP, OKRA, AND WAKAME SEAWEED OVER CRUSHED ICE

TUNA SASHIMI AND GREEN ONIONS WITH MISO

MUSHROOM TOSS

DAIKON RADISH WITH LEMON-MISO (FURO-FUKI-DAIKON)

CAULIFLOWER FLORETS WITH MISO

 JAPANESE PIZZA (OKONOMI-YAKI)

IF, ON MEETING A PERSON FOR THE FIRST TIME, you are presented with a gloomy face and mumbled speech, your relationship is not likely to develop well. So it is with meals. They should begin pleasantly. The appetizer, therefore, is critically important.

My mother assigned me to be the official appetizer maker of the house when I turned fifteen. Since my parents entertained a lot, my role was quite important in the kitchen. Mother requested appetizers to suit her intercultural dishes, such as lasagna and sushi, tempura and galantine, paella and teriyaki. It was a challenge not to duplicate what was to be served later in the main course. I planned appetizers in terms of what drinks were to be served with the meal. With beer, nutty fresh-boiled soybeans often appeared on the table. Sake drinkers always appreciated my simple cucumbers with a dab of miso paste. The seasons also dictated the choice of appetizers. Asparagus with bonito flakes was served in early summer; chestnuts and mushrooms were a must in the fall; daikon radish with miso was served piping hot in the winter; spring was represented by bamboo shoots and ferns. Year-round foods such as celery, carrots, seaweeds, tomatoes, roe, tuna sashimi, etc., were always on my big appetizer platter.

The fun and challenge of making appetizers was especially in their presentation. As they were the very first dish to be nibbled, I paid extra attention to garnishing. Young baby lemon leaves, flower blossoms, and fruits made beautiful decorations. Carved radishes and flowery green onions surprised a lot of guests.

When the appetizers were completed, I would proudly show them to my parents for approval. Mother often made last-minute improvements with her long chopsticks, propping up bamboo shoots, adding a touch of green, or removing a few cucumbers where it seemed overcrowded. Father, on the other hand, insisted on being the first to taste my creations. When one turned out especially well, he would photograph it; sometimes then I would be missing the olive-eye from my fish mold or salmon roe from my celery sticks before the guests arrived, which meant a last-minute rush to make repairs and more appetizers.

Today, I continue to make my big appetizer platters, but I also serve them individually in small plates and dishes. Now Sakai, my husband, is the official nibbler.

SUGGESTIONS: 1. Individual servings are preferred in traditional Japanese cuisine, to give a personal touch. 2. Allow small portions, so as not to spoil the main course. 3. As in all courses, the food must be fresh, crisp, and beautiful. 4. Any Japanese dish served in small portions makes an ideal appetizer.

EGGPLANT WITH CHERRY BLOSSOM SAUCE
4 SERVINGS

The Japanese eggplants called nasu are especially tender and sweet. Served with a pretty cherry-blossom-color sauce made of cod roe, the eggplant becomes an elegant appetizer.

4 small Japanese eggplants
 vegetable oil for deep frying
1 segment cod roe (tarako) encased in its
 membrane (about 1½ tablespoons)
1 tablespoon vegetable oil
1 tablespoon water
2 tablespoons mayonnaise
1 teaspoon rice vinegar
2 tablespoons grated onion
1 tablespoon chopped green onion

Trim ends of eggplant and cut in half. Heat oil in a skillet over medium heat and deep fry eggplant slices until tender, about 3 minutes. Pat dry with paper towels.

Meanwhile, puncture the membrane of roe and scoop roe into a small bowl. Add vegetable oil, water, mayonnaise, vinegar, and grated onion and mix well.

Serve the eggplant piping hot with the tarako sauce on top, garnished with green onion.

ASPARAGUS WITH BONITO FLAKES
(OHI-TASHI)
4 SERVINGS

Serve this appetizer hot in cold weather and chilled on warmer days. Asparagus will vary in price according to the season, but it is available almost all year round. This dish is an all-time favorite of mine and those I've prepared it for.

20 asparagus spears, trimmed

   DRESSING
½ cup dashi
2 tablespoons soy sauce
1 tablespoon mirin

4 tablespoons bonito flakes
 lemon wedges (optional)

Cut asparagus spears in half crosswise. Parboil the thicker, bottom halves in lightly salted water for about 2 minutes, then add the more delicate top halves. Continue parboiling until asparagus is *cooked but still crisp,* a total parboiling of 3 to 4 minutes, depending on the thickness

of asparagus. Plunge into cold water to stop cooking. Chill until serving time if prepared in advance.

Combine dashi, soy sauce, and mirin in a small saucepan and bring to a boil, then remove from heat. If the dish is to be served hot, use immediately or reheat over a low flame. For a refreshing cold dish, cool to room temperature, then refrigerate before serving.

To serve, arrange asparagus on individual salad plates. Pour hot or cold dressing on top and garnish with a mound of bonito flakes (1 tablespoon per serving) or with lemon wedges.

VINEGARED CRAB

4 SERVINGS

Cucumbers can marry with just about any seafood: crab, octopus, shrimp, fish, seaweed. Here's a light cucumber salad with vinegar dressing that goes well with any lunch or dinner, American or Japanese.

1 European cucumber, or 4 kirby
    cucumbers, or large American
    cucumber, peeled and seeded
1 teaspoon salt

DRESSING
¼ cup rice vinegar
½ tablespoon soy sauce
2 tablespoons dashi
1 tablespoon sugar

¼ pound cooked crab meat, shredded, or
    3 "crab sticks" (kani-kamaboko)
1 teaspoon peeled and thinly sliced
    gingerroot
4 small lemon leaves or parsley sprigs

Slice cucumber paper-thin and sprinkle with salt. On a flat plate, knead cucumbers for 30 seconds till water is released, then cover them with another heavy dinner plate to press out more moisture. After 10 minutes remove the heavy plate and briefly rinse cucumbers under running water. Gently squeeze cucumbers with your hands to press out water. Chill.

Combine dressing ingredients in a small pot and bring to a boil. Remove from heat and cool completely.

Combine shredded crab, cucumbers, and ginger in a small bowl. Pour on the vinegar dressing, toss lightly, and place 2 or 3 tablespoons in each small deep bowl. Garnish with lemon leaves or parsley sprigs.

NOTE: "Crab sticks" are made from fish, not crab, but are seasoned to taste like real crab. Some contain MSG and food coloring, so read labels carefully before buying. Fresh or frozen crab is always preferred. Avoid canned crab altogether; it tends to be far too salty.

VARIATION: SHRIMP OR OCTOPUS LEMON BOATS. For an unusually pretty presentation, hollowed-out lemons can be used as a serving dish. Cooked jumbo shrimp are especially good this way. Briefly boil 4 jumbo shrimp, peel, devein, and cut into ¼-inch pieces, then proceed as for Vinegared Crab. Just before serving the salad, cut the tops off 4 lemons and scoop out the pulp. (You may want to shave a bit off the bottom of each lemon so it will sit stably on the table.) Place 2 or 3 tablespoons of shrimp mixture in each lemon boat, placing the lids alongside as decoration.

You may also substitute ¼ pound cooked octopus (sold in Japanese grocery stores) for the shrimp and serve the same way.

BLUSHING PINE NUTS
4 SERVINGS

The female cod lays beautiful ovals of pink roe (eggs), which the Japanese call tarako. This means "the children of cod fish." Millions of small cod eggs are encased in a transparent membrane, which is punctured easily with a knife. I love to sprinkle tarako over steaming rice, and also enjoy serving it as an appetizer with pine nuts. The elegant buttery flavor of pine nuts complements the salty roe. Tarako is sold in most Japanese grocery stores, but almost any kind of fish eggs will do—cod roe, salmon roe, crab roe, Russian or Iranian caviar, etc. But tarako is less expensive than most of these, and at least as delicious. Serve the nuts in empty clamshells and garnish with a little seaweed to remind your guests of a beautiful beach.

⅓ cup dried wakame seaweed (optional)
4 shiso leaves (optional)
   salt
1 segment of cod roe (tarako) encased in its
      membrane (about 1½ tablespoons)
1 tablespoon sake
4 tablespoons raw pine nuts

Soften wakame seaweed for garnish in water for 30 minutes. Drain. Squeeze out water.

Slice shiso leaves into narrow strips, crosswise. Sprinkle with salt and gently knead the strips of shiso leaves to release moisture. Let stand for 2 minutes. Rinse briefly under water and squeeze strips with your hands to press out water. Set aside.

Puncture membrane of roe and scoop roe into a small bowl. Add sake and mix well. Toss in the pine nuts and mix gently. Arrange a tablespoon or more of seasoned pine nuts on a bed of shiso leaf strips.

If you are using clamshells for serving dishes, arrange the filled shells on a tray and surround with strips of seaweed.

SERVE WITH Tuna Sashimi
   Sushi

VARIATION: ROSY ENOKI MUSHROOMS
This recipe is slightly more complex and interesting. Trim ends off 2 bunches of enoki mushrooms and cook with 2 tablespoons each sake and dashi for 2 minutes over medium heat. Blanch the cod roe in boiling water for 30 seconds; drain. Combine roe with mushrooms and their cooking liquid and serve warm or at room temperature, sprinkled with lemon juice.

OKRA AND AVOCADO COCKTAIL
4 SERVINGS

Mother believes avocados are best eaten like ice cream: with a spoon, scooping each mouthful. On the other hand, my husband likes it sliced like sashimi, with lemon and soy sauce. I enjoy this avocado cocktail with a light sesame dressing and so do Mother and my husband.

8 okra pods, washed and trimmed
1 medium avocado
½ medium tomato

DRESSING
1 tablespoon rice vinegar
1 teaspoon sesame oil
1 teaspoon soy sauce
½ teaspoon Dijon mustard
4 tablespoons vegetable oil

salt
pepper

In a medium saucepan bring water to a boil, add a dash of salt, and cook okra for 3 minutes. Drain. Slice each okra pod ⅛ inch thick. Chill.

Peel the avocado, remove the pit, and cut into ¼-inch cubes. Do the same with the tomato. Chill.

Combine dressing ingredients. Add a dash of salt and pepper to season.

Just before serving, toss avocado, tomato, and okra with dressing. Serve in shallow, stemmed glasses or small bowls.

SERVE WITH Pasta with Squid and Cod Roe

OYSTERS WITH GRATED DAIKON RADISH
4 SERVINGS

These tangy oysters look especially appetizing served in hollowed-out citrus rinds or their own shells.

4 ounces daikon radish, peeled and grated
1 dozen fresh oysters, shucked

DRESSING
2 tablespoons dashi
2 tablespoons mirin
2 tablespoons rice vinegar
juice of 1 small lemon
dash of salt
1 tablespoon grated lemon peel
soy sauce

Squeeze the grated radish with your hands to release liquid, then set aside, discarding the liquid.

Bring a large saucepan of salted water to a boil. Remove from heat and drop the oysters into the hot water. Almost immediately, remove the oysters with a slotted spoon, draining excess water. The oysters will be only slightly cooked. Chill.

Just before serving, combine dressing ingredients and pour half of the mixture over the oysters. Toss the other half with the grated radish.

Divide oysters evenly among individual bowls or saucers. Pour a bit of the radish dressing over each. Sprinkle with grated lemon peel to add a bright color and tart taste. Serve chilled, with soy sauce for dipping.

SERVE WITH Honey Squash Salad
Marinated Cod in Miso
Sauce

MATSUTAKE MUSHROOM AND SHRIMP SURPRISE
4 SERVINGS

When you unwrap the foil, the perfume of matsutake mushrooms will make you pleasantly full even before you taste them. You may use any type of mushroom in place of matsutake, but no other mushroom can beat its fragrance. They are available in the fall in Oriental grocery stores.

4 large shrimp
8 mitsuba leaves (optional)
8 ginkgo nuts, water-packed
4 small fresh matsutake mushrooms
    salt
4 teaspoons sake
½ lemon, cut into wedges
    vegetable oil
    soy sauce

Preheat the oven to 350 degrees.

Bring water to a boil in a small saucepan and cook shrimp for just 1 minute. Drain and rinse under running water. Remove shells.

Tie mitsuba leaves into knots. Drain ginkgo nuts and rinse.

Prepare 4 sheets of aluminum foil, each measuring about 8 by 5 inches. Grease each piece lightly with oil. Place a quarter portion of the shrimp, mushrooms, ginkgo nuts, and mitsuba leaves in each sheet of foil. Salt lightly and sprinkle sake. Seal the foil by pinching the ends together.

Put the wrapped mushrooms in the oven for 8 minutes.

Serve the wrapped mushrooms immediately on individual plates with lemon wedges. Pass the soy sauce around.

SERVE WITH Tofu and Wakame
Suimono
Hand-Molded Sushi

SPRING RAIN SHRIMP
4 SERVINGS

Harusame noodles make a light and crispy substitute for tempura batter. This dish is for an elegant evening menu.

8 medium shrimp
2 ounces harusame noodles
    vegetable oil
    salt
    potato starch or cornstarch
1 egg white, beaten
½ lemon, cut into wedges

Wash shrimp, peel away shells, but keep tails intact. Devein and slit the underside of shrimp in a couple of places, about ¼ inch deep, to prevent shrinkage while deep frying.

Cut harusame noodles into ½-inch pieces with a pair of scissors.

Preheat oil for deep frying in a heavy cast-iron pan. Lightly salt a shrimp, dust with potato starch, dip in beaten egg white, and coat it with harusame noodles. Repeat with the remaining shrimp.

Deep fry the shrimp over medium heat, turning the shrimp to cook evenly on both sides until noodles puff up. The shrimp should cook in a minute; do not burn the noodles. Remove from heat and drain on paper towels. Gently transfer 2 shrimp to each individual serving plate, overlapping the tail ends. Place a lemon wedge on each plate.

SERVE WITH Steamed Red Snapper with Lemon Slices
Rice with Peas

SQUID WITH GINGER
4 SERVINGS

Squid may be unfamiliar to you, but it is simple to prepare and tasty, not at all fishy. You may grill the squid on a barbecue grill or in your broiler. This should be eaten piping hot.

4 small fresh squid
2 tablespoons peeled and grated gingerroot
¾ cup chopped green onions (green part only)
soy sauce

Wash the squid. If they were not cleaned at the fish store, remove legs and head and clean the body, carefully removing the sac. Peel off the thin membrane and discard. Clean the legs.

Broil the legs and bodies separately in a heated broiler until they begin to curl and turn opaque, approximately 5 minutes, turning once to cook both sides.

Remove squid from heat. Slice each body into ¼-inch-thick rings. Serve legs whole. Place each serving in a small bowl and garnish with grated ginger and chopped green onions. Serve immediately, passing soy sauce separately.

CHILLED EGGPLANT WITH GINGER SAUCE
4 SERVINGS

I serve this appetizer on hot summer days because it is so light and refreshing. Steamed eggplants are so sweet and tasty that they hardly need a sauce—the fresh grated ginger served on the eggplants gives just a little bite to the flavor.

4 Japanese eggplants
4 ounces boneless chicken breast
¼ cup mild soy sauce
1 tablespoon mirin
1 teaspoon sesame oil
1 tablespoon peeled and grated gingerroot
1 green onion, chopped

Slice eggplants in half lengthwise and make diagonal incisions on the uncut surface, about ¼ inch deep, all the way across. Place cut side up on a dish that will fit inside your steamer.

Heat water in a steamer. Put the dish of eggplant in the steamer and cook for 10 minutes. Cool and chill.

Simmer chicken in water (or chicken broth) until tender and cooked, about 3 minutes on each side. Let cool, then use your fingers to shred it into small pieces.

Combine soy sauce, mirin, sesame oil, and ginger to make sauce.

Just before serving, arrange 2 eggplant halves on each individual serving plate. Garnish each serving with chicken and spoon sauce over each piece.

Sprinkle green onion on top for decoration.

SHIITAKE MUSHROOM MOUNTAINS
4 SERVINGS

My mother's specialty, this appetizer has become our family favorite. Ground chicken is gaining popularity in the U.S., but if you can't find it at your butcher shop, try grinding chicken briefly in your food processor or meat grinder. It's tastier than ground turkey, lighter than pork, beef, or veal. You can make this dish ahead of time, if you wish, and reheat the mushrooms in a steamer just before you serve them. Mother also puts these mushrooms in suimono soups.

8 fresh or dried shiitake mushrooms
  cornstarch
5 ounces ground chicken
1 tablespoon peeled and grated gingerroot
2 teaspoons sake
2 tablespoons soy sauce
2 tablespoons mirin

Rinse fresh shiitake mushrooms in water. Remove stems and pat dry. If using dried mushrooms, soften in water for 30 minutes, remove stems, and pat dry.

Make an incision in the shape of a cross on the cap of each mushroom. The cross should not pierce the mushroom all the way through.

Lightly pat cornstarch on the underside of each cap. Set aside.

Combine ground chicken, ginger, and sake. Mound 1 to 1½ tablespoons of seasoned ground chicken on the underside of each mushroom.

Bring water to a boil over high heat in a steamer and steam mushrooms, meat side up, for 5 minutes.

In the meantime, combine soy sauce and mirin in a small saucepan and bring to a boil. Remove from heat and keep warm.

Place 2 mushrooms on each small serving plate, one cap side up, the other cap side down. Spoon a tablespoon of sauce over each serving. You may serve this hot or at room temperature.

SERVE WITH Vegetarian Nabe

GRILLED TOFU WITH MISO
(DENGAKU)
4 TO 6 SERVINGS

Pressed, firm tofu cubes are skewered and grilled with miso topping. The marriage of the mild, custardlike tofu and seasoned miso paste is perfect. Try it at your next backyard cookout.

1 (19-ounce) cake firm tofu
1 tablespoon black sesame seeds
1 tablespoon white sesame seeds

RED MISO TOPPING
¼ cup red miso paste
1 tablespoon white miso paste
1 tablespoon sake
1 tablespoon mirin
1 tablespoon sugar
1 egg yolk
4 tablespoons water or dashi

Preheat the broiler or prepare coals in an outdoor grill.

Wrap the tofu cake in a clean cotton cloth or towel. Gently place a heavy dinner plate on top. Let stand for half an hour. (The weight of the plate will press out much of the tofu's moisture.) Do not press down on the plate; let weight and time do the job of firming the tofu.

Mix the miso, sake, mirin, sugar, and egg yolk in a small bowl. Set the bowl in a saucepan of boiling water and simmer for 5 minutes. Add water or dashi to the mixture and stir over low heat another 3 minutes. Remove from heat.

Slice pressed tofu into bite-size rectangles.

Grill both sides of tofu until surface is toasted. Remove from heat and spread on a layer of miso topping with a knife, about ⅛ inch thick. Grill or broil the miso-topped side of each piece till it is slightly toasted. Sprinkle with sesame seeds. Skewer each grilled tofu with 2 toothpicks and serve immediately.

ICICLE RADISH WITH LEMON SAUCE
4 SERVINGS

This is a fresh light appetizer that is crisp, hot, and crunchy. The slivered lemon peel adds a necessary touch of color and piquancy to the otherwise plain radish.

   6 icicle radishes
1½ teaspoons salt
   2 tablespoons soy sauce
      juice of 1 lemon
   2 tablespoons thinly *sliced lemon peel*

Slice radishes crosswise, about ⅛ inch thick. Rub radish slices generously with salt; let stand for 10 minutes. The radish will turn slightly limp.

Rinse radishes thoroughly under running water and drain. Chill.

Just before serving, combine soy sauce and lemon juice and pour over radish slices. Toss them together with lemon peel slivers and serve immediately.

ROE ROE ROE YOUR BOAT
4 SERVINGS

An elegant appetizer of salmon roe in little celery canoes, this dish tastes especially good with warm sake.

   6 tablespoons salmon roe
   1 teaspoon sake
   4 celery stalks

   DRESSING
   1 cup grated daikon radish
2½ tablespoons rice vinegar
   1 teaspoon sugar
⅓ teaspoon salt
   1 teaspoon mild soy sauce

Sprinkle salmon roe with sake.

Trim the celery stalks and cut each into 2 or 3 pieces.

Mix dressing ingredients together and add salmon roe.

Scoop 1 or 2 teaspoons of the roe-radish mixture into each piece of celery. Arrange the filled celery on small plates. Serve immediately.

SESAME TOFU
9 SERVINGS

This dish is enjoyed for its sesame fragrance. No soybeans are used to make this "tofu"; it's made from sesame seed paste (atari-goma), arrowroot starch (kuzu), and dashi, and its name is derived from its shape, which resembles a cake of tofu. Both sesame paste and arrowroot starch are treasured for their healthful properties and are available in Japanese grocery stores. My grandmother often makes sesame "tofu" for use as an appetizer before the tea ceremony. My mother serves it as a side dish with seafood dishes.

⅓ cup arrowroot starch (kuzu)
⅓ cup sesame seed paste (atari-goma)
1¼ cups Fragrant Dashi (page 50) or instant
    dashi, cooled
 1 teaspoon sake
¼ teaspoon salt
 1 tablespoon dried wasabi powder
   soy sauce

Sift the kuzu. It is quite lumpy, so use your fingers to crush the lumps. Put starch and sesame seed paste in a medium bowl and gradually add the dashi broth, mixing constantly to achieve a creamy texture.

Strain the mixture through a fine sieve into a saucepan and add sake and salt. Turn heat to low and mix with a wooden paddle until kuzu mixture achieves the consistency of heavy custard cream, about 5 minutes. Be careful not to burn. Remove from heat.

Wet nagashi-bako (metal mold) or a 6-inch square aluminum pan, preferably one with a removable bottom. Pour in kuzu mixture and let stand until firm. Chill.

To serve, dissolve wasabi powder with a few drops of water until it achieves the consistency of a paste. Cut tofu into 2-inch squares. Transfer tofu to small plates with a spatula, and put ½ teaspoon wasabi paste on top of each square. Serve with soy sauce.

NOTE: Before use, sesame seed paste should be mixed with a spoon until oil and paste are thoroughly blended.

SERVE WITH Steamed Buddha's Hands
Just Vegetable Suimono

CARROTS WITH WALNUT SAUCE
4 SERVINGS

The rich flavor of walnuts and the sweetness of carrots make a tasty appetizer for year-round menus. Grandmother found California carrots to be so much sweeter and tastier than Japanese carrots that she often calls them sweets instead of vegetables.

1 large carrot
2 ounces walnuts
1 tablespoon soy sauce
1 tablespoon mirin
1 teaspoon sugar
1 tablespoon dashi
  dash of salt

Peel the carrot and slice into thin rectangles, measuring ⅜ inch by 1 inch. Bring water to a boil in a steamer and cook the carrot for about 5 minutes. Cool.

Roast walnuts in a dry frying pan over medium heat for a couple of minutes. Reserve 4 small whole walnuts for garnish and mash the rest with a mortar and pestle or electric blender. Add the remaining ingredients and mix well.

Combine carrot rectangles with walnut sauce and serve in small individual bowls. Garnish each with a toasted walnut.

SHRIMP, OKRA, AND WAKAME SEAWEED OVER CRUSHED ICE
4 SERVINGS

This appetizer of several tastes is served on a bed of crushed ice. It is light and surprising, and takes the heat off a sweltering summer evening.

8 okra pods, washed and trimmed
½ cup dried or fresh wakame seaweed
8 ounces bay shrimp, peeled and cooked

VINAIGRETTE
5 tablespoons rice vinegar
4 tablespoons soy sauce
3 tablespoons mirin
1 teaspoon peeled and grated gingerroot

crushed ice
4 lemon wedges

Boil okra, uncovered, in lightly salted water for 2 minutes. Rinse under cold water to bring out its color.

Drain. Slice okra crosswise into ⅛-inch-thick rings and chill.

Rinse wakame seaweed and soak in water for 5 to 10 minutes if fresh, 10 to 20 minutes if dried. Discard any hard parts. Cut seaweed into 2-inch pieces and chill.

Combine dressing ingredients.

To serve, combine shrimp, wakame seaweed, and okra in a bowl and pour on the dressing. Toss gently.

Make a bed of crushed ice in 4 individual-size salad bowls. Place a portion of the salad on top of the crushed ice, with lemon wedges on the side.

SERVE WITH Grilled Halibut
String Bean Sesame Toss

TUNA SASHIMI AND GREEN ONIONS WITH MISO
4 SERVINGS

If you have fresh tuna fillet, here is a simple appetizer-salad that tastes heavenly. Tuna is best, but clams, squid, or white fish, if they are fresh, are also delicious with miso dressing. There's a whole section on sashimi later on in this book (see pages 159–167); this recipe is just a succulent sample.

MISO DRESSING
4 tablespoons white miso paste
1 tablespoon mirin
1 tablespoon sake
1 tablespoon sugar
1 teaspoon dry Japanese mustard
1½ tablespoons rice vinegar

salt
1 bunch green onions
8 ounces raw tuna (lean fresh fillet only)

Combine miso, mirin, sake, and sugar in a saucepan. Cook over low heat for 4 minutes, mixing gently. Cool completely; add mustard and vinegar. Chill.

Bring water to a boil in a medium saucepan. Sprinkle in a dash of salt and boil the green onions, putting the white ends into the water first and then gradually lowering the green ends in, as the white ends take longer to cook. Boil for 1½ minutes and drain.

Scrape the green onions with the flat surface of your knife to remove the sticky liquid. Do not smash the white part. Cut into 2-inch pieces. Chill.

Slice tuna into ½-inch cubes. Chill.

To serve, arrange tuna and green onions in individual bowls. Top each serving with 1½ to 2 tablespoons miso dressing. Serve immediately.

SERVE WITH Egg Tofu Delight
Vinegared Crab
Five-Eye Rice

MUSHROOM TOSS
4 SERVINGS

Mrs. Tam, a neighbor, celebrates the arrival of autumn by arranging on her porch some fall-tinted maple leaves that she picks from a tree in her yard. Each time I pass by I take a moment to appreciate these crimson leaves and feel happy for the rest of the day. This dish brings the same autumn spirit to the table.

4 ounces enoki mushrooms
5 ounces button mushrooms
5 ounces shimeji mushrooms
4 fresh shiitake mushrooms
1 teaspoon lemon juice
6 chestnuts, sweetened (canned or
  homemade, page 238)
1 dozen gingko nuts in their shells

DRESSING
3 tablespoons vegetable oil
2 tablespoons rice
⅓ teaspoon salt
  pepper

2 tablespoons vegetable oil
2 tablespoons sake
  salt
  pepper
1 tablespoon chopped parsley
4 red maple leaves (or any leaves that have
  turned colors)

Wash mushrooms and pat dry with a paper towel. Remove stems from shiitake and shimeji mushrooms and discard. Trim enoki and button mushrooms. Sprinkle mushrooms with lemon juice.

Combine ingredients for the dressing.

Cut shiitake mushrooms into quarters. Cut chestnuts in half.

Dry roast unshelled gingko nuts in a skillet until they brown, about 3 to 5 minutes. Crack the shells with a hammer and remove the nutmeats; discard shells.

In clean skillet, heat oil over high heat and stir fry the shiitake, shimeji, and button mushrooms for 2 minutes. Add enoki mushrooms, sake, salt and pepper to taste, and stir fry for 1 more minute. Add gingko nuts and chestnuts, toss gently, and remove from heat.

Pour dressing over the mushrooms while hot and toss gently. Garnish with chopped parsley.

Serve immediately. Garnish each serving with a tinted maple leaf.

DAIKON RADISH WITH LEMON-MISO
(FURO-FUKI-DAIKON)
4 SERVINGS

 My favorite winter appetizer! It is served as you would a one-pot dinner, in a hot pot or electric skillet. (See page 201 for more information.) While sipping sake or beer, your guests scoop the daikon radish out of the simmering broth and eat with a dab of lemon-miso sauce.

2 pounds daikon radish (1 medium)
5 cups liquid reserved from washing rice

LEMON-MISO SAUCE
4 tablespoons red miso
2 tablespoons sugar
½ lemon rind, grated

10 inches konbu seaweed
3 cups warm water

Peel daikon radish and cut into thick slices, ¾ inch to 1 inch. Trim the edges with a beveled cut (page 15). With a knife, slit a cross on one side of each slice.

Pour the rice liquid into a large saucepan and add daikon radish slices. (If you have no plans to serve rice this day and have no rice liquid reserved, use plain water, but the rice liquid helps remove bitterness from daikon, so it is the preferred choice.) Cook daikon over medium heat until the slices are tender, about 10 minutes. Remove from heat. Keep the daikon in the pan until ready to serve.

Mix lemon-miso sauce ingredients except for the lemon rind in a saucepan and cook over low heat for 2 minutes. Transfer the sauce to a small serving bowl. Add lemon.

To serve, place a tabletop cooking unit on the table. Place the sheet of konbu seaweed and the warm water in a cast-iron or clay nabe pot. Add daikon, cover, and simmer for 10 minutes. Serve daikon radish with lemon sauce.

While the pot simmers, put a small plate and a pair of chopsticks at each place. When the dish is ready, the diners scoop a portion of radish out of the pot and onto their plates. Eat while hot, with a bit of sauce.

CAULIFLOWER FLORETS WITH MISO
4 SERVINGS

Sliced thin, fresh raw cauliflower florets make a tasty vegetarian "sashimi."

MISO DIP
3 tablespoons white miso
2 tablespoons mirin
½ teaspoon dry Japanese mustard

1 small carrot
1 kirby cucumber
¼ medium cauliflower

Combine dip ingredients in a small bowl. Chill. Cut the carrot into flower shapes (page 14). Slice the cucumber into 2" x ½" x ½" wands. Slice off the end of each wand on a slant to make peaks. Arrange cauliflower florets on a large plate. Garnish with carrot flowers and cucumber peaks. Serve miso dip on the side.

JAPANESE PIZZA
(OKONOMI-YAKI)
4 SERVINGS, 8 PANCAKES

Japanese love pizzas, Italian and American, but the Japanese version, called okonomi-yaki, is just as popular and is served as an appetizer, lunch, or snack. They are made like pancakes, with fresh eggs, flour and water, soy sauce, tonkatsu sauce, and vegetables. People also like to add chicken, shrimp, crab, beef, and/or pork. It's a perfect brunch dish—invite your friends and make Japanese pizzas in an electric skillet.

1½ cups flour
1 egg
1 teaspoon baking powder
1¼ cups milk
1 cup chopped cabbage
1 green onion, chopped
1 carrot, chopped
½ bell pepper, chopped
½ pound in all boneless chicken and/or
   shrimp, crab, beef, pork, cut into thin
   strips
oil
mayonnaise
tonkatsu sauce or soy sauce
½ cup bonito flakes (optional)
½ cup nori seaweed flakes (optional)

Combine flour, egg, baking powder, and milk. Toss lightly with chopsticks or fork. The batter will be quite thin.

Arrange chopped vegetables and meat or seafood on a plate and bring to the table. Turn on the electric skillet (or griddle if you plan to make it in the kitchen) to medium heat.

Heat oiled skillet and pour enough batter to make a small (4-inch) pancake. Do two or three at a time if you have a large grill. While the bottom of the pancake is cooking, sprinkle on a bit of cabbage, green onion, carrot, bell pepper, and meat or seafood. Turn the pancake over and let it cook 3 or 4 minutes longer.

Remove pancake from grill and brush surface with mayonnaise, tonkatsu sauce, or soy sauce. Sprinkle on bonito flakes and nori seaweed flakes if you wish. Eat while piping hot.

SERVE WITH Basic Miso Soup
Rainbow Salad

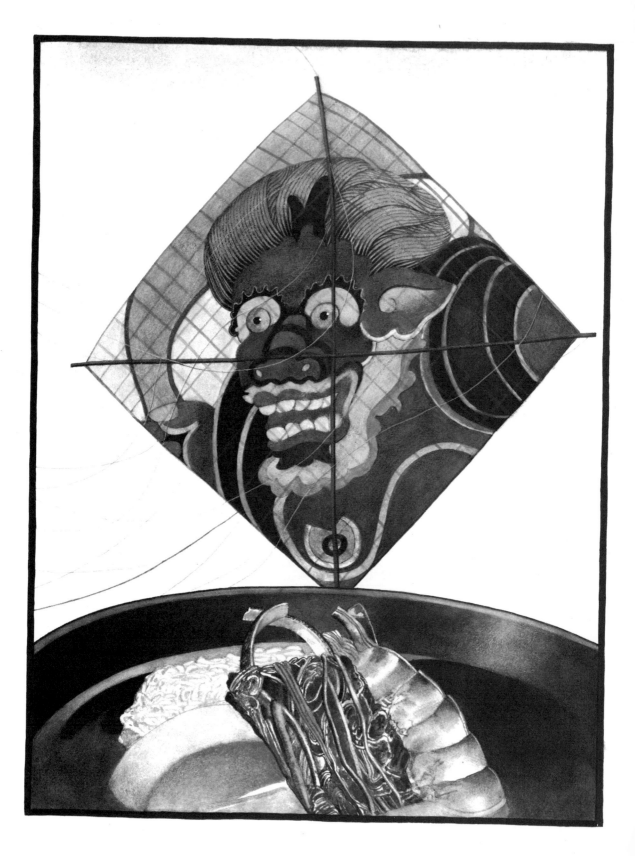

CHAPTER 4
SUCH SOUPS!

EVERYBODY EVERYWHERE SEEMS TO LOVE A GOOD SOUP. It stimulates taste buds and appetite. It tones the tummy for more solid fare to come. It warms and satisfies.

In Japan, making soup for the family is a daily task, for in Japan soup is eaten even with breakfast, often with all three meals. Unlike many Western soups, which become richer and more flavorful the more ingredients you use, Japanese soups are mainly simple in the making, quick to prepare, and require as few as two or three ingredients, in modest amounts. They are served in small lacquer or ceramic bowls. Spoons are not used.

Raising such soup in such a bowl to your lips is itself a pleasurable experience. Your cupped fingers are warmed. The fragrance is directly under your nose. Solid bits of tofu, shrimp, seaweed, or other ingredients may be rescued from the bowl with chopsticks or just nibbled from the bowl's warm edge.

There are two principal types of Japanese soup—miso, derived from protein-rich soybeans, and suimono, more delicate and sophisticated soups, something like fine consommé in French cuisine. Both soups have delicious variations. Both are based on the traditional soup stock, dashi, of which there are several tasty varieties.

Let's consider dashi first. Like chicken soup in Jewish cookery, it is a basic, healthful broth. Dashi, however, derives from the sea, with dried fish, seaweed, and water its usual components.

The most common variety of dashi is made from a mixture of seaweed and flakes of dried bonito. In Japan, many people shave flakes off a large block of dried fish, for a super-fresh flavor, each time they make dashi. These large dried fillets are difficult to come by in this country, though, and it is likely that you will have to use vacuum-packed flakes. These are packed freshly cut and are quite tasty.

Unlike beef and chicken stocks, which require hours of gentle simmering, dashi can be made in less than ten minutes. Don't walk away from the kettle, as you might while cooking up a pot of chicken stock; timing is critical. It is important that you remove the seaweed from the pot just before the water boils, or the stock will turn fishy. I remember how Grandmother would lower her glasses down the bridge of her nose and fixedly study the strands of seaweed dancing in the hot water; just before the water actually boiled she'd snatch them out with her long cooking chopsticks.

It should be mentioned that many traditional Japanese no longer make their dashi from scratch every time. Prepared dashi powders make dashi almost instantly like beef and chicken bouillon cubes, but some contain salt and artificial flavorings. I sometimes use the powder myself and don't hesitate to recommend it to you, but do try making your own dashi from scratch. The fresh flavor and fragrance are worth the few extra minutes needed to assemble the ingredients and cook them together briefly.

The possibilities of dashi understood, let's now consider miso soup. For it, in addition to dashi, you will principally need miso paste. This is a basic ingredient made from soybeans (mostly imported from America).

In Japanese culture, miso enjoys a mystique almost like wine in France. Miso paste too is fermented, for at least a year (best "vintages" may be three years old). Like wine, miso paste also comes in red and white varieties. Red miso (aka-miso) is dark and a bit salty. White miso (shiro-miso), actually yellow in color, is light and slightly sweet. Variations of white miso are Shinshu-miso, a tart miso that comes from the Shinshu area of Japan, and Saikyo-miso, which is quite sweet. Red miso also comes in a variety. Inaka-miso (country-type miso) and Sendai-miso, which comes from the Sendai area of Japan, are generally labeled red miso. Also available is Hatcho-miso, which is chunky and salty. In general, red miso soup is enjoyed during summer months, white miso in wintertimes. But miso paste is the amiable servant of its chef (you). It's quite agreeable to being mixed, red together with white, according to your taste. Also like Western wines (and like sake), miso paste is used in many other dishes besides soup. Note too that some miso pastes, red and white, incorporate grains of wheat, rice, or soybeans to create a variety of crunchy textures and tastes. The possible combinations are infinite. All Japanese families have their favorite. After you experiment a bit, you and your family will, too.

A somewhat more delicate and refined soup is suimono, which literally means "something to sip." It is more sophisticated than miso in the way it's prepared and served. On formal occasions suimono appears after the appetizer as the first course of the meal. But it can also be served at midpoint to clear the palate between dishes. It may also appear toward the end of the meal, together with the final course of rice and pickled vegetables.

Suimono, like miso soups, starts with any of the basic dashi stocks. For suimono, flavor your chosen dashi with just two or three drops of mild soy sauce (to give it a slightly tawny color), plus a hint of sake for fragrance, and a touch of salt.

In each of your empty individual serving bowls you will place a small morsel of cooked chicken, or fish fillet, or egg, tofu, or briefly boiled vegetable. Then you'll want to add a tiny bit of complementary food to enhance the color and flavor of the first one. If a piece of shrimp is the first ingredient, you'll want to counterpoint that pink color—perhaps with something green, like a few little strips of cucumber. A final ingredient might be the pale yellow or orange twist of a thin, decoratively sliced citrus peel.

Now, to complete your suimono, you will gently pour in the hot dashi, trying not to disturb the colorful pattern laid out in each bowl. You may adjust or rearrange the design with chopsticks before serving.

Some final recommendations: Little cooking time is needed—but to make good soups, use only the freshest ingredients. A limp string bean, a fishy fish, is not acceptable.

Dashi stock keeps nicely in your refrigerator for three days, but completed soups should be served immediately. Reheating diminishes the flavor. If your guests want second helpings, have the dashi, miso paste, and other ingredients ready to go, so you can create it at the last minute. It won't take long.

Do serve your soup in small black or red lacquerware bowls or small dark ceramic bowls. It is ideal if they have lids, since flavors and heat will be contained. Moreover, a lidded bowl gives your guests something extra to look forward to—a visual surprise. *Please* avoid shallow, white soup dishes; they cool the soup, spoil the fun, and make the most delicious miso or suimono look bland and taste blah.

FRAGRANT DASHI

6 CUPS

This fragrant stock from the sea, like all varieties of dashi, is basic to making soups and useful for many other Japanese dishes. It's especially good for suimono soup. It will keep well in the refrigerator for 3 days, and takes less than 10 minutes to prepare.

10-inch strip dried konbu seaweed
 6 cups water
¾ cup dried bonito flakes (katsuo-bushi)

With a damp, well-wrung cloth or paper towel, lightly pat the seaweed to remove surface dust. Do not wipe too hard, because the white powdery surface of dried seaweed imparts essential flavor.

With a knife make two or three incisions in the seaweed, so juices come out freely while simmering. Place the seaweed and measured water in a saucepan over medium heat. With a fork or chopsticks, remove the seaweed *just before* water reaches the boiling point, about 8 minutes.

Add fish flakes and let water come to a full boil.

Turn off heat and allow fish flakes to settle naturally to the bottom of the saucepan.

Line a sieve with clean cheesecloth and strain the stock through it. Save the fish flakes and seaweed to make Light Dashi (recipe follows) if you wish, or discard. Used fish flakes and seaweed keep in the refrigerator for 2 days. Flavor diminishes thereafter.

VARIATION: LIGHT DASHI

This stock is suitable for making miso soup, salads, and sauces and for simmering vegetables and seafood. Keeps in the refrigerator for 3 days.

Combine bonito flakes and seaweed reserved from Fragrant Dashi with 6 cups water in a medium saucepan and bring to a boil over medium heat. Remove seaweed and simmer another 5 minutes.

Strain the broth and discard fish flakes. The seaweed may be eaten as is, or with a bit of miso. It makes a unique appetizer that goes well with sake.

Makes 6 cups.

VARIATION: VEGETARIAN DASHI

For a pure vegetarian stock redolent of the sea, try this. It can be used as stock for soup, sauces, and somen noodles.

Make two or three incisions in a 12-inch strip of konbu seaweed and let stand in 6 cups water for 3 to 4 hours. The seaweed will release its juices and naturally turn the water into stock.

Makes 6 cups.

VARIATION: RICHLY FLAVORED DASHI

Here is a robust and healthful dashi with which to make hearty miso soups. It's also good for braising vegetables, meats, and seafood. Don't use it for suimono soup— it's too strong. Tiny dried Japanese sardines (niboshi) provide the flavor. They are available in Japanese markets and in some supermarkets.

With a paring knife remove the heads and entrails of 12 to 15 dried sardines.

Prepare as for Fragrant Dashi, allowing the fish to simmer for 5 minutes.

Makes 6 cups.

BASIC MISO SOUP
4 SERVINGS

This is a classic miso soup that appears on the Japanese family menu at least once or twice a week. It blends wakame seaweed and fresh tofu into an unforgettable flavor that is highly nutritious and nearly fat-free. Do be sure to dilute the miso paste with hot broth before adding it to the broth, or your soup will be lumpy.

½ cup dried wakame seaweed (or 1 cup loosely packed fresh)
1 (6-ounce) cake firm or silken tofu
3 cups dashi (your choice, page 50)
3 tablespoons red miso paste
¼ cup chopped green onions (green part only)

If seaweed is dried, soften in water for 10 to 15 minutes; if fresh, soften in water for 5 minutes.

Cut tofu cake into ½-inch squares. Cut seaweed into 2-inch pieces, discarding any hard parts.

Bring dashi to a boil.

In a small bowl dissolve miso paste with a bit of the stock. Pour dissolved miso solution into the stock. Add tofu and wakame seaweed and bring to a boil.

Remove from heat. Serve topped with chopped green onions.

SERVE WITH Flounder Teriyaki
Okra Plum Salad

VARIATION: MISO SOUP WITH ENOKI MUSHROOMS. Substitute 1 package enoki mushrooms, root ends trimmed and rinsed, for the seaweed and tofu, proceeding as for Basic Miso Soup.

CLAM MISO SOUP
4 SERVINGS

Small live clams are used for this tasty soup. Buy fresh littleneck clams or, if possible, tiny asari or shijimi clams (available in some Japanese-American markets).

8 littleneck clams (or 20 asari or shijimi clams) in their shells
3½ cups Vegetarian Dashi (page 50)
3 tablespoons red miso paste
1 green onion (green part only), finely chopped

Soak clams in lightly salted water 4 to 6 hours (to remove sand), with one rinse and change of water. Clams like a quiet dark place like the bottom of the sea, so do not disturb them too much while soaking.

Clean each clam carefully with a brush or cloth.

Pour dashi over clams and bring to a simmer over medium heat. Cook gently for 5 minutes, or until clams open. Remove any film from surface of soup.

Dissolve miso paste in a few tablespoons of dashi. Pour diluted miso paste into the simmering soup and bring to a simmer. Remove from heat.

Garnish each serving with chopped green onion. Serve at once.

DAIKON RADISH MISO SOUP
4 SERVINGS

3 inches daikon radish
1 medium carrot
1 green onion (green part only)
3 cups Richly Flavored Dashi (page 50)
3 tablespoons white miso paste

Peel daikon radish and cut into 2-inch julienne strips. Do the same with the carrot.

Chop green onion finely.

Pour dashi stock into a medium saucepan. Add radish and carrot. Bring to a boil, then simmer about 5 minutes, until carrot and radish are tender.

Dissolve miso paste with a few table-spoons of stock and add to soup. Bring to a boil once again, then remove from heat and pour into individual bowls.

Sprinkle each serving with chopped green onion. Serve at once.

SERVE WITH Chicken Yakitori on Skewers
Rice with Chestnuts

VARIATION: MISO SOUP WITH WAKAME SEAWEED AND POTATOES. Substitute a small Idaho potato, sliced ¼ inch thick, and ½ cup softened wakame seaweed for the radish and carrot. Proceed as for Daikon Radish Miso Soup.

VEGETABLE AND CHICKEN MISO SOUP
(SATSUMA-JIRU)
4 SERVINGS

This is a satisfying miso soup, great for a cold day. My mother serves it for lunch with homemade bread.

In this recipe yam would be fine, but try instead to find satsuma-imo potatoes. They are available in Japanese markets, have a red skin, and are yellow inside, with a taste that is quite sweet.

8 ounces satsuma-imo potato (or yam)
1 carrot
4 fresh shiitake mushrooms
12 ounces chicken legs or wings
2 tablespoons vegetable oil
4 cups dashi broth (your choice, page 50)
3 tablespoons miso paste (red or white)
⅛ teaspoon Japanese red chili pepper (togarashi). Do not use Mexican chili; it is too strong for this recipe
1 green onion, chopped

Peel satsuma-imo potato and cut into ½-inch cubes. Peel the carrot and cut into ¼-inch cubes. Cut mushrooms in half.

Cut chicken pieces in half with a cleaver. Blanch in hot water and drain. Heat oil in a large skillet and brown chicken over medium heat. Remove from heat.

Bring dashi to a simmer in a large saucepan. Add chicken and vegetables and simmer for 20 minutes, skimming off surface film occasionally.

Dissolve miso paste in a few tablespoons of dashi. Combine this miso solution with the simmering stock and cook over medium-high heat for 3 minutes.

Add a dash of Japanese red chili pepper and serve with chopped onions.

OPTIONAL: You may add ⅓ firm tofu cake cut into 1½-inch cubes after the miso paste is added. Also nice might be placing a decoratively sliced strip of lemon rind (about ½ inch by ⅛ inch) in each bowl just before serving.

BAMBOO AND WAKAME SUIMONO
4 SERVINGS

This soup is so symbolic of springtime. If you can, use fresh cooked bamboo shoots imported from Japan; they are expensive but tastier than canned bamboo. This soup takes me back to the days in Grandmother's kitchen and brings good memories of her kitchen lessons.

6 ounces bamboo shoots, canned or water-
    packed
½ cup dried wakame seaweed
3 cups Fragrant Dashi (page 50)
1 teaspoon salt
1 teaspoon mild soy sauce

Blanch bamboo shoots briefly in hot water. Drain. Slice bamboo shoots lengthwise, about ¼ inch thick.

Soften wakame seaweed in water for 30 minutes. Cut into 2-inch pieces, discarding any hard parts.

Bring dashi to a boil and reduce heat. Gently add bamboo shoots and wakame to stock. Add salt and soy sauce.

Remove from heat. Serve immediately.

SERVE WITH Shrimp Lemon Boats
            Scattered Sushi

TOFU AND WAKAME SEAWEED SUIMONO
4 SERVINGS

In this delicate savory soup, tofu rules. Be sure to buy fresh tofu (of the silken variety), and slice it cleanly into ½-inch cubes.

½ cup wakame seaweed, dried
1 (6-ounce) cake silken tofu
3 cups Fragrant Dashi or Vegetarian Dashi
    (page 50)
1 teaspoon salt
1 teaspoon sake
⅔ teaspoon mild soy sauce
    dash of white pepper

Soften wakame seaweed in water (15 to 20 minutes if dried, 5 minutes if fresh). Discard any hard parts. Cut into 2-inch bits.

Slice tofu carefully into ½-inch cubes.

Bring dashi to a boil and reduce heat. Gently add tofu cubes and wakame to stock. Add salt, sake, and soy sauce while tasting for flavor; make your own adjustments. (Do not use too much soy sauce, because, besides overflavoring, it might turn your soup too dark.)

Remove from heat. Serve immediately, with a final dash of white pepper in each bowl.

CLOUDS-IN-THE-SKY EGG SUIMONO
4 SERVINGS

This suimono is fun to make, since it requires timing and dexterity. It is also pretty to look at just before you enjoy its satisfying fresh taste.

2 eggs
2¾ cups Fragrant Dashi (page 50)
1 teaspoon salt
⅔ teaspoon mild soy sauce
1 teaspoon cornstarch or rice starch
1 tablespoon cold water
4 mitsuba leaves, with stems

Break eggs into a bowl and beat *lightly*.

Bring dashi to a simmer in a saucepan. Add salt and soy sauce.

Combine cornstarch or rice starch with cold water and gently add to the stock. (This will thicken the broth slightly.) Bring stock to a boil, then reduce heat slightly. With a circular motion, carefully pour lightly beaten eggs around the perimeter of your pot. Continue to boil gently until eggs are half cooked; the egg trails will become light yellow clouds in the soup's sky. Swirl once with your chopsticks before the eggs harden.

Remove from heat and pour into individual bowls. Garnish with mitsuba leaves tied into loose knots.

NOTE: Don't pour the eggs in until the stock comes to a boil. Otherwise, the entire soup will become cloudy (like a gray overcast day).

SERVE WITH Japanese Pork Roast
Chilled Eggplant with
Ginger Sauce

JUST VEGETABLE SUIMONO
4 SERVINGS

This is a virtuous soup, full of taste, vitamins, protein (from tofu), and health.

1 (8-ounce) cake firm tofu
1 burdock root (optional)
1 carrot
1 teaspoon vinegar
½ cake konnyaku
2 green onions
1 tablespoon vegetable oil
3 cups dashi (your choice, page 50)
1 teaspoon salt
1 tablespoon mild soy sauce

To remove water, wrap tofu in a clean cotton cloth. Place a dinner plate gently over the tofu and let the weight of the plate press out the water for 20 minutes. Cut tofu into ½-inch cubes.

Wash burdock, wipe or brush to remove dirt, but do not peel. Slice burdock into matchsticks. Do the same with the carrot. Soak burdock and carrot in water to cover and vinegar.

Blanch konnyaku in boiling water for 3 minutes. Rinse under cold water. Slice into ⅛-inch-thick rectangles.

Cut green onions into 1-inch strips.

Heat the oil in a heavy saucepan and sauté the carrot, burdock, and konnyaku for 3 to 4 minutes. Add stock. Bring to a gentle boil and remove surface film. Add salt and soy sauce. Simmer gently for 5 minutes. Add tofu and simmer for an additional minute. Serve hot.

FOUR-MUSHROOM SUIMONO
4 SERVINGS

Enjoy nameko mushrooms for their slippery texture, enokis for their beauty, shiitakes for their fragrance, and shimejis for their flavor. If you happen to encounter edible mushrooms besides these—Italian porcinis, chanterelles, even a slice of truffle—put them in this suimono. It will make the soup more complex and flavorful.

2 ounces fresh shimeji mushrooms
4 dried shiitake mushrooms
2 ounces fresh enoki mushrooms
4 ounces nameko mushrooms (water-packed
    in cans)
2 deep-fried tofu pouches (age)
½ bunch mitsuba leaves or ½ cup chopped
    green onions, green part only
3 cups dashi (your choice, page 50)
1 teaspoon salt
1 tablespoon mild soy sauce

Soften shiitake mushrooms in water for 30 minutes.

Wash all mushrooms and remove roots and hard stems. Separate the bunches of enoki mushrooms into bite-size pieces, trimming off root ends.

Cut each shiitake mushroom into 4 pieces.

Blanch tofu pouches briefly in boiling water. Cut each into 4 pieces.

Cut mitsuba leaves in half.

In large pot, combine stock and tofu pouches. Bring to a boil over medium heat. Add mushrooms and seasonings and return to a boil. Add leaves, remove from heat, and serve immediately.

SNAKE EYE SUIMONO
4 SERVINGS

Serve this soup in the summertime, chilled or hot. Light somen noodles make a nest for the shrimp, and the cucumbers make the eyes of a snake.

4 small shrimp, peeled and deveined
⅛ European cucumber
1 ounce dried somen noodles
3 cups Fragrant Dashi (page 50)
1 teaspoon salt
1 teaspoon mild soy sauce
1 teaspoon sake

In a medium pot, bring water to a boil. Add shrimp and a dash of salt and simmer for 1 minute. Drain the shrimp and rinse under water.

Slice cucumbers in "snake eye" shapes (page 15).

In a medium pot, bring water to a boil. Add somen noodles and cook for 3 to 5 minutes, or until tender but not mushy. Drain and rinse under cold water.

Heat dashi in a large pot. Add salt, soy sauce, and sake. While heating the dashi, place one quarter of the somen noodles in each soup bowl. Place a shrimp on top of the noodles, and finally arrange 2 cucumber pieces slightly overlapping each other. Gently pour the dashi into the bowls and serve immediately.

SPRING CLAM SUIMONO
4 SERVINGS

Two shells tightly clasped together make a clam. Children in Japan are taught that husband and wife are also like a clam joined tightly together, and no two couples are alike. This soup is served at weddings and on Girl's Day in honor of this belief.

8 medium littleneck or cherrystone clams, in shell
3 cups Vegetarian Dashi (page 50)
1 teaspoon salt
2 teaspoons sake
1 green onion (green part only), chopped
1 tablespoon lemon rind, cut into decorative strips

Soak clams in water 4 to 6 hours to remove sand. Clean each clam well with a brush or cloth.

In a medium pot, combine stock and clams. Simmer over medium heat till clams open (about 5 minutes).

Remove clams and filter stock through a cheesecloth-lined sieve.

Pour filtered stock back into pot and season with salt and sake. Bring to a boil, then remove from heat.

To serve, place an open shell in each empty serving bowl. Use the meat of 2 clams for each opened clam, so that both top and bottom shells are filled. Carefully fill each bowl with hot broth. Sprinkle on onion and lemon rind as garnish. Serve hot.

NEW YEAR CELEBRATION SOUP

(MOCHI SOUP)

4 SERVINGS

This is a festive soup to celebrate the incoming year. Variations of it are traditional all over Japan. My Tokyo family's version—usually served three days in a row—features chicken, steamed fish cake, spinach, carrots, scallions, and above all mochi.

Mochi makes this soup special, especially for the children. Mochi is steamed sweet rice pounded to the consistency of a dumpling. It stretches like bubble gum (fun!) when boiled or broiled. The texture is smooth and the taste is wonderful.

Mochi can be bought ready-made in Japanese-American grocery stores and in some health food stores.

Warning: Don't stuff your mouth full of mochi. It's so delicious and so elastic you might choke. Eat mochi in small well-chewed bites, and swallow before nibbling more.

4 ounces boneless chicken
4 ounces steamed fish cake (kamaboko)
½ bunch spinach (about 4 ounces)
4 pieces mochi
3 cups dashi (your choice, page 50) or
   chicken stock
1 teaspoon salt
2 teaspoons soy sauce
4 strips lemon peel

Preheat the broiler.

Cut boneless chicken into bite-size pieces. Slice steamed fish cake crosswise into quarters.

Wash spinach. Boil for 2 minutes. Rinse under cold water. Drain. Bunch the ends together, remove roots, and cut spinach into 4 pieces, crosswise. Squeeze water out of each small bunch.

Broil mochi, turning it frequently until it softens and begins to rise like bread. Toast a little on both sides. Remove from heat. Rinse mochi briefly under hot water. Drain.

Heat stock in a pot over medium heat till it begins to simmer. Drop in chicken slices and cook for 2 minutes. Add salt, soy sauce, and steamed fish cake. Cook for another minute only.

To serve, put a small bunch of cut spinach and a piece of mochi in each individual small soup bowl. Pour the hot dashi over the spinach and mochi. Make sure each bowl gets some chicken and steamed fish cake. Garnish with slices of lemon peel. Serve hot. Happy New Year!

FISH BONE SOUP
4 SERVINGS

Grandmother taught me not to waste anything. Fish bones and heads make a wonderful soup. Americans might use them in a chowder or bouillabaisse; Japanese would make a clear suimono. You may use almost any type of fish bones: perch, cod, mackerel, bonito, red snapper, etc. Use the fillet for sashimi or other fish recipes.

1 fish head and fish bones, gills removed
  salt
3 cups water
1 piece konbu seaweed, 5 inches long
  salt
2 teaspoons sake
1 green onion (green part only)

Wash fish head and bones and cut bones as shown below. The fish bones should be cut into 3-inch pieces, crosswise.

Generously salt the fish bones (about 1 tablespoon) and let stand for 15 minutes.

Blanch in boiling water for 10 seconds and drain.

In a large pot, bring water and seaweed to a boil. Add the fish bones, reduce heat, and simmer for 4 minutes. Remove surface film with a slotted spoon. Add 1 teaspoon salt and sake.

Carefully arrange 2 or 3 segments of fish bones in each bowl and gently pour hot soup into the bowl. The bones can be picked up with chopsticks for nibbling at the flakes of fish left on them. Garnish with green onions.

SALMON SOUP WITH SAKE LEES
4 SERVINGS

This is an aromatic soup. Sake lees is a by-product of sake. It is sweet, pasty, and white in color. It adds a creamy texture to the soup, yet it is much lighter than Western soups made of rich creams and butter. Like miso paste, lees must be diluted before being added to hot broth. Sake lees is available in Japanese grocery stores.

3 (6-ounce) salmon fillets, sliced in thirds
4 ounces daikon radish
1 small carrot
1 (4-ounce) cake firm tofu
½ cake konnyaku
2 ounces fresh spinach
3½ cups dashi (your choice, page 50)
4 ounces sake lees
1 teaspoon salt
1 tablespoon mild soy sauce

Sprinkle salt lightly on both sides of salmon pieces.

Cut radish in half lengthwise and slice each half ¼ inch thick. Peel carrot and slice ¼ inch thick.

Cut tofu into 1-inch cubes.

Boil konnyaku for 5 minutes. Drain and rinse under cold running water. Slice crosswise into ¼-inch cubes.

Boil spinach for 1 or 2 minutes. Rinse

under cold water and drain. Bunch the ends together, remove roots, and cut spinach into 4 pieces, crosswise. Squeeze water out of each small bunch.

Combine stock, radish, carrot, and konnyaku in a pot and bring to a boil. When vegetables become tender (about 7 minutes) add salmon and tofu, and reduce heat to a simmer.

Dilute sake lees with stock to make a smooth paste. Add to stock.

Season soup with salt and soy sauce. Add spinach and bring back to a boil. Remove from heat immediately and serve hot.

RICE SOUP WITH EGG AND VEGETABLES
(OKAYU)
4 TO 6 SERVINGS

Here's a hearty soup made with leftover rice and greens. It will remind you of oatmeal because it gets quite thick as it simmers. It makes a nice breakfast, lunch, snack, or dinner. Any green vegetable, such as zucchini, broccoli, or Chinese cabbage, can take the place of spinach.

½ bunch spinach (about 4 ounces)
2 cups cooked brown or white rice
4 cups dashi (your choice, page 50) or
   chicken broth
2 teaspoons mild soy sauce
½ teaspoon salt
2 eggs, lightly beaten
½ cup chopped green onions

Boil spinach for 1 or 2 minutes. Rinse under cold water and drain. Bunch the ends together, remove roots, and cut spinach into 4 pieces, crosswise. Squeeze water out of each small bunch.

Pour cold water over rice to soften it. Drain.

Combine dashi, soy sauce, and salt in a pot and bring to a boil.

Add the rice and mix gently with chopsticks or a wooden spoon.

When rice mixture begins to bubble and boil, add eggs, spinach, and green onions. Cover and simmer until eggs look lightly cooked. Remove from heat. Toss gently with chopsticks or a spoon.

Serve immediately in individual bowls, with pickled vegetables on the side.

OPTIONAL: Add a cup of sliced boneless chicken, or more vegetables.

SERVE WITH Asparagus with Bonito
   Flakes
   Pickled vegetables

CURRIED GINGER CUCUMBER

SNOW PEAS WITH ALMOND DRESSING

CELERY AND CARROT SALAD

LOTUS ROOT WITH PLUM SAUCE

SUMMER SALAD

C H A P T E R 5

SALADS

BLACK-AND-WHITE TRIFLE

RAINBOW SALAD

BIRD'S NEST SALAD

CABBAGE PATCH SALAD

SEAWEED AND CUCUMBER SALAD

AUTUMN SALAD

BURDOCK SALAD WITH SESAME DRESSING

KIWI DELIGHT

OKRA PLUM SALAD

HONEY SQUASH SALAD

SNOW PEA PODS WITH HOT MUSTARD

JAPANESE-AMERICAN POTATO SALAD

SNOW-COVERED MOUNTAIN SALAD (SHIRA-AE)

THE DIFFERENCES IN STYLE BETWEEN JAPANESE AND WESTERN CUISINES are nowhere more evident than in their salads.

Japanese salads are served in quite small portions, as appetizing taste treats rather than bowlsful. Secondly, the Japanese do not use dressings heavy with oil, cream, cheese, or buttermilk. Finally, Japanese salads are *composed*—they must harmonize aesthetically as well as nutritionally with the main dish.

For instance, if your entree is a white fish, you might make a salad of string beans or spinach (both with sesame seed dressing), which would complement your main dish in color, flavor, and texture as well as nutrition. If your main dish is vegetarian, you might want to use seafood, meat, egg, and/or dried fruits in your salad—each chosen as a painter chooses and places adjacent colors.

All internationally favored ingredients may be used—the familiar lettuces, other vegetables, seafood, meat, and fruit—plus any readily available Japanese ingredients, such as seaweed, tofu, and sesame seeds.

Japanese salad dressings are of two basic types: a light vinegar-based dressing and thicker miso, tofu, egg yolk, or seed dressings. Oil is not much used (though I have included in the following recipes a Chinese salad popular in Japan that uses a light sesame seed oil).

It is traditional and important to try to use *seasonal* foods in your salads. *Bring the taste of the seasons to your table.* In spring, shop for fresh green asparagus, fresh varieties of lettuce, small new tomatoes, fresh cabbage, peas. In summer, look for fresh new cucumbers, fine garden tomatoes, string beans, eggplant, abalone. In fall, find new pumpkins, field mushrooms (careful!), chestnuts, persimmons, apples, and fresh salmon. In winter, chrysanthemum leaves, daikon radish, Chinese cabbage, burdock, oysters, crab, tuna.

And, of course, these days lots of useful, fresh, out-of-season foods are imported all year round—from Mexico, Australia, New Zealand,

Morocco, and other countries. Fresh beautiful blueberries from New Zealand in winter are a special pleasure. Perennial nonseasonal foods like eggs, shiitake mushrooms, hijiki seaweed, wakame seaweed, fried tofu pouches, tofu, potatoes, salmon caviar, cod eggs, squid, and shrimp are always welcome.

Keep your eyes wide open to fresh foods that appear in the markets. Always choose the most perfect. There is a direct relationship of freshness to both attractiveness and nutritional health.

Some of these salad recipes require parboiling or blanching of some vegetables. Do not overcook, so the vegetables remain firm and crisp. *Always place blanched vegetables immediately into cold water.* This stops the cooking, cools them for serving, keeps their colors bright, and locks in fresh flavors.

Some of the fresh vegetables are to be sliced thinly, rubbed with salt, and pressed or squeezed. Don't hesitate to use a lot of salt; it acts as a brine to bring out the flavor. The final step is to rinse them *thoroughly,* so the dish will not end up too salty.

All ingredients must be as dry as possible before they are tossed with the dressings. Wet foods make soggy salad. Shake your salad materials gently over the sink and then use paper towels to pat dry each segment of leaf. Mechanical salad spinners are of no use here. These recipes do not require vigorous shaking; besides, salad spinners distort the shape of vegetables and require rather large quantities to work well.

Dressings should be tossed with the salad *just before* serving. And never drown the salad with the dressing; use moderate amounts. Dressing is only to complement the natural goodness and tastiness of your ingredients.

Finally, serve your salads in quite small dishes or bowls. Don't stuff the bowl. Leave open dish space around your salad by arranging each portion into a small mound—like a miniature Mount Fuji.

CURRIED GINGER CUCUMBER
4 SERVINGS

Cucumbers appear in the Japanese menu almost every day for breakfast, lunch, and dinner. Ginger is a spicy accompaniment. In America, both vegetables are easily available at your supermarket, so this dish can be whipped up without going to much trouble. Try to find long, seedless, unwaxed cucumbers (known as European or "hothouse") or firm, unblemished kirby cukes.

½ *European cucumber or 4 small kirby*
   cucumbers
1 *celery stalk*
½ *red onion*

DRESSING
1 *teaspoon ginger juice*
4 *tablespoons salad oil*
2 *tablespoons rice or white vinegar*
½ *teaspoon pepper (sansho or black)*
¾ *teaspoon salt*
½ *teaspoon sugar*
½ *teaspoon curry powder*

Slice cucumbers diagonally and thinly. Do the same with the celery. Slice the red onion thinly and let it stand in chilled water for 5 minutes. Drain.

Make the ginger juice by peeling and grating a 1- to 2-inch length of ginger root into a small bowl (or use a Japanese grater, which has a small box attached to catch the gratings). With your fingers, press the juice from the grated ginger; discard the fibrous gratings.

Combine 1 teaspoon of the ginger juice with the remaining dressing ingredients in a small bowl.

Combine cucumbers and celery and toss with dressing just before serving. Sprinkle red onion on top. To catch the eye and appetite of your eaters, make sure the red onion is visible on each serving.

SNOW PEAS WITH ALMOND DRESSING
4 SERVINGS

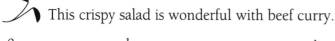

This crispy salad is wonderful with beef curry.

8 *ounces snow pea pods*
3 *tablespoons sliced blanched almonds*
1 *tablespoon raisins*
1 *tablespoon rice vinegar*
3 *tablespoons vegetable oil*
⅓ *teaspoon salt*
  pepper

Remove strings from snow pea pods and parboil for 1 minute. Rinse and chill under cold water.

Roast sliced almonds in a dry frying pan over medium heat for 1 minute. Remove from heat and mince the almonds and raisins. Combine vinegar, vegetable oil, salt, and pepper with the almonds and raisins to make the dressing.

Place small mounds of snow peas in individual bowls, and top with a spoonful of almond dressing.

SERVE WITH Japanese Beef Curry
      Steamed rice

CELERY AND CARROT SALAD
4 SERVINGS

In Japan, where it was only recently introduced, celery is considered a gourmet vegetable. The Japanese do not eat it as a casual snack, as in the West. Each stalk of celery is used as carefully as possible, without waste. Here is a delicious, crunchy celery and carrot salad.

2 large celery stalks
1 small carrot

DRESSING
1 Japanese dried chili pepper
3 tablespoons rice vinegar
1 tablespoon soy sauce
2 teaspoons sesame seed oil
1 teaspoon mustard
½ teaspoon salt

Trim celery tops and bottoms. Slice celery thinly on the diagonal. Let stand in chilled water for 5 minutes. Drain. Repeat for peeled carrots.

Discard seeds from chili pepper and chop it up coarsely. Combine chopped pepper with remaining dressing ingredients.

Mix celery, carrots, and dressing together and let stand for 10 minutes, tossing occasionally to let flavors mingle.

Serve cold.

SERVE WITH Crab Sushi Loaf
Basic Miso Soup

LOTUS ROOT WITH PLUM SAUCE
4 SERVINGS

Lotus root is a curiously structured vegetable, with open canals running through it. Sliced, it looks like tiny wheels ready to roll on. Lotus root is crunchy. Served with plum sauce, it is full of nutrients and tastes like nothing else in the world. Serve this salad as a side dish with sashimi.

6 ounces raw lotus root
1 teaspoon rice vinegar
3 pitted salted plums (large ones)
1 teaspoon soy sauce
1 teaspoon sugar

Wash and peel the lotus root. Slice into wheels, about ⅛ inch thick.

Bring a medium-size pot of water to boil. Put in the vinegar and lotus pieces and simmer until the lotus becomes almost transparent, about 2 minutes. Drain. Rinse under cold running water. Pat dry with paper towels. Chill.

In a small bowl, mash salted plums with a fork. Add soy sauce and sugar and blend well.

To serve, combine chilled lotus root with seasoned plum sauce. Toss well to coat the lotus root evenly. Serve in small individual bowls.

SUMMER SALAD
4 SERVINGS

Although tomatoes are not native to Japan, once introduced there, they became very popular, especially for use raw in salads. Japanese tomatoes are very red and juicy. Use fresh beefsteak tomatoes in this recipe for the same bright tomato taste.

4 Japanese eggplants
8 ounces green beans
5 red radishes
2 medium tomatoes

SESAME DRESSING
3 tablespoons vegetable oil
2 teaspoons sesame oil
1 tablespoon water
3 tablespoons rice vinegar
1 teaspoon sugar or honey
3 tablespoons soy sauce

Peel eggplants and boil them in water for 4 minutes, till tender. Drain off boiling water and soak eggplants in ice water till they cool. Remove from water and with your hands gently press out liquid from eggplants. Slice each eggplant lengthwise into 4 pieces.

Boil green beans until tender but crisp. Rinse under cold water. Cut each green bean in half.

Slice radishes thinly and soak in ice water until ready to use. Slice tomatoes.

Combine all ingredients for the dressing.

On a large platter arrange eggplant, tomatoes, and green beans in rows. Sprinkle sliced radishes on top. Chill.

Pour dressing over the vegetables just before serving.

SERVE WITH Chilled Pork Roast
Braised Japanese Potatoes
and Carrots

BLACK-AND-WHITE TRIFLE
6 SERVINGS

Visually, there is nothing like this black-and-white dish in Western cuisine. Furthermore, it will lead you by the tongue into a new world of taste and textures. Serve this jet-black seaweed tossed with a pure white tofu sauce as side dish or appetizer.

⅔ cup dried hijiki seaweed
1 teaspoon vegetable oil
2 teaspoons mirin
1 teaspoon sugar
1 tablespoon soy sauce

TOFU SAUCE
1 (6-ounce) cake firm tofu
2 tablespoons sesame seeds
2 teaspoons sugar
½ teaspoon mirin or sake
1 teaspoon rice vinegar
1 teaspoon soy sauce

Soften hijiki seaweed in water for at least 30 minutes. In a fresh pot of water, boil seaweed for 3 minutes. Drain.

Heat vegetable oil in a skillet and sauté seaweed. Add seasonings and simmer until most of the liquid is absorbed by the seaweed. Remove from heat. Let cool.

Wrap the tofu in a clean cotton cloth and place a heavy dinner plate on top for 20 minutes to press out the moisture.

Roast sesame seeds for 3 to 4 minutes in a dry frying pan, then grind them using a Japanese mortar and pestle. When seeds are well ground, add tofu and mash it, mixing into the sesame seed paste. Add remaining sauce ingredients and mix well.

Toss seaweed with tofu sauce; refrigerate for 20 minutes. Serve small portions, about 2 tablespoons per serving, in small cups or bowls.

Will keep 1 day refrigerated, but it's best eaten the same day.

SERVE WITH Tofu and Wakame
Seaweed Suimono
Seafood Tempura

RAINBOW SALAD
4 SERVINGS

Seven colors, textures, and flavors are combined in this salad, with a light vinegar dressing. Slice all ingredients into julienne strips to achieve uniformity (important for efficient chopsticking). This salad complements all foods.

4 dried kikurage mushrooms
2 tablespoons dried fruit (apricot, peach, or persimmon)
5 ounces shirataki noodles (canned or fresh)
6 ounces daikon radish
1 small carrot
2 kirby cucumbers
1 tablespoon salt
1 teaspoon vinegar

DRESSING
4 tablespoons sesame seeds
1 tablespoon sugar
¼ teaspoon salt
3 tablespoons rice vinegar
4 lemon rind strips, 1 inch by ⅛ inch

Soften mushrooms in water for 20 minutes. Remove stems and slice into julienne strips. Do the same with dried fruit. Chill.

Cut shirataki noodles into 2-inch pieces. Blanch in boiling water for 2 minutes and drain. Set aside.

Peel and slice daikon radish and carrot into julienne strips about 1½ inches long, and place in a bowl. Do the same with the cucumbers.

Rub radish, carrot, and cucumbers with 1 tablespoon salt until vegetables become slightly limp. Rinse salt off thoroughly under running water and drain. Sprinkle with vinegar. Chill.

Roast sesame seeds until fragrant, about 1 minute over medium heat in a dry frying pan. Remove from heat and pound sesame seeds with a mortar and pestle for 3 minutes. Add remaining dressing ingredients and mix well.

Toss dressing lightly with vegetables just before serving and garnish with lemon strips.

BIRD'S NEST SALAD
4 SERVINGS

Small quail eggs are served on a bed of delicate green beans, carrots, and daikon radish, and a ring of alfalfa sprouts. Watercress surrounds the bed to resemble a beautiful nest. This is a lovely all-year-round salad or appetizer.

1 dozen fresh or canned quail eggs
1 small carrot
4 ounces daikon radish
2 ounces green beans
1 package alfalfa sprouts
1 bunch watercress

GINGER DRESSING
4 tablespoons rice vinegar
6 tablespoons vegetable oil
2 teaspoons ginger juice (page 64)
1 teaspoon salt
  pepper

Boil quail eggs until hard-boiled, about 5 minutes. Cool and shell. If using canned eggs, drain and rinse with water.

Peel carrot and daikon radish and slice into matchstick pieces, about 2½ inches long. Remove string from green beans and slice into matchstick pieces, about 2½ inches long.

In a medium saucepan, bring water to a boil. Add a dash of salt, green beans, carrots, and daikon radish and cook over medium heat for 3 minutes. Drain and rinse under cold water. Cool completely and refrigerate.

Wash alfalfa sprouts and watercress. Pat dry with paper towels. Cut watercress into small pieces, discarding tough stems.

Combine ingredients for dressing. Chill.

To serve, place one quarter of the green beans, carrot, and daikon radish on the center of each salad plate. Put 3 boiled quail eggs on top. Surround the vegetables with a ring of alfalfa sprouts and watercress to resemble a bird's nest. Serve the dressing on the side.

SERVE WITH Grilled Salmon
Basic Miso Soup

CABBAGE PATCH SALAD
4 SERVINGS

The ruffly Chinese cabbage leaves are crispy and sweet and look very pretty with orange wedges, apples, and cucumbers. Kids especially love this salad.

4 Chinese cabbage leaves
½ Golden Delicious apple
1 navel orange
1 kirby cucumber
½ lemon

HONEY DRESSING
4 tablespoons vegetable oil
1 tablespoon rice vinegar or cider vinegar
¼ teaspoon salt
2 teaspoons honey
  pepper

Wash cabbage leaves. Tear off the ruffly tips of the leaves and use only these tips for the salad. Reserve the hard parts for Steamed Buddha's Hands or other recipes. Crisp the tips in a bowl of ice water.

Slice apple crosswise, about ⅛ inch thick. Soak in lightly salted water to prevent discoloration while preparing the other vegetables. Drain and chill. Peel orange and separate into wedges. Peel the membrane of each wedge carefully and cut in half. Chill.

Slice cucumber ⅛ inch thick. Slice lemon ⅛ inch thick. Chill.

Combine ingredients for the dressing.

In a large salad bowl, combine all the salad ingredients. Add the dressing and toss lightly. Serve in individual salad bowls or plates. Garnish with lemon.

SERVE WITH Steamed Buddha's Hands
Snake Eye Suimono

SEAWEED AND CUCUMBER SALAD
4 SERVINGS

Seaweed and cucumber go wonderfully well together, especially when tossed in toasty sesame oil dressing. This salad was served frequently at the cafeteria of my grade school in Japan. While I didn't care for most dorm food, this was an exception. I usually helped myself to two servings.

½ *European cucumber or 3 to 4 small kirby*
   cucumbers
1 *tablespoon sesame seed oil*
1 *cup bean sprouts*
¾ *cup fresh wakame seaweed or ½ cup dried*
   wakame seaweed

DRESSING
4 *tablespoons soy sauce*
1 *teaspoon sugar*
2 *tablespoons sake*
2 *tablespoons rice vinegar*
¼ *teaspoon Japanese chili pepper powder*
½ *garlic clove*
¼ *teaspoon salt*
1 *tablespoon sesame seed oil*

1 *teaspoon peeled and chopped gingerroot*

Wash cucumber and slice thinly, about ¼ inch thick. Sauté in sesame oil over medium heat for 2 minutes.

Boil bean sprouts until crisp and tender, about 1 minute. Drain and rinse under cold water.

Wash salt off fresh wakame seaweed and soak for about 5 minutes. Chop into 1-inch pieces. If you use dried seaweed, soak it in water for about 20 minutes, remove the hard parts, and chop into 1-inch pieces.

Arrange cucumber, seaweed, and bean sprouts on a platter.

Combine dressing ingredients and mix well. Toss with salad just before serving. Garnish with chopped ginger.

SERVE WITH Daikon Radish Miso Soup
Pork Cutlets

Autumn Salad
4 SERVINGS

Persimmons, a sweet and succulent fruit symbolic of autumn in Japan, make an ideal salad ingredient. Use only the sweet Japanese-type persimmons (Fuyu); the sour ones won't do. Japanese persimmons are available in season in Japanese grocery stores and gourmet health food stores. Toss in walnuts, if you like, for extra flash and texture.

*3 sweet, firm Japanese persimmons (Fuyu-
   type)*
4 dried kikurage mushrooms
1 (5-ounce) cake firm tofu
3 tablespoons sesame seeds and/or walnuts
1 tablespoon sugar
½ teaspoon salt

Peel persimmons and cut each into ¼-inch wedges.

Soften kikurage mushrooms in water for 20 minutes. Slice thinly into strips.

Wrap tofu in clean cheesecloth or a dish towel and press out water by placing a dinner plate on top. Let stand for 20 minutes. Pat dry with paper towel.

Roast sesame seeds in a dry frying pan over medium heat until fragrant, about 1 minute. When you see 3 seeds bounce in the pan, remove from heat. (Walnuts need no roasting.)

Pound sesame seeds or walnuts with a Japanese mortar and pestle to make a paste. (You may use store-bought sesame seed paste instead.) Add tofu, sugar, and salt and mix until well blended. If you prefer a very creamy texture, put the tofu mixture in an electric blender.

Set aside 1 tablespoon of kikurage mushroom strips for decoration. Mix the rest of the mushrooms with the persimmons and toss with the dressing.

Put the salad in a serving bowl and adorn the top with the reserved mushrooms, placing them in an attractive design in the center of the bowl.

SERVE WITH Moon-Gazing Taro
Potatoes
Rice with Chestnuts
Japanese Fried Chicken in
Ginger Sauce

VARIATION: FIDDLEHEAD FERN SALAD
Fiddlehead (or bracken) ferns are a springtime delicacy in Japan. As a child I used to hunt for the wild variety in the mountains above Kamakura. Its special bitter flavor makes it exotic and tasty, and it is a good springtime alternative to the persimmon salad. To prepare, substitute 4 ounces fiddlehead ferns, boiled until just tender and cut into 2-inch pieces, for the persimmons and mushrooms. Proceed as for Autumn Salad.

BURDOCK SALAD WITH SESAME DRESSING

4 SERVINGS

Burdock is the longest root vegetable that exists on earth. Some grow to twenty-four inches. It is eaten in Japan all year round but especially during New Year's "to prolong happiness." The burdock available in Japanese and Chinese grocery stores is actually grown in America.

2 large burdock (gobo) roots
1 tablespoon rice vinegar
  dash of salt

DRESSING
4 tablespoons sesame seeds
1 tablespoon rice vinegar
1½ tablespoons soy sauce
½ tablespoon sugar

1 teaspoon nori seaweed powder (optional)

Scrub burdock roots with a clean brush. Do not peel off the skin, because it contains the woodsy flavor (and vitamins!). Wash it just enough to remove dirt.

Slice into thin matchsticks. Soak in water for 10 minutes, changing the water twice to rid them of dirt.

Boil burdock with vinegar for 5 minutes or until tender. Rinse in cold water and add a dash of salt. Cool completely. Chill.

In a dry frying pan, roast sesame seeds over medium heat until fragrant, about 1 minute. (When 3 seeds bounce in the pan, that is the sign to remove the seeds from heat.)

Using a Japanese mortar and pestle, pound the sesame seeds until well ground and oily, about 3 minutes. Add the remaining dressing ingredients. Chill.

To serve, combine the dressing with the burdock strips and sprinkle nori seaweed powder on top, if you wish. The green seaweed powder adds color and calcium. You can find nori seaweed powder in the condiments section of Japanese grocery stores.

NOTE: Use any type of root vegetable, such as carrot or rutabaga, in the place of burdock.

KIWI DELIGHT
4 SERVINGS

This is a pretty salad, slightly untraditional but completely delicious.

*3 tablespoons sesame seeds or 1 tablespoon
    sesame seed paste*
6 ounces firm tofu
2 tablespoons mayonnaise
½ teaspoon salt
1 teaspoon sugar

1 avocado
1 kiwi fruit
1 pear, Japanese-type preferred
⅓ lemon
    peppermint leaves

Roast sesame seeds in a dry frying pan over medium heat until fragrant, about 1 minute. When the seeds become toasty, remove from heat.

Grind roasted sesame seeds with a Japanese mortar and pestle for 3 minutes, or use sesame paste. Wrap tofu in a clean cotton cloth and place a dinner plate on top to press out water for 20 minutes. Press tofu through a fine sieve to purée.

Add ground sesame seeds, mayonnaise, sugar, and salt to the puréed tofu.

Peel avocado, kiwi, and pear. Cut into bite-size pieces. Sprinkle lemon juice on avocado to prevent discoloration.

Toss the avocado and pear with the dressing. Garnish each serving with peppermint leaves and decorate with kiwi slices.

SERVE WITH Steamed Buddha's Hands
Everything-in-It Custard

OKRA PLUM SALAD
4 SERVINGS

There is an old Japanese saying that an ume-boshi (plum) a day keeps the doctor away. In any case, Japanese salted plums contain vital enzymes that are good for your digestive system. Besides, this dish is delicious. I often serve it as a side dish or appetizer.

8 ounces fresh okra
2 or 3 Japanese salted plums (ume-boshi)
2 tablespoons bonito flakes (optional)

Blanch the okra in boiling water for 3 minutes. Rinse under cold running water. Drain. Cool.

Slice each pod thinly and neatly, discarding stems. As you cut the okra you will find it stringy and sticky. Set aside.

Discard seeds from salted plums and chop well.

With chopsticks, lightly toss okra and salted plums together as you would toss a salad. The more sticky the okra gets the tastier it is, so you may toss well. Once okra is mixed with plum sauce its color turns brown, so do not toss the okra with the sauce until the very last minute.

Serve in small deep bowls. Garnish with bonito flakes if you wish.

HONEY SQUASH SALAD
4 SERVINGS

Japanese squash (kabo-cha) is widely grown in California and has become available in many American supermarkets. Compared to Western squash, kabo-cha is less watery and more like a potato or pumpkin in texture. It is sweet and full of vitamin A and fiber. If kabo-cha squash is unavailable, use acorn squash or butternut squash.

12 ounces Japanese squash (kabo-cha) or
    butternut or acorn squash
½ onion
5 red radishes

MISO DRESSING
2 to 3 tablespoons red miso paste
⅔ cup vegetable oil
⅓ cup rice vinegar
2 teaspoons lemon juice
½ teaspoon pepper
1 tablespoon honey or sugar

With a cleaver or heavy knife cut squash in half. Remove seeds and cut squash into 2½-inch cubes. Heat water in a steamer and steam squash for 5 minutes, or until it can be easily pricked with a toothpick. Remove from heat and cool.

Chop the onion. Slice red radishes thinly. Slice squash cubes diagonally in half. Combine all vegetables in a salad bowl and chill.

In a blender, combine dressing ingredients until smooth.

Toss vegetables with the dressing. Serve immediately.

SERVE WITH Matsutake Mushroom and
Shrimp Surprise
Flounder Teriyaki

SNOW PEA PODS WITH HOT MUSTARD
4 SERVINGS

Snow pea pods are naturally sweet and crisp. This is a tasty cold and spicy dish for a hot summer day.

5 ounces snow pea pods
½ teaspoon salt
½ tablespoon mirin

DRESSING
1 teaspoon dry Oriental mustard mixed
    with 2 tablespoons water
2½ tablespoons mild soy sauce
2½ tablespoons dashi

1 tablespoon bonito flakes (optional)

Remove strings from snow pea pods. Slice in half crosswise and parboil for 1 minute. Rinse and cool. Sprinkle with salt and mirin. Chill.

Combine dressing ingredients. The mustard powder must be dissolved in the measured water before being mixed with other ingredients (check instructions on package).

To serve, toss dressing with snow pea pods. Garnish each serving with a dusting of bonito flakes.

JAPANESE-AMERICAN POTATO SALAD
4 SERVINGS

When Grandmother and Mother both visited us in the U.S. we prepared steaks for the welcome dinner. I had made steamed rice, but Grandmother insisted on having potatoes with the steaks. "Let's be Americans tonight," she said. So I had to send my husband out to the supermarket. Sakai is a great artist but no cook. He didn't know which potato to buy, so he came back with five bags—russet potatoes, red potatoes, Idaho potatoes, yams, etc. I realized I hadn't been specific enough.

Potatoes can be fun and varied in taste. Here's a potato salad that is Japanese in flavor but still American enough to serve with steaks or Southern-fried chicken. Use any of your favorite potatoes (although yams might be a bit too sweet).

1 pound potatoes (any type)
1 small carrot
2 ounces string beans
1 boneless chicken breast (optional)
1 tablespoon sake
1 tablespoon cornstarch
  salt
  pepper

DRESSING
2 tablespoons roasted sesame seeds
4 tablespoons mayonnaise
2 teaspoons rice vinegar
2 teaspoons soy sauce
1 teaspoon sugar

Peel potatoes and carrot and cut into strips, about ½ inch by 2½ inches by ¼ inch.

Remove ends of string beans and cut them into pieces 2½ inches long.

In a medium-size pot, boil water over high heat. Boil string beans for 2 minutes, then add carrot and potato strips. Boil for 4 more minutes and remove from heat. Drain. Chill.

Slice chicken thinly into pieces the same size as the vegetables. Sprinkle with sake and cornstarch and toss to coat. Bring water to a boil in a medium-size pot. Drop the chicken into the hot water and cook for 2 minutes. Remove from water and season with salt and pepper. Chill.

To make dressing, pound roasted sesame seeds with a Japanese mortar and pestle for 3 minutes to make a paste (or use the store-bought variety). Add mayonnaise, vinegar, soy sauce, and sugar.

To serve, toss chilled chicken and vegetables with dressing. Serve in a medium-size bowl.

SERVE WITH Red Wine Steaks
Icicle Radish with Lemon
Sauce

SNOW-COVERED MOUNTAIN SALAD

(SHIRA-AE)
4 SERVINGS

The gentle taste of tofu makes a wonderful dressing for salads. This dish uses carrot, shiitake mushrooms, and konnyaku, but you can combine just about any raw or cooked vegetables on earth. The ingredients are tossed with the white tofu dressing and mounded to resemble a snow-covered mountain.

3 *deep-fried tofu pouches (age)*
3 *large dried shiitake mushrooms*
½ *cake konnyaku*
1 *medium carrot*
1½ *cups dashi*
2 *tablespoons mirin*
1 *tablespoon mild soy sauce*

TOFU DRESSING
1 *(12-ounce) cake firm tofu*
2 *tablespoons white sesame seeds*
1 *tablespoon sugar*
2 *tablespoons mirin*
½ *tablespoon mild soy sauce or*
   ½ *tablespoon white miso*
   salt

Blanch deep-fried tofu in hot water. Drain and slice ⅛ inch thick.

Soften shiitake mushrooms in water for 20 minutes. Remove stems and slice thinly, about ⅛ inch thick.

Blanch konnyaku in hot water. Drain and slice ⅛ inch thick.

Peel carrot and slice into rectangles, about the same size as the konnyaku pieces.

In a medium saucepan, combine dashi, mirin, and soy sauce and bring to a boil. Add konnyaku, mushrooms, and carrot and simmer until most of the liquid is absorbed by the vegetables. Remove from heat and cool completely.

Blanch tofu in hot water. Drain and pat dry with paper towels. Wrap tofu in a clean cotton cloth and place a dinner plate on top to press out water. Let stand under the plate for 20 minutes. Press tofu through a fine sieve to purée.

Roast sesame seeds in a dry frying pan over low heat, moving the pan to keep the sesame seeds from burning. When the sesame seeds begin to pop, remove from heat and transfer to a Japanese mortar. Grind sesame seeds to make paste. Add puréed tofu and remaining dressing ingredients and mix well. (You may make this dressing up to 3 hours ahead of time.)

Just before serving, combine the vegetables with the dressing and toss well. Arrange small mounds of salad in individual dishes or bowls and sprinkle with black sesame seeds.

BASIC WHITE RICE

BROWN RICE

RICE WITH PEAS

RICE WITH CHESTNUTS (KURI-GOHAN)

BROILED MOCHI CAKES

CHAPTER 6

RICE & NOODLES

PANDA'S DELIGHT (TAKENOKO-GOHAN)

FIVE-EYE RICE (GOMOKU-GOHAN)

RICE WITH CRAB AND SHIITAKE MUSHROOMS

RICE WITH HIJIKI SEAWEED (HIJIKI-GOHAN)

BETTER-THAN-EVER FRIED RICE

FRIED RICE WITH TOFU AND VEGETABLES

HAND-WRAPPED SOMEN NOODLES

CHILLED KISHIMEN NOODLES

MORI-SOBA

HOT MOON-GAZING SOBA

YAKI-SOBA NOODLES

NABE-YAKI-UDON

KAMO-NAMBAN

SUMMER NOODLES (CHUKA-SOBA)

PASTA WITH CLAM SAUCE

PASTA WITH SQUID AND COD ROE

IN THE WEST, rice and noodles are generally served as side dishes. In Japan they are often the basis of a satisfying main dish. In Japan, rice is usually offered toward the end of a meal, perhaps with a small salad or a taste of marinated vegetables. So rice becomes something delicious to look forward to, a final satisfying taste to clear the palate. "Gohan, gohan, Mama!" we kids would yell. And she would bring the rice.

My grandmother used to tell us kids: "If you leave one grain of rice in your bowl, you'll go blind." We knew we wouldn't go blind if we wasted a little rice. Now that I'm grown up, somewhat, I can see that Grandmother was speaking the truth, at least metaphorically.

Three kinds of Japanese rice grow in California and are generally available in American supermarkets. They are brown rice, medium- or short-grain white rice, and sweet rice. All are of superior quality. My mother used to take California-grown rice back to Japan as a special gift. Americans can definitely get the finest kinds of Japanese rice.

The pearly-white short-grain rice is preferred by most Japanese; it is shiny, tasteful, and fluffy. For health, a minority of Japanese, including my parents, insist on brown rice—which is nutty in flavor, unpolished, and therefore richer in vitamins. Sweet rice is not sweet, as its name suggests. Rather, it is opaque in color and a bit more sticky than short-grain white rice. Pounded sweet rice (mochi-gome) is served in Japan on happy occasions like birthdays, weddings, and anniversaries. It stretches like bubble gum and is fun to eat.

You can enjoy Japanese steamed rice plain, like American long-grain rice, or with a variety of colors and aromas from seasonal vegetables, meats, and seafood. For blustery winter days you don't necessarily have to resort to a can of cream of chicken or tomato soup. With leftover rice you can cook a wonderful Japanese rice soup called okayu. It is made by simply simmering day-old rice with broth, soy sauce, and sake. A raw egg dropped in, with chopped vegetables, adds rich flavor. Okayu was a special meal I looked forward to when sick in bed, or when I selfishly wanted to be treated better than my brothers and sisters.

Noodles in Japan are what hamburgers and hot dogs are to Americans. They are easy to make, fast to eat, nutritious for the body, and one seems never to tire of them. Besides the several native types, the Japanese are also partial to Chinese noodles and to Italian pasta of all kinds—especially spaghetti—which is lovingly transmogrified into delicious, very Japanese dishes.

At Japanese train stations you see rows of people at noodle stands, slurping these hot delicacies for breakfast. In school cafeterias, ramen (Chinese) noodles are one of the most common and best-liked dishes among schoolkids. At night in the cities, portable shops on wheels, with glowing red lanterns, invite customers to munch a snack of noodles before they go home.

The Japanese theory of noodle eating differs from most other ethnic noodle practices. Japanese noodles are generally served plain, without any sauce on top, unlike, for instance, Italian spaghetti dishes. Instead, a separate bowl of dipping sauce is served on the side. The dipping sauce may be made of such ingredients as soy sauce, mirin, broth, and vegetable condiments. Or the noodles may be served in a hot broth, as a soup, to be eaten quickly before they have time to go limp.

Unlike Western noodles, Japanese noodles rarely contain eggs. These are the principal varieties of Japanese noodles:

SOBA NOODLES: Made of buckwheat flour, wheat flour, and potato starch. They are thin and brown in color. They are available in the

U.S. in dried or fresh forms. Noodles are a serious matter in Japan. Good soba restaurants are found by word of mouth. Soba noodles are much eaten in northern Japan. The people of Tokyo are particular soba lovers, and the best soba can be found there. Soba noodles are traditionally eaten on New Year's Eve for good luck.

CHA-SOBA NOODLES: Part of the soba noodle family, but green in color because they are flavored with green tea. Marvelous!

UDON NOODLES: These come from the southern part of Japan. Made of wheat flour, they are white, thick, and round. Udon noodles are wonderful winter food, served mostly in a hot broth with egg, meat, vegetables, and seafood.

KISHIMEN NOODLES: Like udon noodles but wide and flat. They are prepared much the same way as udon noodles.

HIYAMUGI NOODLES: Fine and white, used mostly in cold summer dishes.

SOMEN NOODLES: The finest and thinnest of all noodles. Served mostly in cold summer dishes, often afloat in ice water with ice cubes (nothing more seasonal than that). My associate Lou Stoumen thought his first bowl looked strange. But after tasting, he slurped up two portions.

CHINESE NOODLES: Japanese love Chinese noodles, which are somewhat richer in flavor. Ramen noodles, the most common Chinese noodles, are served in a broth. Chinese yaki-soba noodles are also popular in Japan. They are the equivalent of chow mein noodles. You can buy both types of Chinese noodles in the U.S., fresh or dried. There are also packaged ramen noodles that are pre-seasoned and precooked. They steal the fun out of cooking, but sometimes when you are not up to the task they will suffice.

ITALIAN NOODLES: They are as popular as Chinese noodles but slight modifications are made, in seasonings, to suit the Japanese taste. Soy sauce and sake can be the main seasoning, in place of oregano, garlic, and tomato. Shiitake mushrooms may be used instead of regular mushrooms.

Tips on Preparing Noodles

In wintertime, Japanese enjoy eating noodles that are piping hot—so hot you have to blow at the noodles each time you carry them to your mouth and then maybe grab for cold water. So hot that you end up making a big slurping sound when bringing the noodles to your mouth with chopsticks. Sipping and slurping, however, are permitted. Making noise is inevitable, and fun. In summertime, you would want just the opposite—cold noodles. Put ice cubes in the serving bowl to chill the dish and the noodles.

There are two basic methods for cooking Japanese noodles. Most fresh noodles (udon, chow mein, or yaki-soba) can simply be cooked in rapidly boiling water until just tender. To test for doneness, take a noodle out of the water and cut it in half. If there is a hard, opaque core it needs another minute or two. To cook dried noodles, like udon, soba, or somen, place the noodles in a large pot of boiling water. When the water returns to a boil, add half cup of cold water (this keeps the water from boiling over). When the water boils again, check for doneness, repeating the process once again if more cooking time is still needed. Whichever method is used, do be sure not to overcook the noodles; they should be *al dente,* never mushy.

Preheating or prechilling the bowls in which the noodles are served is a good way to prevent them from going limp. Noodles are eaten quickly and consumed in generous quantities, with lots of condiments such as grated gingerroot, sesame seeds, Japanese horse-radish (wasabi), shiso plant, and chopped green onions.

BASIC WHITE RICE
3 CUPS COOKED RICE

1½ cups short-grain white rice
1½ cups plus 4 tablespoons water

Wash the rice with water by swishing and swirling with your hands or a wooden spoon. Drain the opaque water. This washing removes the powdery surface film from the rice.

Pour the rice and measured water into a medium flat-bottomed pot with a tight-fitting lid. Let stand for 20 minutes to 3 hours.

Cover the pot, turn on the heat, and bring to a full boil. *Don't uncover while cooking.* You will hear the rice dancing.

Reduce heat to low and simmer for 15 minutes. Keep the lid on. You will hear the rice hissing.

Remove the pot from the heat and let stand, *covered,* for 10 minutes. This allows the rice to steam itself.

Now remove the lid. With a damp wooden spoon, or Japanese shamoji paddle, toss the rice lightly in the pot. This gentle tossing is important. It allows steam and air to circulate through the pot, giving uniform texture to each portion.

Serve in individual rice bowls.

NOTE: Automatic electric rice cookers are now available in most Oriental food markets and American cookery stores. Most Japanese now cook rice in these devices to save time and work. I use one myself.

To make rice in an electric rice cooker, follow the same steps of washing and soaking the rice as you would for cooking in a pot. Turn on the switch and forget about it until the switch goes off. If you are a rice lover, invest in an electric cooker. They cost about as much as a good electric toaster but pretty nearly guarantee properly cooked rice every time.

BROWN RICE
3 CUPS COOKED RICE

1 cup short-grain brown rice
2½ cups water

Combine brown rice and water in a heavy flat-bottomed medium-size pot. Let the rice soak for 1 to 3 hours.

Turn on the heat and bring to a boil. Keep the lid on tightly while cooking. You will hear the rice dancing.

Reduce the heat. Simmer for 40 minutes. You will now hear the rice hissing.

Remove from the heat. With the lid on the pot, let the rice steam itself for 10 minutes.

With a damp wooden spoon or a Japanese shamoji paddle, toss the rice lightly in the pot. Serve in individual bowls.

OPTIONAL: Sprinkle a mixture of sea salt and black sesame seeds over the rice for added flavor and color.

RICE WITH PEAS
6 SERVINGS

When you are bored with plain white rice and want something cheerful and simple, mame-gohan can be a perfect dish. Use fresh peas if at all possible, or substitute fresh lima beans for the peas.

¼ cup sweet rice
2 cups short-grain white rice
2½ cups water
2 teaspoons mirin
½ teaspoon salt
1 cup fresh or frozen (thawed) peas

Wash the rice and drain. Let the rice soak in measured water at least 1 hour.

In a medium, lidded, heavy pot, combine all ingredients except the peas. Bring to a boil over medium heat.

Reduce the heat. Simmer for another 12 minutes. Then raise the heat to high again for 20 seconds, while adding the peas. Stir lightly. Remove from the heat immediately and let stand, *covered,* for 10 minutes.

Serve in individual rice bowls.

SERVE WITH Salmon Teriyaki or
Teriyaki Okra Chicken

RICE WITH CHESTNUTS
(KURI-GOHAN)
4 TO 6 SERVINGS

As a child I was nicknamed "Kuri-chan," which means "chestnut girl." I love chestnuts. A big chestnut tree still grows in front of the main entrance to my grandmother's house. During fall chestnut season, Grandmother would sweep the entrance area and water it. Then she would gently shake the chestnut tree to drop a few chestnuts to the ground. When guests came to visit, they would admire the beautifully fallen chestnuts on the ground and exclaim, "Fall has really come!" It was during that season that Grandmother made my favorite Rice with Chestnuts. This recipe is hers.

12 raw chestnuts
¼ cup sweet rice
2 cups short-grain white rice
1 teaspoon salt
2½ cups water
2 tablespoons mirin
1 tablespoon lemon peel strips

Soak chestnuts in water for 3 hours; this helps soften the chestnuts and makes them easier to peel. Carefully peel each chestnut, cut them in half and soak in salted water overnight to remove bitterness. Drain off the water.

Wash rice in water. Drain. Let soak in fresh water 30 minutes to 1 hour.

Pour rice, salt, drained chestnuts, and measured water into a large heavy pot. Cover and bring to a boil. Reduce heat. Add mirin and simmer for 6 minutes.

Lower heat further and simmer for another 10 minutes. Turn heat to high for 15 seconds, then remove from heat immediately and let stand, *covered,* to steam for 10 minutes.

Garnish with thinly sliced lemon peel, used sparingly. Serve in individual rice bowls.

SERVE WITH Basic Miso Soup
Black-and-White Trifle
Steak Miso

BROILED MOCHI CAKES
4 TO 6 SERVINGS

On ear-freezing winter days, Grandmother would broil mochi cakes on an indoor hibachi while we children gathered around the kotastu (a foot warmer) to watch and salivate. The mochi—a specially prepared sweet rice available in Japanese shops—would puff up like popcorn and stretch like toasted marshmallows. Great fun for kids—and adults, too.

2 sheets nori seaweed (raw or toasted)
6 to 8 mochi patties
1 cup grated daikon radish
   soy sauce

Cut toasted nori seaweed into 4 by 4-inch squares. If your nori sheets are raw, first toast them by gently moving each sheet by hand over a medium flame of the gas range until nori turns slightly green. Toast both sides. This takes only about 10 seconds.

Broil the mochi patties. Turn them occasionally until they begin to soften and toast. Allow them to puff up.

Remove patties from the broiler while steaming hot. Flatten gently with chopsticks and wrap each patty with a square of nori seaweed.

Serve immediately with grated daikon radish and, to taste, a bit of soy sauce.

Broiled mochi cakes must be eaten piping hot.

The first time you make this recipe, *please* do it with nori seaweed. I want you and your eaters to enjoy that special mochi-nori taste. On later occasions, when your kids are already hooked on mochi, you might want to experiment with variations. Instead of using nori seaweed, try wrapping your mochi cakes with pieces of fried bacon—or ham—or smoked salmon.

PANDA'S DELIGHT
(TAKENOKO-GOHAN)
4 TO 6 SERVINGS

Bamboo shoots are spring vegetables, edible only until the tenth day after they have emerged from the ground. After that, they grow green, hard, and tall and become beautiful trees in Oriental paintings. Bamboo shoots are the special diet demanded by the Chinese pandas, which also know they must be eaten in their earliest growing season or not at all. Here's a delicious bamboo shoots and rice dish for humans. Serve it, if you wish, with a clear suimono broth and Steamed Buddha's Hands (page 196).

2 cups short-grain white rice
1½ cups water
½ cup dashi
1 tablespoon sake
1½ tablespoons soy sauce
1 teaspoon sugar

SEASONED BAMBOO SHOOTS
¾ cup boiled bamboo shoots
½ cup dashi
1 teaspoon soy sauce
¼ teaspoon salt
1 teaspoon sugar

Wash the rice and let stand in measured water for 20 minutes to 2 hours.

To prepare seasoned bamboo shoots, slice the shoots into thin strips about 1 inch long. Combine dashi, soy sauce, salt, and sugar, and bring to a boil. Reduce heat and add the bamboo shoots. Simmer until the liquid is almost completely absorbed by the shoots, about 5 minutes.

In a medium-size heavy pot, combine rice, seasoned bamboo shoots and their liquid, dashi broth, soy sauce, and sugar, and stir the rice mixture with a wooden spoon or chopsticks.

Cook as for Basic White Rice (page 82).

FIVE-EYE RICE

(GOMOKU-GOHAN)
4 SERVINGS

Almost every rice-loving country has its own version of paella—rice cooked with vegetables, meat, and seafood. The Japanese version is called gomoku-gohan, which can be translated into five-eye rice. The vegetables and chicken are cut into chopstick pieces, all approximately the same size. The chopping process can be rhythmic and contemplative. You will want five eyes to enjoy this colorful dish.

2¼ cups short-grain white rice
1½ cups water
 ½ medium carrot
 3 dried shiitake mushrooms
 4 ounces bamboo shoots
 ½ cup burdock root or ½ small rutabaga
 1 teaspoon rice vinegar
 ½ cake konnyaku
 5 ounces boneless chicken breast or thigh
 1 tablespoon vegetable oil
 1 cup dashi
 2 tablespoons soy sauce
 1 tablespoon sugar
 ⅓ teaspoon salt
 2 tablespoons sake
 1 ounce peas
 1 sheet nori seaweed, toasted

Wash the rice in water. Drain and let stand with the measured water in an electric rice cooker or a heavy, medium-size saucepan for 30 minutes.

Cut the carrot into ¼-inch cubes. Soften shiitake mushrooms in water for 30 minutes. Drain and cut shiitake mushrooms into ¼-inch slices.

Blanch the bamboo shoots and cube. (Canned bamboo shoots are already cooked; blanching freshens them and removes odor.)

Wash the burdock root or rutabaga and shave it with a vegetable peeler to achieve 1-inch strips. (If using burdock, do not discard the skin, because it is delicious.) Soak shavings in water with vinegar for 15 minutes. Drain.

Cut the chicken into ¼-inch pieces.

Blanch the konnyaku and slice into ¼-inch rectangles. (The blanching freshens it and removes odor.)

In a medium saucepan, heat the oil over medium heat. Combine bamboo shoots, carrots, mushrooms, burdock, chicken, and konnyaku and stir fry for 2 minutes. Add dashi and bring to a boil. Remove surface film and add soy sauce, sugar, and salt; simmer for 5 minutes. Remove from heat and drain, reserving liquid.

Add water to the reserved liquid to measure 1 cup. Add liquid, chicken, seasoned vegetables, and sake to the rice and cook as you would Basic White Rice (page 82). Add the peas during the last 3 to 5 minutes of cooking.

Cut seaweed into thin 2-inch strips.

Serve in individual rice bowls, garnished with strips of nori seaweed.

RICE WITH CRAB AND SHIITAKE MUSHROOMS

4 SERVINGS

This is a very colorful dish that, with a simple soup, makes a filling, simple-to-prepare meal.

2¼ cups short-grain white rice
  6 ounces cooked crab, fresh or frozen
  2 tablespoons sake
  5 medium dried shiitake mushrooms
2¼ cups dashi
  1 teaspoon salt
  1 teaspoon soy sauce
  1 konbu seaweed strip, 2 inches long

EGG GARNISH

2 eggs
1 tablespoon sugar
¼ teaspoon salt
1 tablespoon sake
1 teaspoon vegetable oil

Wash rice in water and let stand in water for 30 minutes. Drain and let stand for an additional 30 minutes.

Shred crab meat and sprinkle with 1 tablespoon sake.

Soften shiitake mushrooms in water for 30 minutes. Remove stems and slice into thin strips.

Transfer the rice to a heavy medium-size pot or electric rice cooker. Add dashi, remaining sake, salt, soy sauce, and konbu as well as the crab and shiitake mushrooms, and cook as you would Basic White Rice (page 82).

In the meantime, make egg garnish. Beat the eggs in a bowl and add sugar, salt, and sake. Heat a lightly oiled frying pan and scramble the eggs over medium heat, using 5 or 6 chopsticks bunched together, so that the eggs become as fine as cookie crumbs.

Just before serving, remove konbu from the rice. Toss and serve in individual rice bowls, garnished with a sprinkling of egg.

SERVE WITH Bamboo and Wakame
        Suimono

RICE WITH HIJIKI SEAWEED

(HIJIKI-GOHAN)
4 TO 6 SERVINGS

This dish is a surprise delight for those not accustomed to eating seaweed. The flavor of hijiki seaweed is tasty and mild, and it is very high in nutrients. My mother says, "Hijiki seaweed helps you stay young and always have shiny black hair." It's supposed to be especially good for the complexion.

2 cups short-grain white rice
2 cups plus 3 tablespoons water
⅓ cup dried black hijiki seaweed
2 slices deep-fried tofu pouches (abura-age or usu-age)
1½ cups dashi or chicken broth
1 tablespoon sugar
2 tablespoons soy sauce
1 tablespoon sake
red pickled ginger (optional)

Wash rice and let stand in measured water for 20 minutes. Cook it following the recipe for Basic White Rice (page 82).

Wash hijiki seaweed in water. Soak it for 10 minutes, then transfer to a medium-size pot and boil for 15 minutes over medium heat; drain.

Cut fried tofu into thin strips about 1 inch long.

In a medium pot, combine fried tofu strips, broth, hijiki seaweed, and the seasonings. Simmer over low heat for 15 minutes, until the tofu and hijiki seaweed have absorbed most of the liquid.

Toss the cooked rice with hijiki seaweed and fried tofu mixture and serve hot.

A pretty and delicious finishing touch is to sprinkle with red pickled ginger diced into 1-inch bits.

BETTER-THAN-EVER FRIED RICE

4 TO 6 SERVINGS

There are dishes in all national cuisines that are said to taste better on the second or third day. Here is such a recipe, which uses leftover rice. It's easy on the budget, quick to prepare, and has its own special tastiness. My mother used to cook 5 cups of rice a day to feed seven of us. If any was left over, she'd serve fried rice the next day, or as a fine after-school snack. Often she would cook extra rice so she could plan for sure on Better-Than-Ever Fried Rice the next day.

4 tablespoons light vegetable oil
½ cup minced green onions or plain onions
1 cup boneless chicken or pork (or beef,
    crab, or shrimp), cut into ¼-inch cubes
½ cup peas, fresh or frozen
3 cups day-old cooked rice
1 egg
2 tablespoons soy sauce
    pepper
2 tablespoons sake
    salt

Heat oil in a frying pan (or in a wok; this was originally a Chinese dish). Add green onions and sauté over medium heat until they are limp and bright green. Add meat and peas. Continue stirring for 1 minute.

Mix in the rice. Stir lightly. Beat the egg and swirl it into the mixture with a fork or chopsticks. Add soy sauce, pepper, sake, and salt. Cook 1 minute. Toss lightly.

Serve hot.

FRIED RICE WITH TOFU AND VEGETABLES
4 SERVINGS

The addition of tofu to fried rice makes this dish more nutritious than plain fried rice.

1 (6-ounce) cake firm tofu
3 fresh mushrooms
¼ bell pepper, seeded and membranes
    removed
1 tablespoon sesame oil
2 tablespoons salad oil
½ cup chopped green onions
2 tablespoons soy sauce
1 tablespoon sake or mirin
3 cups cooked rice (freshly cooked or
    day-old)
    salt

Press water from tofu, following instructions on page 102. Dice tofu into ½-inch cubes. Dice mushrooms about the same size as tofu. Do the same with the bell pepper.

Heat sesame oil and salad oil in a skillet. Sauté tofu, mushrooms, onions, and bell pepper. Add soy sauce, sake, and rice. Stir well over medium heat.

Salt to taste. When thoroughly heated, remove from heat and serve immediately.

HAND-WRAPPED SOMEN NOODLES
4 SERVINGS

Fine noodles need no mask. They can be tasty plain, cold or hot. This noodle dish is distinguished by its special presentation. The cooked noodles are taken from the pot in small bunches and wrapped gently around the back of your hand, then gently transferred to a large serving platter. Your eaters take their own servings from the platter with chopsticks, bunch by bunch, dipping each bunch into an individual bowl of delicious dipping broth, and then right into their mouths.

Seafood and vegetables go perfectly with these wrapped somen noodles. Together they make a special feast for a summertime lunch or brunch. The broth can be kept chilled in the refrigerator for a week.

DIPPING BROTH

⅔ cup bonito flakes or 2 teaspoons instant dashi powder
⅜ cup soy sauce
⅜ cup mirin
1½ cups water

12 medium shrimp
   salt
   lemon
½ European cucumber
2 small fish fillets (flounder, sole, cod, or snapper)
2 tablespoons sake
   potato starch or cornstarch
1 pound dried somen noodles
1 lemon
½ cup chopped green onions

To make broth, bring bonito flakes, soy sauce, mirin, and measured water to a boil and then simmer for 4 minutes. Filter the broth through a sieve. Discard bonito flakes. Chill until ready to use.

Clean shrimp, removing shells and veins. Bring water to a boil in a small saucepan and add shrimp. Let cook for 2 minutes and then transfer to chilled water to cool. Drain, sprinkle shrimp with salt and lemon juice, and chill.

Slice cucumber into matchsticks.

Slice fish fillets into bite-size pieces. Marinate them in sake for 10 minutes. Pat dry, then coat lightly with potato starch. Bring water to a boil in a medium saucepan and add the fish. Let simmer for 4 minutes, or until cooked, then transfer to chilled water to cool. Drain and chill.

Cook noodles. Rinse in cold water; drain well.

To arrange noodles, wrap a small bunch gently around your hand as you would yarn. Gently transfer the noodle skeins to a large plate or bowl. Repeat this process with another bunch of noodles, one set of wrapped noodles slightly overlapping the next. Chill in the refrigerator if you do not plan to serve immediately.

Just before serving, put some ice cubes on top of the noodles as decoration. Slice the lemon thinly and scatter the slices over the noodles.

Serve each diner ½ cup broth in a small dipping bowl. Let them help themselves to teaspoons of chopped green onions to add to the broth. Take some noodles, dip them in the broth, and slurp. Serve family-style the cucumbers, shrimp, and fish, to be alternated between mouthfuls of noodles. You may dip them in the sauce, too.

SERVE WITH Honey Squash Salad

CHILLED KISHIMEN NOODLES
4 SERVINGS

Here's a summer dish that is balanced in nutrition. It is served with a sesame dipping sauce.

SESAME DIPPING SAUCE
 3 tablespoons sesame seeds
 ¾ cup dashi
 ¼ cup mirin
 ¼ cup soy sauce

 1 pound dried kishimen noodles
 1 pound boneless chicken
 2 tablespoons sake
 2 medium tomatoes
 ½ European cucumber or 2 kirby cucumbers
 ½ cup chopped green onions (green part only)
 4 to 6 shiso leaves (optional)

To make sesame seed sauce, roast sesame seeds in a dry frying pan until fragrant and grind them with a mortar and pestle. Combine liquid ingredients in a saucepan and bring to a boil over medium heat. Cool broth and add the ground sesame seeds. Chill.

Boil kishimen noodles for 4 to 6 minutes, until cooked—al dente, of course.

Marinate chicken in sake for 10 minutes. Put the chicken in a bowl and steam over high heat for 20 minutes. Cool completely and shred the chicken into 2-inch pieces.

Slice tomatoes ¼ inch thick and arrange in a large basket or on a plate. Do the same with the cucumber. Arrange green onions next to tomatoes and cucumber—on the shiso leaves, if you wish. Put the cooked noodles next to the vegetables. Place chicken on a serving dish.

Provide a small bowl with ½ cup sauce for each diner. Pass around the serving platter of noodles, chicken, and vegetables. The morsels and noodles should be dunked in the sauce and eaten.

MORI-SOBA
4 SERVINGS

These beige buckwheat noodles are so tasty that they do not need any elaborate accompaniments. Just a few strips of crisp toasted nori seaweed and chopped green onions are enough. This is a traditional summertime dish that Japanese eat in large quantities. Cha-soba (tea noodles), made with green tea powder, also work well in this recipe.

1 pound dried or 1½ pounds fresh soba
  noodles
½ sheet nori seaweed, toasted

BROTH
1⅛ cups water
¾ cup bonito flakes
1 tablespoon sugar
¼ cup soy sauce
1½ ounces mirin

GARNISH
⅔ cup chopped green onions
2 tablespoons peeled and grated gingerroot
1 tablespoon wasabi paste

Cook noodles. Rinse well and chill.
  Cut nori seaweed into thin strips, ⅛ inch by 2 inches.

In a medium saucepan, combine all the ingredients for the broth and bring to a boil. Then lower heat to medium and cook for an additional 3 minutes. Remove from heat and cool. Strain broth through a sieve. Chill.

To serve, place a quarter portion of the noodles on each basket or plate. Serve the broth in small deep bowls, about ⅓ cup per serving. Serve the garnishes on the side, to be passed around while slurping.

OPTIONAL: You may add 1 teaspoon sesame oil to the broth, for fragrance.

HOT MOON-GAZING SOBA
4 SERVINGS

A raw egg is broken into the middle of this hot noodle dish just before serving so your guests may gaze at the beautiful egg yolk moon before it disappears in the dark broth. The heat of the broth will partially cook the egg as you eat. Try it!

1 pound dried or 1½ pounds fresh soba
  noodles
4 dried shiitake mushrooms
8 ounces spinach
  Kamo-namban broth (page 95)
2 green onions, chopped
4 eggs

Cook noodles; drain and rinse under cold water. Drain well.
  Soften shiitake mushrooms in water for 30 minutes. Remove stems and slice thinly.
  Cook spinach in boiling water for 1 minute and rinse under cold water. Gently

squeeze out the water and cut the bunched leaves into 4 sections.

Heat noodle broth.

Arrange noodles, spinach, mushrooms, and green onions in individual soup or donburi bowls, leaving room in the center of the bowl for the egg.

Pour the piping-hot broth carefully over the noodles and vegetables, then drop an egg into the middle of each serving. Serve immediately.

YAKI-SOBA NOODLES
4 SERVINGS

When the annual summer festivals are held in Japanese temples, the delicious smell and smoke of yaki-soba noodles takes over. Kids dress up in yukata (a summer cotton kimono) and indulge themselves, trying the delicacies at each food stand. They take home goldfish, paper balloons, and other prizes from the games they play.

2 dried shiitake mushrooms
8 ounces boneless pork, chicken, or beef
2 cabbage leaves
1 carrot
1 green pepper
1½ pounds fresh Chinese-style chow mein noodles or yaki-soba noodles
4 tablespoons vegetable oil
1 tablespoon peeled and chopped gingerroot
½ green onion, chopped
1 cup bean sprouts
4 to 6 tablespoons tonkatsu sauce

Soften shiitake mushrooms in water for 30 minutes, remove stems, and slice thinly into julienne strips.

Cut meat, cabbage, carrot, and green pepper into julienne strips, about 2½ inches long.

Boil noodles in a large kettle for 4 to 8 minutes, depending on the thickness of the noodles. They should be *al dente*, of course. Drain and rinse under cold water.

Heat 2 tablespoons oil in a large skillet. Add ginger and noodles and sauté for 2 minutes. Remove the noodles with a slotted spoon and set aside.

Heat remaining 2 tablespoons oil in the same skillet. Sauté all the vegetables and meat except bean sprouts. Add noodles and bean sprouts and mix all ingredients together over high heat, about 1 minute. Add the sauce and mix over high heat for an additional minute. Remove from heat and serve immediately.

NABE-YAKI-UDON
4 SERVINGS

You can put anything you wish in this versatile noodle broth. This recipe uses tempura leftovers from the night before. The tempura gets dunked in the hot broth, spreading its flavor and toasty aroma. It is a wholesome dish.

4 dried shiitake mushrooms
4 servings of fresh udon noodles, about 6
    ounces each, or 1 pound dried udon
    noodles
4 deep-fried tofu pouches (usu-age)
3 ounces steamed fish cake
1 green onion
12 pieces Shrimp Tempura (see page 171)
    or Vegetable Tempura (see page 131)
4 eggs

BROTH
4½ cups dashi
4 tablespoons soy sauce
1½ tablespoons sugar
1 tablespoon mirin
½ teaspoon salt

Soften shiitake mushrooms in water for 30 minutes. Remove stems and make a cross on the cap with a knife.

Cook the noodles until they begin to look translucent. Drain and rinse under cold water.

Blanch tofu pouches in hot water. Slice each piece in half.

Slice steamed fish cake ¼ inch thick, using the wave cut (see page 14).

Slice green onion into quarters.

Bring all the broth ingredients to a boil over medium heat.

Serve udon noodles in large, deep individual bowls, preferably donburi bowls.* Arrange tempura shrimp, shiitake mushrooms, steamed fish cake, tofu pouches, and green onions in each bowl. Pour hot broth. Drop an unbeaten egg into the center of the broth. Serve immediately.

* Deep bowls, called "donburi," are ideal for noodles in broth, cereal, and salads. You can buy donburi bowls in Japanese hardware and grocery stores.

KAMO-NAMBAN
4 SERVINGS

Noodle delivery service is as common in Japan as pizza delivery in America. The noodle man carries the noodle bowls on a tray tied to the back of his bicycle and rides through the busy streets of Tokyo to deliver the noodles before they become cold. I was always amazed at how the noodle man could manage this trip without spilling any of the delicious hot broth. The noodles are served in donburi bowls.

BROTH
4½ cups dashi broth
1 tablespoon sake
2 tablespoons mirin
4 tablespoons soy sauce
½ teaspoon salt

8 ounces boneless chicken breast
1 carrot
4 servings of fresh udon noodles, about 6
    ounces each, or 1 pound dried udon
    noodles
2 green onions, chopped
    Japanese dried chili pepper (optional)

Bring all the broth ingredients to a boil in a medium saucepan. Drop in chicken and carrots and simmer for 3 minutes. Keep warm.

Cut chicken into bite-size morsels. Peel and slice carrot diagonally, about ¼ inch thick.

In a separate saucepan, cook the noodles until they begin to look translucent. Drain and rinse under cold water. Serve in large individual bowls.

Pour hot broth, chicken, and vegetables over the noddles. Sprinkle with green onions and chili pepper and serve immediately.

SUMMER NOODLES

(CHUKA-SOBA)
4 SERVINGS

A summertime delight. Chinese chow mein noodles are used in this dish. While authentic Chinese cold noodles are commonly served with a thick sesame paste sauce, Japanese-style Chinese summer noodles are served with a much lighter broth that contains a dash of fragrant sesame oil. This dish is a nice substitute for chef's salads and cold pastas.

1½ pounds fresh chow mein noodles
1 large squid
12 ounces boneless steamed chicken (page 184)
1 carrot
½ European cucumber
3 ounces steamed fish cake (kamaboko)
1 Egg Pancake (page 158)

BROTH
1 cup chicken or beef broth
6 tablespoons rice vinegar
6 tablespoons soy sauce
3 tablespoons sugar
2 teaspoons sesame oil
2 teaspoons ginger juice (page 64)

1 tablespoon Oriental or regular prepared mustard

Cook the noodles. Drain and rinse under cold water. (If you plan to serve the noodles later, sprinkle with a teaspoon of sesame oil and refrigerate.)

Wash squid and remove innards, legs, and the flaps that resemble ears. Peel off membrane, rubbing it with a dry cloth. Slit the body open lengthwise. Cut off about 2 inches from the top and discard. Score the outer side diagonally, then turn the squid 90 degrees and score again, to make a grid pattern.

Bring water to a boil in a medium saucepan and cook the squid pieces in rapidly boiling water for 30 seconds. Drain and cut the squid into 2½-inch squares. Cut each square diagonally to make triangles. Chill.

Shred the chicken. Peel carrot and slice into matchsticks, about 2½ inches long. Bring water to a boil in a small saucepan. Cook carrot for 2 minutes. Drain and chill.

Slice cucumber into matchstick pieces and chill. Do the same with steamed fish cakes. Chill.

Slice egg pancake into thin strips, about 2½ inches long. Chill.

Mix all the broth ingredients and chill.

To serve, put the noodles in individual serving plates. Decorate the noodles with the squid, cucumbers, steamed fish cake, chicken, and carrot to make a colorful pattern. Garnish the center with a mound of egg strips. Serve with mustard and chilled broth on the side.

PASTA WITH CLAM SAUCE
4 SERVINGS

The noodles are Italian but the flavor is Japanese. The combination makes a delicious surprise. Use kishimen noodles instead of spaghetti, if you wish.

4 dried shiitake mushrooms
2 green onions
1 green pepper
2 tablespoons vegetable oil
30 littleneck clams, shucked (reserve liquid)
½ cup bamboo shoots
1½ cups clam, dashi, or chicken broth
3 tablespoons soy sauce
3 tablespoons sake
1 teaspoon salt
2 tablespoons cornstarch mixed with 2 tablespoons water
1 pound spaghetti

Heat a large pot of water for cooking the spaghetti.

Soften shiitake mushrooms in water for 30 minutes. Remove stems and slice thinly. Chop green onions and green pepper into small pieces.

In a large skillet over medium heat, heat oil and sauté onions for 1 minute. Then add green pepper, clams, mushrooms, and bamboo shoots and sauté for one more minute.

Add enough broth to the reserved clam liquid to make 1½ cups. Add broth to the vegetables and clams and reduce to a simmer. Add soy sauce, sake, salt, and cornstarch paste. The sauce will become thick when you add the cornstarch. Simmer over low heat for 3 minutes.

Meanwhile, cook the spaghetti in boiling water until *al dente*, approximately 8 to 10 minutes. Ladle the sauce over the hot noodles and serve immediately.

PASTA WITH SQUID AND COD ROE
4 SERVINGS

This is a unique spaghetti dish that has become popular in Japan. It is a great dish for those who want to cut down on the fat and stick to seafoods.

½ sheet nori seaweed, toasted
2 segments cod roe (tarako)
2 tablespoons sake
1 large squid
1 pound spaghetti
2 tablespoons vegetable oil

Heat a large pot of water for cooking spaghetti.

Cut nori seaweed into thin strips, about 2 inches long. Set aside.

Puncture the membrane of the roe and scoop the roe into a small bowl. Add sake and mix with roe. Set aside.

Prepare squid as for Summer Noodles, opposite.

Cook spaghetti in boiling water for 8 to 10 minutes. Drain and rinse under cold water.

Heat a large skillet with oil over medium heat, add spaghetti, and sauté for 2 minutes. Remove from heat and mix with seasoned roe, squid, and nori. Serve immediately.

CHILLED TOFU WITH GINGER SAUCE

BRAISED KOYA-DOFU WITH PEA PODS

COLD-DAY TOFU

VEGETARIAN "CHICKEN" TOFU

DRAGON'S HEAD (HIRYOZU)

CHAPTER 7

TOFU & EGG DISHES

TOFU FROM THE SEA (KENCHIN-MUSHI)

TOFU GRATINÉE

STUFFED TOFU

SCRAMBLED TOFU

TOFU TREASURE BAGS

VEGETARIAN "BURGER"

HEAVENLY OMELETTE

HEAVENLY OMELETTE WITH CHICKEN

EGG TOFU DELIGHT (TAMAGO-DOFU)

EVERYTHING-IN-IT CUSTARD (CHAWAN-MUSHI)

EGG WHITE CUSTARD WITH SHRIMP

POACHED EGGS WITH SNOW PEA PODS

SCRAMBLED EGGS WITH CRAB MEAT

PARENT AND CHILD (OYAKO-DONBURI)

TOFU AND EGGS ARE PERHAPS THE MOST VERSATILE, economical, and healthy foods in Japanese cuisine. Eggs are already your old friends. Tofu is still a wonderful surprise to many cooks and eaters in the West.

Sometimes called bean curd or bean cake, tofu is a pure white food something like yogurt in texture, but more firm, with a gentle mild flavor. It is sold in water-packed containers and is available in most supermarkets as well as ethnic and health food shops. Tofu is made from soybeans that have been pureed, cooked, curdled, and pressed into soft cakes. The nutritional beauty of tofu is that nothing artificial has been added. It is pure protein, full of minerals and vitamins. Unlike meat, tofu is extremely low in fats and cholesterol. And because tofu tends to take on the flavors of the foods it's cooked with, it can marry with many different ingredients. I've even substituted tofu for beef in a winy "tofu bourguignon."

My hometown of Kamakura is an ancient town of strong Zen Buddhist tradition. There is just about one tofu shop for every temple in Kamakura, and there are nearly a hundred temples, so not only the vegetarian monks but people who live in this town get good tofu. Each tofu shop takes pride in the temple it provides with tofu.

Tofu is made at dawn, just as Western-world bakers bake their bread, for early-morning distribution. In Japan, the tofu man comes around each neighborhood on his bicycle (or motorcycle, these days), announcing his coming with a gentle toot of his horn. As kids, we would rush out when he signaled, with an empty bowl in our hands. The tofu man would gently put the tofu in the bowl with water. I felt I was carrying something alive, like a goldfish, when making the short run back to my house.

Tofu should be absolutely fresh. Try to get tofu made on the day of purchase, just like bread. It keeps in the refrigerator for 3 to 4 days, but the flavor does not improve with time. A bad tofu turns sour in taste and cheeselike in texture. After you have opened the sealed water-packed container, drain off the liquid and replace it with fresh water. Change the water daily, as fresh, pure water prolongs tofu's life. Seal the tofu again to keep it free of refrigerator odors. When using deep-fried or broiled tofu, keep it in plastic bags or sealed containers and use as quickly as possible. Here are the various forms in which it can be found:

SILKEN TOFU (kinugoshi-dofu): This is a very soft, smooth tofu used in salads and soups. You must not cook silken tofu for a long time because it is too delicate. The smooth, tapered cakes are available in water-packed 8- to 19-ounce containers. Keeps for several days in the refrigerator.

FIRM TOFU (men-dofu): This is the most popular tofu, a bit firmer, denser than the silken kind. It is also called "cotton-type" tofu and is widely used in sukiyaki and other one-pot dinners. Available water-packed in 8- to 19-ounce containers, it keeps for 3 to 4 days in the refrigerator.

GRILLED TOFU (yaki-dofu): This is firm tofu that has been briefly grilled. It can be used for sukiyaki dishes and casseroles that require long cooking time. Comes in water-packed containers, 8 to 12 ounces. Keeps in the refrigerator 3 to 4 days.

TOFU POUCHES (abura-age or usu-age): Like pita bread, these can be used for many dishes; you slit one end open and it becomes a "pillow," ready to be stuffed with vegetables, rice, or meat. Since they have been deep-fried, blanch them to remove excess oil before cooking. Keeps for 3 to 4 days. Refrigerate in a plastic bag.

DEEP-FRIED TOFU (nama-age or atsu-age): This is a firm tofu that has been deep-fried. Blanch in hot water before use, to remove excess oil. Keeps for 3 to 4 days. Refrigerate in a plastic bag.

TOFU FRITTERS (ganmodoki): This is a deep-fried tofu that contains seaweed and vegetables. Used in one-pot dishes or braised with meat and seaweed. Delicious in salads. Keeps for 3 to 4 days. Sold in plastic wrap. Refrigerate in a plastic bag.

FREEZE-DRIED TOFU (koya-dofu): This is dehydrated tofu that is to be softened in warm water and used pretty much in the same manner as other tofu products. It is slightly spongy and does not have much flavor, but is a great convenience in the kitchen. Cook it with seasonings such as soy sauce, sake, sugar, broth. Since this tofu is freeze-dried, it will keep for years in a cool place. Sold in the U.S. in Japanese stores. The price is high, but it's handy stuff to have when you need it.

How to Press Tofu

Many recipes call for removing some of the moisture from tofu, especially when making dressing for salad or when you plan to simmer it for an extended period. Since tofu contains a lot of moisture, you must press it gently to extract the water. Do not attempt this by hand, as the tofu will crumble. The proper method is to place a flat dinner plate on top of the tofu and let its weight alone press down lightly for about 30 minutes. For even faster results, wrap the tofu in a clean dish or cheese cloth, then place the weight of the dinner plate on top of it. As a result of this pressure, the tofu will become firm, less moist, and easier to cut, cook, and serve.

CHILLED TOFU WITH GINGER SAUCE
4 SERVINGS

This is an instant, refreshing side dish or appetizer that proclaims the spirit of summer. The icy-cold tofu soothes a parched spirit on a hot day.

1 (8-ounce) cake silken tofu
1 tablespoon peeled and grated gingerroot
1 tomato
½ lemon, cut into wedges
1 kirby cucumber
 soy sauce

Cut the tofu into quarters and place the cubes in individual small bowls. Put a dab of grated ginger on top of each cube.

Cut the tomato into 8 wedges. Arrange 2 tomato wedges and 1 lemon wedge in each bowl. Slice the cucumber in half, then lengthwise into quarters, and arrange 2 in each bowl.

Surround the tofu and vegetables with small cocktail ice cubes or cracked ice.

Have a bottle of soy sauce available.

SERVE WITH Okra and Avocado
Cocktail
Chilled Pork Roast

BRAISED KOYA-DOFU WITH PEA PODS
4 SERVINGS

Once an apprentice monk left tofu out overnight in the snow. When he returned the next day , the tofu was frozen. Feeling shameful, the monk tried to figure out a way to use the thawed frozen tofu, and this dish is proof that he succeeded. Today, freeze-dried tofu (koya-dofu) is one of the most delicate tofus of all. You will find it in Japanese grocery stores.

4 cakes freeze-dried tofu (koya-dofu)
1½ cups dashi
1 tablespoon sugar
1 teaspoon salt
1 teaspoon mild soy sauce
2 tablespoons sake
2 tablespoons mirin
20 snow pea pods

Soften koya-dofu in hot water for 30 minutes. Drain and place in cold water. Press out water and cut into quarters.

In a large saucepan combine dashi, sugar, salt, soy sauce, sake, and mirin and bring to a boil. Add tofu and simmer for 15 minutes.

In the meantime, remove strings from pea pods and add to the tofu pot for the last minute of cooking. Remove from heat and let both tofu and pea pods steep in the liquid until ready to serve.

To serve, place 2 or 3 pieces of tofu in a deep bowl for each person. Garnish with pea pods.

SERVE WITH Sashimi
Hijiki Seaweed with Tofu

COLD-DAY TOFU
4 SERVINGS

On a wintry day, serve this dish as you would fried fritters—very hot! It will take the chill away.

2 (8-ounce) cakes deep-fried tofu (atsu-age
    or nama-age)
1 tablespoon peeled and grated gingerroot
½ cup chopped green onions
½ cup grated daikon radish
    soy sauce

Broil the tofu cakes in the broiler or a toaster oven until they are sizzling hot and slightly toasted on both sides.

Cut each cake into 1-inch cubes. Garnish with ginger, green onions, and grated daikon radish.

Serve piping hot with soy sauce on the side.

SERVE WITH Clouds-in-the-Sky Egg
        Suimono
        Watercress Ohi-tashi

VEGETARIAN "CHICKEN" TOFU
4 SERVINGS

When tofu spends a night in your freezer it becomes very firm—almost like chicken in texture. With the right preparation and vegetable accompaniment, your frozen tofu becomes the basis for a delicious alternative to meat.

1 (19-ounce) cake firm tofu
6 small taro potatoes or 3 new potatoes
1 large carrot
1 cake konnyaku
3 tablespoons vegetable oil
4 cups dashi
½ teaspoon salt
3 tablespoons soy sauce
2 tablespoons sugar
2 tablespoons sake

Press water from tofu (see page 102). Place drained tofu cake in a bowl, cover, and freeze overnight.

Defrost tofu the following day till soft. Wrap tofu in cotton cloth or a towel to press out more water, being careful not to crumble tofu. Cut into 1-inch cubes.

Peel potatoes and carrot and slice, using a random cut (see page 15).

Blanch konnyaku in hot water. Cut into 5 pieces crosswise, then cut each piece diagonally to make triangles.

Heat oil in a large pot and sauté potatoes, carrot, and konnyaku for 5 minutes over medium heat. Combine dashi, salt, soy sauce, sugar, and sake and simmer vegetables until they are cooked, about 8 to 10 minutes. Add tofu and simmer with the lid on until the liquid is absorbed.

Serve the stewed tofu and vegetables with their broth in deep bowls, hot or at room temperature.

SERVE WITH Just Vegetable Suimono
        Asparagus with Bonito
        Flakes

DRAGON'S HEAD

(HIRYOZU)

4 SERVINGS

A little work is involved in making the head of this mythical creature, but there is no secret—just tofu, vegetables, and delicate seasonings. The dragon's head is served in a broth and eaten while very hot.

1 (19-ounce) cake firm tofu
5 dried kikurage mushrooms
16 ginkgo nuts, fresh or canned
4 ounces raw shrimp
1 taro potato or 2 ounces yama-no-imo potato
1 egg yolk
½ teaspoon salt
½ teaspoon soy sauce
2 teaspoons sugar
vegetable oil for deep frying

BROTH

1½ cups dashi
2 tablespoons sake
1 tablespoon soy sauce
1 tablespoon mirin
1 tablespoon sugar
¼ teaspoon salt

2 tablespoons peeled and grated gingerroot

Press tofu (see page 102).

Soften mushrooms in water for 30 minutes. Remove stems and mince.

Crack the white shells of the ginkgo nuts and discard. Blanch the nuts in hot water, rinse under cold water, and peel away the brown inner skin. Mince the nuts. If using canned ginkgo nuts, simply blanch them in hot water, rinse in cold water, and mince.

Peel and devein shrimp. Also mince finely.

Peel potato and grate it. It will produce a soupy liquid, which should be reserved for this dish.

Purée tofu in a blender or food processor. Blend in minced mushrooms, ginkgo nuts, shrimp, grated potato and its liquid, egg yolk, salt, soy sauce, and sugar.

To assemble patties, make 8 to 12 equal patties from the tofu mixture, using a large spoon to shape them.

Heat oil in a heavy-bottomed skillet and deep fry patties over medium heat on both sides until they are well browned, about 5 minutes. Drain on paper towels.

While the patties are cooking, combine all broth ingredients in a medium saucepan and bring to a boil over medium heat.

Blanch the deep-fried patties briefly in boiling water to remove excess oil. Drain on paper towels.

Serve 2 to 3 patties per serving in a deep bowl and pour several tablespoons of broth gently into each bowl. The dragon's head must be exposed from the broth. Put a dab of grated ginger in the center of each patty. Repeat with the remaining patties.

SERVE WITH Matsutake Mushroom and
Shrimp Surprise
Spinach Sesame Toss

TOFU FROM THE SEA

(KENCHIN-MUSHI)
4 SERVINGS

Squid, stuffed with finely chopped vegetables and tofu and steamed, makes a beautiful white pillow. This pillow is then sliced into rings to expose the tofu stuffing. This dish is not fishy at all and will surprise your guests when they taste it.

1 (19-ounce) cake firm tofu (men-dofu)
2 tablespoons dried hijiki seaweed
2 large squid, each measuring about 12 inches long
½ medium carrot
8 snow pea pods
½ cup bamboo shoots
⅓ cup dashi
2 tablespoons soy sauce
1½ tablespoons mirin
½ teaspoon salt
2 teaspoons sugar
½ tablespoon cornstarch or potato starch
1 egg

SOY SAUCE DRESSING
⅔ cup dashi
⅓ teaspoon salt
2 teaspoons soy sauce
1 teaspoon mirin
1 teaspoon cornstarch or potato starch
1 teaspoon peeled and grated gingerroot

parsley

Press tofu (see page 102). Pat dry with cloth or paper towel.

Soak hijiki seaweed in water for 30 minutes. Drain.

Clean squid, removing innards, legs, and the flaps that resemble ears. To peel off the skin, try rubbing it with a dry cloth. It works!

Peel carrot and mince finely. Mince the snow pea pods and bamboo shoots. Combine dashi, soy sauce, and mirin in a medium saucepan and bring to a boil. Add chopped vegetables and simmer until most of the liquid is absorbed, about 10 minutes. Cool.

Put the tofu in a blender with salt, sugar, and cornstarch and purée. Blend in the egg and vegetables. Stuff each squid with tofu mixture and pin the end closed with a toothpick. Pack the stuffing as tightly as possible.

Bring water to a boil in a steamer and cook the squid for 12 minutes over high heat.

While the squid are steaming, make the soy sauce dressing, by combining dashi, salt, soy sauce, and mirin and simmer for 3 minutes in a small saucepan.

Dissolve cornstarch with an equal amount of water. Add cornstarch to the dressing, along with the grated ginger. Simmer for another minute. Remove from heat.

To serve, slice each squid into ⅛-inch rings while still hot. Put 3 slices of squid on each plate and gently pour 2 or 3 tablespoons of dressing over each serving. Garnish with a small sprig of parsley.

SERVE WITH Clam Miso Soup
Healthy Roots

TOFU GRATINÉE

4 SERVINGS

This is tofu cooking that will please cheese and sauce lovers. It totally breaks the rules of Japanese cooking, but never mind, it's wonderful.

2 (8-ounce) cakes grilled tofu (yaki-dofu)
  salt
  pepper
3 tablespoons white flour
2 tablespoons vegetable oil
2 tablespoons sake
12 medium shrimp, peeled and deveined
1 small onion
12 mushrooms
4 tablespoons butter

WHITE SAUCE

2½ tablespoons butter
2½ tablespoons white flour
1½ cups milk
1 egg yolk, beaten
¼ teaspoon nutmeg
  salt
  pepper
½ cup grated Swiss cheese
1 tablespoon grated Parmesan cheese

Slice tofu crosswise, about ¼ inch thick. Season with salt and pepper and pat with flour. Heat oil in a large skillet and fry tofu over medium heat until browned on both sides. Remove from heat and arrange in a lightly oiled platter or gratin dish.

Sprinkle sake over shrimp and let stand for 5 minutes. Chop onion and mushrooms. Heat butter in another skillet over medium heat. Sauté onion for 2 minutes, then add the mushrooms and shrimp and continue sautéing for 1 minute. Arrange the shrimp mixture over the tofu in the platter.

To make the white sauce, melt the butter in a saucepan, and when it is hot, add the flour, mixing well with a whisk. Cook for about 30 seconds. Add the milk, beaten egg yolk, nutmeg, and salt and pepper to taste. Lower the heat and let the sauce simmer for about 1 minute. Pour the sauce over the tofu-shrimp mixture.

Sprinkle the sauce with the grated Swiss and Parmesan cheese, and bake in a 350-degree oven for approximately 15 minutes. Serve immediately.

SERVE WITH French bread
　　　　　Anytime Steamed Chilled
　　　　　Chicken

STUFFED TOFU

4 SERVINGS

One culinary delight common to many ethnic cuisines is the small pyra-midal mouthful, baked or fried and stuffed with ground meat, known in Chinese cuisine as wonton and in Jewish cuisine as kreplach. The tasty, healthy Japanese version uses firm cakes of deep-fried tofu as its base.

8 green beans
4 (8-ounce) cakes deep-fried tofu (atsu-age or nama-age)
4 ounces ground pork, chicken, or beef
1 green onion, chopped
1 tablespoon peeled and grated gingerroot
⅓ teaspoon salt
pepper
1⅓ cups dashi
2 tablespoons sugar
3 tablespoons soy sauce

Halve green beans and cook in boiling water for 4 minutes, or until tender but still crisp. Drain and rinse under cold water. Set aside.

Blanch tofu in hot water and cut diagonally to make triangles. Gently make an incision in the cut side of each triangle and, without breaking the tofu, scoop out the insides with a spoon to form a pocket. Reserve the tofu removed from each pocket. Repeat for all 4 tofu cakes.

Combine meat, chopped green onion, ginger, scooped-out tofu centers, salt, and pepper and mix well. Stuff each empty pocket of tofu carefully with this mixture.

Bring dashi, sugar, and soy sauce to a boil in a medium saucepan. Reduce heat and gently add stuffed tofu. Simmer, covered, for 20 minutes.

Serve hot with the cooking broth in small deep bowls and garnish with the green beans.

SERVE WITH Tofu and Wakame
Seaweed Suimono
Vinegared Crab

SCRAMBLED TOFU

4 SERVINGS

For a simple, light dinner, accompany this dish simply with steamed rice.

1 (19-ounce) cake firm tofu (men-dofu)
3 dried shiitake mushrooms
1 small carrot
2 tablespoons vegetable oil
4 ounces ground chicken, pork, or beef
3 tablespoons chopped green onions
1 egg, lightly beaten
3 tablespoons soy sauce
1 teaspoon sugar

Press water from tofu (see page 102). Mash tofu with a fork.

Soften shiitake mushrooms in water for 30 minutes; discard stems and chop finely. Chop the peeled carrot into small pieces.

Heat the oil in a heavy skillet and sauté meat until browned, about 1 minute. Add mushrooms, carrot, green onions, mashed tofu, and beaten egg and sauté over medium heat for 2 minutes. Stir in soy sauce and sugar and continue sautéing for 3 minutes. Remove from heat and serve in medium-size bowls.

SERVE WITH Snake Eye Suimono
Flounder Teriyaki

TOFU TREASURE BAGS
4 SERVINGS

This is another version of stuffed tofu, which uses deep-fried tofu pouches as pockets. They are gently braised and served hot or at room temperature. Everyone enjoys biting into these little treasure bags.

8 deep-fried tofu pouches (usu-age)
1 (8-ounce) bag shirataki noodles
5 inches burdock root
8 ginkgo nuts, fresh or canned
4 ounces ground beef
1 green onion, chopped
1 tablespoon soy sauce
1 tablespoon mirin

BROTH
1⅓ cups dashi
1 tablespoon mirin
1 tablespoon sugar
1 tablespoon sake
3 tablespoons soy sauce

Blanch tofu pouches in hot water. Slit one end carefully to make a pocket.

Blanch shirataki noodles in hot water. Cut into 2-inch pieces. Wash burdock and shave with a carrot peeler to achieve 2-inch-long shavings.

Crack the white shells of the ginkgo nuts and discard. Blanch the nuts in hot water, rinse under cold water, and peel away the brown inner skin. If using canned ginkgo nuts, simply blanch them in hot water and rinse with cold water.

Combine burdock root, beef, shirataki noodles, green onion, soy sauce, and mirin and divide into 8 portions. Stuff each pocket with the beef filling. Put a ginkgo nut in each pocket.

Seal the pocket with toothpicks.

In a medium saucepan, bring all broth ingredients to a boil. Add the treasure bags and simmer over low heat until most of the liquid is absorbed, about 20 minutes.

Serve 2 pouches in each medium-size bowl.

SERVE WITH Vegetable and Chicken
Miso Soup
Autumn Salad

VEGETARIAN "BURGER"

4 SERVINGS

Here is a salubrious "burger" that can be eaten on a bun or dipped in very hot broth. Serve leftovers cold the next day or crumble them into a salad. If you are a strict vegetarian, omit the crab meat and use carrots instead. This is one gourmet dish that kids like, too.

2 (8-ounce) cakes firm tofu
2 eggs, beaten
½ teaspoon salt
3 dried shiitake mushrooms
3 green onions
8 ounces cooked crab (or cooked carrots)
  vegetable oil

BROTH (optional)
⅓ cup mirin
⅓ cup soy sauce
1½ cups dashi
1 tablespoon sake

GARNISH
1 cup grated daikon radish
1 tablespoon peeled and grated gingerroot

Press tofu (see page 102). Put tofu in a mortar and mash. Add beaten eggs and salt. (You can use a food processor for this step if you wish.) Transfer to a mixing bowl.

Chop mushrooms, green onions, and crab (or carrots) and add to tofu. Divide tofu mixture into 10 to 12 patties.

Fry patties over medium heat in a lightly oiled skillet till they are browned. Remove from heat.

If desired, bring all broth ingredients to boil in a saucepan, then pour over tofu patties.

Serve patties with hot broth or on a roll or bun, and garnish with grated radish and ginger.

SERVE WITH Celery and Carrot Salad
Bamboo and Wakame
Suimono

HEAVENLY OMELETTE
4 SERVINGS

American omelettes are usually crescent or oval in shape and heavy with butter. Japanese omelettes are light and slightly sweet and have a rectangular shape. The rectangle is achieved with a rectangular or square pan, but these pans are available only in Japanese hardware stores. Buy such a pan if you like. It will serve you well. However, you can use your regular round omelette pan or a skillet with a nonstick surface.

Another distinct characteristic of the Japanese omelette is its beautiful layers. The egg is not scrambled; instead, while it is frying, chopsticks are used to roll it into a tube. When it is cut into slices, a swirl pattern emerges. The omelette is allowed to cool and is usually served at room temperature, cut into 1 by 2-inch fingers. Served plain, with soy sauce and grated daikon radish, it makes a great breakfast with hot rice and miso soup. It can be served anytime as an appetizer or with sushi.

5 eggs
3 tablespoons dashi
1 tablespoon sake
½ teaspoon salt
1 to 2 tablespoons sugar
1 teaspoon mild soy sauce
    vegetable oil

Beat eggs well in a medium-size bowl. Add dashi, sake, salt, sugar, and soy sauce.

Lightly grease a nonstick frying pan over medium heat.

Pour in one third of the egg mixture. Tilt the pan back and forth to allow the egg mixture to spread thinly and evenly. When the mixture is slightly set, pop any air bubbles that appear. Then with chopsticks fold the omelette into thirds, lifting the far end of the omelette and folding it toward you.

Push the omelette to the far end and lightly grease the pan, which should still be heated evenly. Pour in another third of the egg mixture, lifting the first omelette to allow the new layer of egg to seep under it. Let the new layer of omelette cook briefly and then roll it toward you, wrapping the first omelette entirely. Cook *briefly*.

Pour in the last third of the egg mixture, lifting the omelette to allow the last layer of egg mixture underneath. Let it set again and repeat the folding process. Cook until slightly browned; turn omelette over onto a plate.

You may wrap the omelette in a clean cloth or bamboo mat and press gently to achieve a nice shape (as rectangular as possible) until ready to serve. Cut into ½-inch slices and arrange 3 or 4 in a fan shape on each plate.

HEAVENLY OMELETTE WITH CHICKEN
4 SERVINGS

This is a variation of Heavenly Omelette. Any chopped vegetables, meat, and seafood can be incorporated into the omelette, making it more colorful and richer in flavor.

2 ounces boneless chicken
½ small carrot
5 tablespoons dashi
½ teaspoon soy sauce
2 tablespoons sugar
⅔ teaspoon salt
2 teaspoons sake
5 eggs
1 parsley sprig
1½ tablespoons sesame oil or vegetable oil

Slice the chicken thinly. Peel the carrot and chop. Combine chicken and carrot in a small saucepan. Add dashi, soy sauce, sugar, salt, and sake and cook over medium heat until most of the liquid is absorbed. Cool.

Beat the eggs and add the chicken mixture. Chop parsley and add to the egg-chicken mixture.

Lightly grease a nonstick frying pan over medium heat.

Make egg omelette as you would Heavenly Omelette.

EGG TOFU DELIGHT
(TAMAGO-DOFU)
4 SERVINGS

Sometimes language is obscure. Especially Japanese. Especially English. In the case of this delightful recipe, the dish is called tofu because it has a tofulike consistency, but no tofu is used at all; only eggs, plus a delicate broth. This one works best chilled in the summertime or warm in winter. Efficient metal molds for steaming custards, called nagashi-bako, are available in Japanese stores, but any small square baking pan will do.

1⅓ cups dashi or chicken broth
½ teaspoon salt
1 tablespoon mirin
⅓ teaspoon soy sauce
4 large eggs

SAUCE
⅔ cup dashi or chicken broth
2 teaspoons soy sauce
2 teaspoons mirin
¼ teaspoon salt

GARNISH

½ cup grated daikon radish
¼ cup chopped onions
½ cup peeled, seeded, and sliced cucumber
1 teaspoon seven-spice mixture (shichimi-
    togarashi) (optional)
    lemon rind strips

Put broth, salt, mirin, and soy sauce in a pot over medium heat and cook for 2 minutes. Remove from heat and cool completely.

In a bowl beat eggs very gently, so as not to make any bubbles. Pour eggs into the broth and mix gently once more. Strain the egg mixture through a fine sieve.

Heat water in a steamer. Meanwhile, line an 8-inch square baking pan with aluminum foil without creasing it. (Any wrinkle will make a crease on the custard's surface.) Allow the aluminum foil to extend beyond both ends to make lifting out easy. (If using a Japanese metal mold, you do not need to line it with foil.) Pour egg mixture gently into the pan. If bubbles form on the surface, wipe or scoop them off.

Place the pan in the steamer. Place a piece of cloth over the steamer to catch moisture, and cover, leaving the lid slightly ajar to let steam escape. Steam over high heat for 2 minutes, then lower the heat and simmer for 15 to 18 minutes, until the custard sets. Remove from heat and let custard cool in the pan completely. Refrigerate custard until just before serving.

To make sauce, combine broth, soy sauce, mirin, and salt in a pot and bring to a boil. Remove from heat and serve chilled, or warm.

Carefully unmold the custard by lifting the aluminum sheet out of the pan and transfer to a cutting board. Cut into 3-inch squares. Serve 1 square per serving with sauce and garnishes on the side, or put each tofu in a deep bowl and pour the sauce over it and garnish the top.

Another attractive way to serve this dish is to float the squares in water with ice cubes and lemon or cucumber slices. In that case, serve the sauce and garnishes in separate bowls.

NOTE: Be careful not to steam the custard on high heat for longer than 2 minutes, as it will lose its smooth surface and become bubbly. Turn the heat to a simmer as soon as the surface of custard becomes opaque.

SERVE WITH Tuna Sashimi and Green
                Onions with Miso
                Grilled Salmon

EVERYTHING-IN-IT CUSTARD

(CHAWAN-MUSHI)

4 SERVINGS

This classic custard is not a dessert. It is an unsweetened custard served at the start of many Japanese meals—a smooth delicious dish containing bits of everything: vegetables, chicken, fish cakes, and shrimp. Other possible ingredients: cooked ginkgo nuts, crab meat, water chestnuts, mitsuba leaves, mushrooms of all types, etc. Everything-in-It Custard is colorful to look at—a rainbow spectrum of interesting flavors. A lovely tasty dish to be served chilled in summer and piping hot in winter.

Individual portions are prepared by steaming in special lidded cups called chawan-mushi. These cups are readily available in Japanese stores. Alternately, use ovenproof glass or ceramic cups and cover the cups with a clean cotton cloth to prevent moisture from dripping into the custard.

1½ cups dashi or chicken broth
½ teaspoon salt
¼ teaspoon soy sauce
1 teaspoon mirin
3 large eggs
2 medium dried shiitake mushrooms
    (softened in water for 20 minutes)
4 medium shrimp, shelled and cooked
4 slices fish cake (kamaboko), each about
    ¼ inch thick
3 ounces boneless chicken, cooked and
    shredded
½ cup cooked spinach, cut into 2-inch pieces

Combine broth, salt, soy sauce, and mirin in a pot and cook over medium heat for 2 minutes, stirring occasionally. Remove from heat and cool completely.

Beat eggs very gently without making any bubbles. Pour egg mixture into the cool broth and mix well but gently. If bubbles form on the surface of the liquid, pop them with a spoon.

Cut the softened mushrooms in half.

Divide the shrimp, fish cake, chicken, and mushrooms between the 4 cups and gently pour the egg mixture over the solid ingredients. Each cup should be three quarters filled. Finally, add the spinach.

Set the cups, uncovered, in a hot steamer. Place a cotton cloth on the steamer and then cover, leaving the lid slightly ajar to allow steam to escape. Steam over high heat for 2 minutes, or until the surface of the custard turns opaque. Reduce heat and cool for 15 to 20 minutes, until the custard sets. Test custard with a toothpick. If it comes out clean, the custard is ready.

Serve immediately, or chill and serve cold.

SERVE WITH Octopus Lemon Boats
          Vegetable Tempura
          Flounder Teriyaki

VARIATION: CLAM AND VEGETABLE CUSTARD. Place 1 raw clam, half of a softened shiitake mushroom, and 1 parboiled snow pea pod in each chawan-mushi cup. Prepare as in the preceding recipe, reducing the dashi to 1¼ cups and adding the liquid saved from the clams to the egg mixture.

EGG WHITE CUSTARD WITH SHRIMP

4 SERVINGS

This is a custard that uses egg whites and milk to give a pearly hue. It is garnished with shrimp and mitsuba leaves for color. If you cannot find mitsuba leaves you may substitute mint or parsley. Serve chilled.

5 egg whites, lightly beaten
¾ cup milk
⅓ teaspoon salt
1 teaspoon mild soy sauce
12 medium raw shrimp
4 mitsuba leaves

BROTH
¾ cup dashi
1 teaspoon sake
1 teaspoon mirin
1 teaspoon mild soy sauce
¼ teaspoon salt
2 teaspoons cornstarch or potato starch
1 teaspoon ginger juice (page 64)

Filter egg whites through a cheesecloth-lined sieve. Add the milk, salt, and soy sauce and mix gently without making any bubbles.

Heat a steamer with water. Pour the egg white mixture into a 6-inch square baking pan lined with aluminum foil. The foil should extend over the ends to make lifting out easy. (If you use a Japanese metal mold, foil is unnecessary.) Pour the egg mixture into the baking pan. Put it in the steamer and place a cotton cloth over the pan. Cover, leaving the lid slightly ajar. Steam over high heat for 2 minutes, then lower the heat and simmer for 18 to 20 minutes, until the custard sets. Remove from heat and cool completely. Refrigerate.

Peel and devein shrimp and boil in salted water until they turn pink, about 1 minute. Drain, rinse under cold water, and chill.

Cut mitsuba leaves into 2-inch pieces and blanch in hot water. Refresh and chill.

In a small saucepan combine ingredients for the broth except for the cornstarch and ginger juice. Cook over medium heat for 2 minutes. Dissolve the cornstarch with 2 tablespoons water and pour slowly into the broth from the side. Add ginger juice. Cool.

Cut the custard into 3-inch squares. Serve each square on a medium-size plate. Sprinkle mitsuba stems and scatter 4 shrimp on top and around the tofu. Gently pour the sauce over it.

POACHED EGGS WITH SNOW PEA PODS
2 SERVINGS

When crispy snow pea pods make their spring appearance, create this dish to celebrate the season. Remember to boil pea pods only till they are slightly tender. And do not overcook the eggs. Keep everything light. Good morning!

4 ounces snow pea pods
2/3 cup dashi or chicken broth
1 teaspoon sugar
1 tablespoon soy sauce
2 large eggs

Remove strings from pea pods and boil in salted water for just 1 minute, until crispy and tender. Rinse under cold running water.

In a medium frying pan, bring broth, sugar, and soy sauce to a boil. Reduce heat to low, add the pea pods, and simmer for 3 minutes.

Scramble the eggs in a bowl and carefully pour them into the frying pan from the side.

Cover frying pan and cook until eggs are delicately done.

Serve hot over rice.

SCRAMBLED EGGS WITH CRAB MEAT
4 SERVINGS

Japanese, like Americans, are egg lovers, and scrambled eggs appear typically on their breakfast tables. Here's a seafood–scrambled egg dish that makes a nice Sunday brunch entree.

1 tablespoon oil
1/2 tablespoon peeled and chopped gingerroot
1 green onion, cut into 2-inch strips
5 eggs
1/2 cup cooked and shredded crab meat
   salt

In a medium frying pan, heat oil. Stir-fry ginger and green onion.

Scramble eggs in a bowl and add to the green onion mixture. Stir and scramble over medium heat. Add crab meat. Cook quickly until eggs are fluffy. Season with salt.

Serve hot.

PARENT AND CHILD
(OYAKO-DONBURI)
4 SERVINGS

This is a wholesome omelette served over a bowl of steaming-hot rice. It makes a satisfying lunch and a great dinner. Serve this hot dish in medium-size bowls with lids. When you open the lid your glasses may be momentarily fogged, but when your vision returns you'll see before you a beautiful yellow mountain.

½ pound boneless chicken
2 green onions
1 bunch trefoil (mitsuba) or mint leaves
8 ounces bamboo shoots
6 eggs

BROTH
1½ cups chicken or dashi broth
3 tablespoons mirin
3 tablespoons sake
2 teaspoons sugar
3½ tablespoons soy sauce

4 cups steamed rice (brown or white)
½ sheet nori seaweed (dried or toasted), chopped

Dice boneless chicken into 1½-inch pieces. Slice green onions diagonally into 1½-inch pieces. Cut trefoil, or mint, into 1½-inch pieces. Cut bamboo shoots into 1½-inch pieces.

Break eggs into a bowl. Divide the beaten eggs into 4 small cups, since you will cook each serving separately.

Mix all ingredients for the broth in a bowl. Pour one quarter of the broth into a heated, nonstick, small frying pan. Bring to a boil over high heat. Add one quarter of the chicken, bamboo shoots, and onions and let the foods cook in the broth for 2 minutes over medium heat.

Pour one portion of beaten eggs into the pan and add a portion of trefoil leaves. Cover and remove from heat. Let stand for 10 seconds. Then shake the covered pan gently (to keep egg from sticking to the pan). Slip the omelette onto a warmed plate and keep warm. Do not overcook the eggs; the steam from their piping-hot rice bed will complete the job. Repeat this process four times. (If you have two small frying pans, you can do two at a time.)

Put a portion of the steamed rice in a bowl and place an omelette on top of the rice. Top with chopped nori seaweed.

Serve with some pickled vegetables for a sharp taste contrast. Even a small strip of American dill pickle would provide zip for your eaters' tongues.

ASPARAGUS CELEBRATION

ALMOST-INSTANT SNOW PEA PODS

 CURRIED CABBAGE

FAN-CUT EGGPLANT

WATERCRESS OHI-TASHI

SPINACH SESAME TOSS

C H A P T E R 8

VEGETABLE & SEAWEED DISHES

BEANS FOR BREAKFAST (NATTO)

BRAISED JAPANESE POTATOES AND CARROTS

SPICY STRING BEANS

BROILED EGGPLANT WITH GINGER

BRAISED HIJIKI SEAWEED WITH MUSHROOMS AND CARROTS

CARROTS WITH BONITO FLAKES

BRAISED KONBU SEAWEED, SOYBEANS, AND KONNYAKU

MOON-GAZING TARO POTATOES (SATO-IMO)

HIJIKI SEAWEED WITH TOFU

HEALTHY ROOTS (KIN-PIRA-GOBO)

VEGETABLE TEMPURA

HOLIDAY POTATOES WITH CHESTNUTS (KIN-TON)

BRAISED SQUASH AND OKRA

BRAISED DAIKON RADISH (KIRI-BOSHI-DAIKON)

THERE WAS A TIME, CENTURIES AGO, when practically the entire population of Japan was vegetarian, in accordance with Buddhist scriptures. Today Japanese eat meat—but meatless meals are preferred by many. *Shojin* vegetarian cuisine, commonly practiced throughout Japan, is a Zen Buddhist tradition; its dishes are especially attractive, tasty, and healthful. A totally vegetarian cuisine is practical, enjoyable, and healthful using Japanese foods and recipes.

I myself prefer a vegetarian diet, though my family and I do enjoy occasional meat and fish dishes.

There are a great variety of vegetarian possibilities in Japanese cuisine which can make a meatless diet interesting and never tiresome. Seaweed, vegetables, tofu dishes, and occasional eggs provide plenty of protein; one small serving of each of these foods plus a bowl of rice make a most satisfying meal.

If you are moving toward a totally vegetarian diet, try to have several dishes of fresh seasonal vegetables prepared in a variety of ways at each meal. Try braising, deep frying, sautéing produce fresh from the field. Experiment with varied color combinations and decorative cuts and arrangements. Make several dishes in large quantities and serve them in small portions for several days. The variety of colors and flavors will entertain your eyes and encourage tastiness on the tongue.

At our house in Tokyo we had a farm lady who visited twice a week carrying a huge woven basket full of fresh produce—a portable vegetable store on her back. Whatever she pulled out of that basket amazed us kids: heavy vegetables such as daikon radish, Chinese cabbage, carrots, and potatoes. Delicate offerings such as spinach, small Japanese eggplants—even eggs wrapped in old newspaper. She offered us fermented soybeans wrapped in bamboo husks, sweet rice patties stuffed with azuki beans and dried seaweeds, and yam cakes made in her hometown.

In Los Angeles, where I now live, I do not have such a sweet farm lady, nor even a friendly neighborhood grocer. I must drive to a supermarket and push a shopping cart, or visit an Oriental market.

Still, I do usually manage to find Japanese vegetable products such as konnyaku cakes and fermented soybeans, and of course a great variety of attractive fresh vegetables. In Los Angeles (and in most other large American cities) there are also many health food stores and ethnic Japanese shops that carry an abundance of fresh and dried seaweeds, such as konbu, nori, hijiki, and agar-agar. These seaweeds are extremely rich in healthful minerals.

In most of these stores, dried delights such as shiitake mushrooms, "cloud ear" mushrooms (kikurage), gourd strips (kampyo), and daikon strips (kiri-boshi-daikon) are commonly available. If your kitchen is far from urban centers, check my geographical list of American shopping sources (page 284).

ASPARAGUS CELEBRATION
4 SERVINGS

The celebration, of course, is for the coming of summer, when the bold green shoots of asparagus appear. This beautiful delight, freshly picked and tenderly cooked, is a perfect vegetable for saluting the happy new season. (School's out! Vacation time!) The egg yolk dressing in this recipe is slightly "hot" from a hint of mustard. Please don't spoil this excellence by using canned asparagus.

¾ pound fresh asparagus
2 tablespoons soy sauce
2 tablespoons rice vinegar
1 egg yolk
½ teaspoon dried mustard powder, softened
    with 1 tablespoon water
½ teaspoon sesame seeds

Boil or steam asparagus in lightly salted water till shoots are tender but still firm, about 4 minutes. Make sure the thicker base of each stalk gets more cooking than the tender tips. One way to do this is to insert the asparagus vertically into a pot only half filled with water—the tougher bases will boil and the delicate tips will steam. Tie the tips *loosely* together if necessary to hold them up out of the water.

Meanwhile, combine soy sauce, vinegar, egg yolk, and mustard in a small saucepan and simmer for 2 minutes. Remove from heat and chill.

When asparagus is cooked, rinse under cold water and drain. Cut into 2-inch pieces and chill.

Just before serving, toss asparagus and dressing. Garnish with sesame seeds.

ALMOST-INSTANT SNOW PEA PODS
4 SERVINGS

Pea pods should be crisp and tender when eaten, so pay special attention when they start to dance in the boiling water. They should stay there for only a minute.

8 ounces snow pea pods
2 tablespoons salad oil
1 teaspoon soy sauce
1 teaspoon sake

Bring water (with a dash of salt) to boil in a medium saucepan. Add pea pods and cook for just 1 minute. Drain and rinse under running cold water—to keep their cheerful green color. Drain water and pat dry on a paper towel.

Heat salad oil in a frying pan. Over medium heat, gently stir-fry the pea pods for 1 minute. Add soy sauce and sake to flavor.

Serve hot.

SERVE WITH Beef Croquettes
    Bird's Nest Salad

CURRIED CABBAGE
4 SERVINGS

Cabbage was introduced to Japan from China about two centuries ago. Its tight, beautiful leaves taste best during early summer, when they are thick, green, tender, and sweet. Enjoy unwrapping this gift of nature and serving it up for the summer season.

5 large cabbage leaves
1 small carrot
1 green pepper
1 medium onion
3 dried shiitake mushrooms (softened in water 20 minutes) or 3 fresh shiitake mushrooms
1½ tablespoons salad oil
1 teaspoon curry powder
salt
pepper

Cut cabbage into ¾-inch squares.

Peel carrot and slice it on the diagonal (see random cut, page 15). Remove the seeds and membranes from the green pepper and cut as you did the carrot. Slice onion into wedges. Remove mushroom stems and cut caps in half.

Boil carrot in salted water for 3 minutes, until slightly tender.

In a medium frying pan, heat the oil and sauté all the vegetables together, stirring constantly, for 3 minutes. Add curry powder and salt and pepper to taste and continue sautéing for an additional 2 minutes.

Remove from heat. Serve hot.

SERVE WITH Ginger Pork
Basic White Rice

FAN-CUT EGGPLANT
4 SERVINGS

To prepare this eggplant dish takes two steps, first deep frying, then cooking in a soy sauce–base stock.

4 Japanese eggplants
vegetable oil for deep frying
1 cup dashi
3 tablespoons soy sauce
2 tablespoons mirin
bonito flakes (optional)

Fan-cut eggplants following the instructions on page 15. This allows the eggplants to cook evenly and looks decorative. Wipe off moisture with a paper towel before frying.

Deep fry until tender, about 5 minutes in medium heat. Drain on paper towels.

Bring dashi broth, soy sauce, and mirin to a boil. Add the eggplant and simmer for 20 minutes, stirring lightly to let the broth soak into the eggplants.

Arrange eggplants in a deep bowl. Sprinkle with bonito flakes if desired.

SERVE WITH Just Vegetable Suimono
Sashimi

WATERCRESS OHI-TASHI
4 SERVINGS

"A meal without ohi-tashi is a bachelor's meal," my brother says. He works in Osaka, three hours away from Tokyo, where my parents live. When he gets a holiday from work he calls my mother to ask her for a big bowl of ohi-tashi, which she gladly provides. Ohi-tashi is plain vegetables briefly blanched in hot water just to make them tender. Their minerals and vitamins do not have time to escape, so this dish is very healthy and gives balance to a meal. You may use asparagus, spinach, bean sprouts, chrysanthemum leaves, cabbage, etc., in place of watercress.

1 bunch watercress
½ teaspoon sesame seeds or 2 tablespoons
    bonito flakes
  soy sauce

Wash watercress, discarding any very thick stems. Bring a large pot of water to a boil. Add a dash of salt and boil watercress for 1 minute; drain. Rinse under cold water and drain. Bunch the stems together and gently squeeze the water out with your hands. Cut the bunch into 3-inch pieces. Chill.

Stand a bunched piece of watercress in each small deep bowl and top with a sprinkle of sesame seeds or bonito flakes and soy sauce.

SPINACH SESAME TOSS
4 SERVINGS

This is a straightforward, refreshing, and healthful salad, easy to prepare. Sesame seeds make this salad come alive.

1 bunch spinach (about 10 ounces)
3 tablespoons roasted sesame seeds or 1½
    tablespoons sesame seed paste
1 tablespoon dashi
1 to 2 teaspoons sugar
2 teaspoons soy sauce

Boil spinach for 1 minute, then rinse under cold water. Wring out the water with your hands and bunch stem ends together. Cut into 3 parts.

Grind sesame seeds with a mortar and pestle (or use a commercial sesame seed paste). Add broth, sugar, and soy sauce.

Mix spinach with dressing, Serve chilled.

VARIATION: STRING BEAN SESAME TOSS
Cook 1 pound string beans cut into 2-inch pieces just until tender-crisp. Grind 4 tablespoons roasted sesame seeds and combine with 1 tablespoon sake, 1 tablespoon sugar, and 1 tablespoon soy sauce. Proceed as for Spinach Sesame Toss.

BEANS FOR BREAKFAST
(NATTO)
2 SERVINGS

Like yogurt, fermented soybeans are rich in protein, calcium, and other minerals, and are slightly sour. Mixed with a raw egg and chopped green onions, they make a traditional breakfast meal for the Japanese. Serve over a steaming bowl of hot rice. I also like them on top of my toast. Fermented soybeans are available in Japanese grocery stores, and will stay fresh for 3 to 4 days in the refrigerator.

1 small package fermented soybeans (natto)
1 chopped green onion
1 egg
¼ teaspoon dry Oriental mustard powder
1 tablespoon soy sauce
  hot steamed rice

Mix together (with chopsticks or a fork) soybeans, chopped green onion, egg, mustard, and soy sauce. Pour mixture over individual bowls of hot rice and serve immediately.

BRAISED JAPANESE POTATOES AND CARROTS
4 SERVINGS

Like a stew, this dish tastes better the next day. Serve in small portions in pretty little dishes.

1 pound potatoes
1 large carrot
1 medium green pepper
4 dried shiitake mushrooms, softened in
    water for 20 minutes
1 Japanese dried chili pepper
2 tablespoons salad oil
4 tablespoons mild soy sauce
1 tablespoon mirin
1 teaspoon sesame seeds
½ teaspoon salt

Peel potatoes and cut them into matchsticks. Soak in water for 5 minutes; drain.

Cut carrot, green pepper, and shiitake mushrooms into pieces the same size as the potatoes. (Even size enables the vegetables to cook in the same amount of time.)

Cut red chili pepper into 4 pieces and discard seeds.

Heat oil to medium hot in a large frying pan and sauté first the green pepper, then the carrot, mushrooms, and potatoes for approximately 3 minutes, maintaining the heat at medium high. When the potatoes begin to look slightly transparent but still crisp, add soy sauce, mirin, and salt and cook a few seconds longer. Add sesame seeds and toss lightly.

Serve in a deep, medium-size dish.

SERVE WITH Lotus Root with Plum
            Sauce
            Daikon Radish Miso Soup
            Chicken Yakitori on
              Skewers

SPICY STRING BEANS
4 SERVINGS

Serve this dish with something that needs to be pepped up. Roast beef or chicken is a good companion.

12 ounces string beans
1 Japanese dried chili pepper
1½ tablespoons salad oil
3 tablespoons dashi or water
1 teaspoon sugar
3 tablespoons soy sauce
1 tablespoon sake
2 teaspoons white sesame seeds

Cut string beans into 3-inch pieces. Cut chili pepper into 4 pieces and discard seeds.

In a frying pan, heat oil until medium hot and sauté the chili pepper until it turns golden; discard.

Add string beans and sauté for 3 minutes. Add broth, sugar, soy sauce, and sake and stir gently with chopsticks until all the liquid is absorbed by the beans (about 4 minutes).

Serve family-style in a small bowl and sprinkle sesame seeds on top. Let everyone help themselves.

BROILED EGGPLANT WITH GINGER
4 SERVINGS

This dish is surprising in look, taste, and temperature. Americans and Italians are accustomed to thick slices or chunks of large eggplants. The Japanese grow small eggplants, about the size of a zucchini. It will be worth your while to visit a gourmet supermarket or an Oriental market to find Japanese small eggplants. They taste sweet and cool as a cucumber, and are available only in summertime. This dish is most tasty when eaten chilled.

6 to 8 Japanese eggplants
1 cup chopped green onions
2 tablespoons peeled and grated gingerroot
4 tablespoons bonito flakes (optional)
   soy sauce

Broil eggplants with skin on. Turn occasionally until all sides are brown and inside flesh is tender. Test tenderness by piercing with a fork.

Rinse eggplants under cold running water as soon as you remove them from

heat. This process makes them easier to peel. Peel gently so that you do not strip off any flesh. Chill.

To serve, slice each eggplant lengthwise. Arrange on a plate.

Sprinkle chilled eggplant with chopped onions, ginger, and bonito flakes.

Serve with soy sauce on the side, which eaters can apply as their tongues decide.

SERVE WITH Stuffed Tofu
         Miso Soup with Enoki
         Mushrooms

BRAISED HIJIKI SEAWEED WITH MUSHROOMS AND CARROTS
4 SERVINGS

This is a dish I serve almost every day. Seaweed is so full of minerals, especially calcium, that a daily ritual of this food makes me and my family feel healthy. It is delicious over hot steamed rice. Serve with roasted sesame seeds.

⅓ cup dried hijiki seaweed
1 dried shiitake mushroom
1 small carrot
1 tablespoon vegetable oil
½ cup dashi or chicken broth
2 teaspoons sugar
1 teaspoon sake
1 tablespoon mirin
1½ tablespoons soy sauce
½ teaspoon roasted sesame seeds

Soak seaweed in water for 20 minutes. It should almost triple in size. Drain. Cut seaweed in half if longer than 2 inches.

Soak shiitake mushroom in water for 20 minutes. Drain. Cut off stems and slice thinly into ¼-inch-thick strips. Peel the carrot and cut into matchsticks.

Heat oil in a frying pan over medium heat. Sauté seaweed until it is well coated with oil, about 1 minute. Add carrot, mushrooms, broth, sugar, sake, and mirin. Simmer another 5 minutes. Then add soy sauce and simmer for another 5 minutes, until most of the liquid is absorbed.

Let cool 6 hours to overnight. Tightly covered, it will keep in the refrigerator up to 1 week.

Serve small portions (¼ cup) in individual dishes. Garnish with sprinkles of roasted sesame seeds.

CARROTS WITH BONITO FLAKES
4 SERVINGS

Bonito flakes are unfishy and make a wonderful light condiment to any steamed or boiled vegetables and rice. A little soy sauce will give the vegetables extra flavor, but it's the bonito flakes that make the vegetable important. They are extremely high in calcium and recommended for daily consumption.

2 medium carrots
1½ cups water
1 tablespoon sugar
2 tablespoons soy sauce
⅔ cup bonito flakes

Peel carrots and cut crosswise into ¼-inch pieces. In a medium saucepan combine carrots and measured water. Add sugar and cook over low heat for 10 minutes. Add soy sauce and simmer for 10 minutes longer. Remove from heat. Toss carrots with bonito flakes and serve immediately or at room temperature.

BRAISED KONBU SEAWEED, SOYBEANS, AND KONNYAKU

4 SERVINGS

Konbu is the king of seaweeds. It is thick and wide and dark green, nearly black. It is full of minerals and flavor. Konbu is the essential ingredient for dashi stock and makes other foods such as soybeans and konnyaku taste better. For this dish buy konbu strips, which are available in dried form. Because the dried beans need overnight soaking, always start this dish a day before you plan to serve it.

⅓ cup dried soybeans
1 cup water
⅓ cup dried konbu seaweed strips
¼ cake konnyaku
1 medium carrot
2 ounces bamboo shoots
1½ tablespoons sugar
1½ tablespoons soy sauce
1½ tablespoons sake

Wash soybeans and soak in the measured water overnight. The next day, cook the soybeans in the same water over low heat for 30 minutes. Make sure that the soybeans are always covered with water while simmering; add more as needed. Remove from heat and drain. Set aside.

Wash seaweed strips under water. Drain and soak seaweed in 1 cup water for 30 minutes.

Blanch the konnyaku for 1 minute in water. Cut into ¼-inch cubes. Peel the carrot and dice into 2-inch cubes. Do the same with bamboo shoots.

Combine soaked seaweed and liquid with soybeans in a medium pot. Add carrot, konnyaku, and bamboo shoots. Bring the mixture to a boil, then reduce heat to medium; remove surface film. When carrot becomes tender (5 to 7 minutes) add sugar and simmer for 3 minutes. Then add soy sauce and sake and simmer until half of the liquid has been absorbed, about 6 to 7 minutes longer.

Remove from heat. Let cool 6 hours to overnight. Keeps in the refrigerator for a week. Serve in small individual dishes, about ¼ cup per serving.

SERVE WITH Tuna Sashimi
Clam and Vegetable
Custard

MOON-GAZING TARO POTATOES

(SATO-IMO)

4 SERVINGS

The autumn full moon is appreciated in Japan with a special culinary ritual—steamed taro potatoes (available here in Oriental grocery stores), roasted chestnuts, tea cakes, and persimmons, all served outside (picnic style or at a table) where the moon can be seen. Autumn flowers and pampas grass are arranged near the foods. Family and friends gather for a pleasant evening.

1½ pounds taro potatoes
2 cups dashi
2 tablespoons sugar
2 tablespoons sake
½ teaspoon salt
1 tablespoon lemon peel strips, ½ by ⅛ inch

Wash potatoes in running water to remove dirt. Peel them and put in a medium-size saucepan with water. Simmer potatoes over medium heat for 7 to 10 minutes, until potatoes can be pierced with a toothpick but are still firm; drain. Combine dashi and seasonings in a separate saucepan and bring to a boil. Add potatoes and simmer for 10 minutes, covered. Rotate potatoes occasionally so they cook evenly. Remove from heat and cool.

Sprinkle with lemon strands. Serve at room temperature.

HIJIKI SEAWEED WITH TOFU
4 SERVINGS

Hijiki seaweed is high in calcium and minerals and a good substitute for dairy products. Serve small portions, about ¼ cup each. I suggest you double this recipe so you can keep it on hand to serve often. Covered, it will keep for 4 to 5 days in the refrigerator.

⅓ cup dried hijiki seaweed or ¾ cup fresh
2 fried tofu pouches (usu-age or abura-age)
1½ tablespoons vegetable oil
½ cup dashi or chicken broth
1 to 2 tablespoons sugar
1 teaspoon mirin
1 teaspoon peeled and grated gingerroot
2 tablespoons soy sauce
roasted sesame seeds, white or black

Wash mass of dried seaweed in water. Drain. Soak seaweed in fresh water for 20 minutes. Drain. If using fresh seaweed, rinse with water and soak for 5 minutes. Drain. Boil seaweed in water for 2 minutes. Drain.

Cut tofu pouches into thin strips, about ¼ inch thick.

Heat oil in a medium frying pan over medium heat. Sauté seaweed until it begins to shine and look well coated with oil, about 1 minute. Add tofu strips, broth, sugar, mirin, and ginger. Reduce heat and simmer for 5 minutes. Add soy sauce and simmer another 7 minutes.

Remove from heat and let cool 3 hours or overnight. Keep in refrigerator, tightly covered.

Top with sprinkles of roasted sesame seeds.

SERVE WITH Spring Clam Suimono
Stuffed Tofu Sushi

HEALTHY ROOTS

(KIN-PIRA-GOBO)

4 SERVINGS

Burdock and carrots both belong to the root family. Burdock is a long root vegetable, full of woodsy fragrance, with a brown skin. While carrots can be eaten raw, burdock must be cooked. This is one of my favorite dishes. The recipe is from my mother.

2 large burdock (gobo) roots
1 teaspoon vinegar
2 carrots
1 Japanese dried chili pepper
3 tablespoons vegetable oil
1½ tablespoons mirin
1 tablespoon sake
1 tablespoon sugar
3 tablespoons soy sauce

1 tablespoon roasted sesame seeds

Wash burdock roots with a nylon scrub brush. Do not peel, because the flavor is in the skin. Cut the roots into matchstick-size pieces. Soak burdock pieces in water with vinegar and let stand 15 minutes. Drain.

Peel carrots and cut into matchstick-size pieces. Remove seeds from chili pepper and slice thinly.

Heat oil in a medium skillet and sauté burdock for 2 minutes over medium-high heat. Add carrot pieces and cook till both vegetables become tender, about 4 minutes total. Add seasonings and chopped chili pepper. Simmer until most of the liquid has been absorbed into the vegetables. Sprinkle with roasted sesame seeds just before serving. Keeps in refrigerator for 1 week.

Serve hot the first time, cold thereafter.

SERVE WITH Rice with Chestnuts
Vegetarian "Burger"

VEGETABLE TEMPURA
4 SERVINGS

Seasonal vegetables are all ideal for tempura—except for very juicy vegetables such as tomato. If you plan to serve tempura in the summer, when there are so many beautiful vegetables around, I recommend an accompaniment of cold somen noodles.

8 fresh mushrooms (any type)
1 bell pepper
1 zucchini
2 carrots
2 Japanese eggplants
1 yam or satsuma-imo potato
8 string beans
1 medium lotus root
1 teaspoon vinegar
1 cup water
* fresh vegetable oil*

* Basic tempura batter (page 173)*
* Dipping Sauce (page 173)*

1 cup grated daikon radish

Cut mushrooms in half. Slice bell pepper into 8 pieces. Cut zucchini and carrots into matchstick-size pieces. Cut eggplants crosswise into ¼-inch slices; soak in salt water for 15 minutes. Drain and pat dry with paper towels. Dice yam or satsuma-imo potato into ¼-inch cubes. Cut ends off the string beans, then cut in half. Peel lotus root, slice ¼ inch thick crosswise. Soak in vinegared water for 10 minutes. Drain and pat dry with paper towels.

Arrange vegetables on a platter. Heat oil in a large heavy skillet.

Deep fry vegetables according to basic tempura instructions (page 171).

Serve tempura hot, with a warm bowl of broth and grated radish.

SERVE WITH Chilled Pork Roast
Basic White Rice

HOLIDAY POTATOES WITH CHESTNUTS
(KIN-TON)
4 SERVINGS

Here is a traditional New Year's dish that is very, very sweet. It is like a dessert and must be served in spoon-size portions. Since satsuma-imo potatoes and chestnuts are both available in fall, I often make this dish to serve with turkey for Thanksgiving. It's delicious. Satsuma-imo potatoes resemble yams but the skin is much redder and the meat is yellow. They can be found in Japanese grocery stores. Sweetened chestnuts can be bought in cans or jars at gourmet stores or made at home by cooking boiled chestnuts in a simple sugar syrup until soft and sweet (see page 238).

1 pound satsuma-imo potatoes
1 cup sugar
4 tablespoons mirin
  dash of salt
8 ounces sweetened chestnuts, drained

Wash and peel potatoes. Slice crosswise, about ¼ inch thick. Put potatoes in a medium-size pot and pour in enough water to cover. Boil potatoes over medium heat until they can be easily pierced with a toothpick, about 7 minutes. Remove from heat.

Mash potatoes in the pot, add sugar, and mix with a wooden paddle over low heat for 5 minutes. Add mirin, a dash of salt, and the chestnuts. Cook for another 2 minutes over low heat. Remove from heat and let stand to cool. Serve at room temperature.

SERVE WITH New Year Celebration Soup
Broiled Mochi Cakes
Scattered Sushi

BRAISED SQUASH AND OKRA
4 SERVINGS

With any hearty fall or winter menu, try this dish for a change. While Japanese squash (kabocha) is recommended here, you may substitute acorn or butternut squash.

1 pound kabocha (or acorn or butternut)
  squash
1½ cups dashi
2 teaspoons mild soy sauce
3 tablespoons sugar
2 tablespoons mirin
  dash of salt
8 okra pods

Wash squash with a brush to remove dirt. Cut squash in half, remove seeds, and cut each half into 2-inch spheres, following instructions for sphere cut on page 15. Peel skin, leaving a few strips of skin on the meat for appearance. Bevel the edges (see beveled cut on page 15).

In a medium saucepan, combine dashi

and sugar. Cook over medium heat for 10 minutes. Add soy sauce, sugar, mirin, salt, and the squash. Reduce heat to low and simmer for 5 minutes, until most of the liquid is absorbed by the squash. Cool.

Heat a steamer with water. Wash okra pods and remove ends. Steam for 4 minutes, then rinse under cold water. Drain and chill.

Serve family-style, with the braised squash at one side of the dish and the okra on the other.

BRAISED DAIKON RADISH
(KIRI-BOSHI-DAIKON)
4 SERVINGS

Kiri-boshi-daikon is dried daikon radish. It is highly nutritious. Available in the dried-food section of Japanese grocery stores, the radish comes shredded, so it is quite manageable. Makes a healthy side dish or salad.

2 ounces dried daikon radish (kiri-boshi-
    daikon)
2 deep-fried tofu pouches (age)
1 Japanese dried chili pepper
2 tablespoons vegetable oil
2 tablespoons sugar
2 tablespoons soy sauce
1 cup dashi
    roasted sesame seeds (optional)

Wash daikon radish in water. Soak in water for 1 hour. It will expand to five times its original size, so allow plenty of water. Drain.

Blanch tofu in hot water. Slice each pouch into ⅛-inch-thick pieces. Remove seeds from chili pepper and slice thinly.

Heat oil in a skillet and sauté daikon over medium heat for a couple of minutes. Add tofu and continue sautéing for 4 minutes more. Add seasonings and dashi and simmer until most of the liquid is absorbed.

Serve in small portions, about ¼ cup each, sprinkled with roasted sesame seeds if desired.

NOTE: Best eaten cold the next day. Keeps for a week in a well-sealed container in the refrigerator.

SERVE WITH Everything-in-It Custard
        Yellowtail Teriyaki

BASIC SUSHI RICE (SHARI)

SUSHI ROLLED IN NORI (HOSO-MAKI-ZUSHI)

CALIFORNIA ROLL

FUTO-MAKI-ZUSHI (GIANT SUSHI ROLL)

HAND-MOLDED SUSHI (NIGIRI-ZUSHI)

CHAPTER 9

SUSHI, SASHIMI & OTHER WAYS WITH SEAFOOD

SHRIMP SUSHI (EBI-NO-NIGIRI-ZUSHI)

CRAB SUSHI LOAF (KANI-NO-OSHI-ZUSHI)

SUSHI HAND ROLLS (TEMAKI-ZUSHI)

SCATTERED SUSHI (CHIRASHI-ZUSHI)

STUFFED TOFU SUSHI (INARI-ZUSHI)

EGG SUSHI BLANKETS (CHAKIN-ZUSHI)

SMOKED SALMON SASHIMI

RED SNAPPER SASHIMI

FLOUNDER SASHIMI

TUNA SASHIMI

SQUID SASHIMI

YELLOWTAIL TERIYAKI

SQUID TERIYAKI WITH SWEET POTATOES

FLOUNDER TERIYAKI

SALMON TERIYAKI

SEAFOOD TEMPURA

KAKI-AGE

SNAPPER TEMPURA WITH ASPARAGUS AND MISO

STUFFED MUSHROOM TEMPURA

GRILLED SALMON

WRAPPED COD WTH MUSHROOMS

STEAMED RED SNAPPER WITH LEMON SLICES

STEAMED PERCH WRAPPED IN SOBA NOODLES

HOKKAIDO-STYLE BAKED SOLE

MARINATED COD IN MISO SAUCE

THE BEACH WAS LIKE MY BACKYARD when I was growing up in
Kamakura. Grandmother and I made frequent walks to the beach at
dawn to buy fish just out of the fishermen's nets. Usually we got to
the beach just as they were reaching the shore or sorting the fish.
The prices seemed to depend on the fisherman's mood. If he had had
a good day, 100 yen would get us enough fish to feed our whole
family, plus a few extra fish of odd sizes and kinds for free. If the day
hadn't gone so well, we would still get fish for a reasonable price, but
no extras. Either way we always got a good deal. I enjoyed going
there to catch crabs and baby octopus hiding under the rocks and
smell the ocean, but Grandmother had a specific reason. When she
made a trip to the beach for fish, she had sashimi—fresh, uncooked
fish fillets—in mind for dinner. We could buy very fresh fish from
the many fish shops in our neighborhood, but she insisted that there
was a difference in the freshness of a fish flipping over with life and
one in an ice box at the shop. Grandmother made a lot of sense. I
soon became just as picky when it came to buying fish. The fish
needed an AAA rating to qualify for sashimi. A simple A was good
enough only for dishes in which the fish was cooked.

Supermarket fish often fail the freshness test for sushi and sashimi,
but specialty fish shops and Japanese grocery stores as well as
fishermen's wharves carry high-quality fish. The key is to get to
know the shop owner, who will honestly tell you how fresh the fish
is.

Learn not to be afraid of handling a fish with eyes, scales, and fins.
I recommend that you be daring and try starting with a whole fish.

But any good fish market, American or Japanese, will bone or fillet a fresh fish for you and save you this part of work.

In this chapter we will consider the delectable matters of sushi (seasoned rice combined with fish, seafood, and other ingredients), sashimi (fresh, uncooked fish fillets), teriyaki (braised fish), tempura (light deep-fried seafood and vegetables), and other ways with seafood (including broiled, steamed, and marinated food from the sea).

This chapter includes instructions for preparing an unfilleted fish for sushi or sashimi. A lot of technical detail is given. If you're not ready to tackle a whole, unfilleted fish, just be sure to buy very fresh fillets. Later, as you get more proficient, you will want to return to these pages as a useful and accurate resource. Meanwhile, have fun in your kitchen as you prepare and serve your first sashimi dinners from market-cut fillets. Just make sure they are really firm and fresh.

SUSHI

Sushi is the celebrated Japanese version of an open-faced sandwich. Each piece is quite small, only one or two bites big, and instead of bread, the fish, vegetables, egg, or fruit rests on a compact oval of prepared rice. Chopsticks may be used, but sushi is one food it is quite proper (and fun) to eat with your fingers. The hand-rolled, hand-molded kinds of sushi described in this book require the use of absolutely fresh fish, which has no odor and tastes as "sweet" as fresh vegetables. This is "fast" sushi food, designed for the impatient and busy metropolitan people of Tokyo. It seems to me it also fits the American temperament perfectly.

The varieties and possibilities of sushi are endless. It's an artful finger food limited only by the availability of ingredients, the appetite of your eaters, and your own imagination. You are not locked into Japanese tradition here. Anything goes. American chefs have already brought into general use in sushi such non-Japanese foods as California avocados and New Zealand kiwi fruits. I don't doubt that some precocious American child, when his or her parents weren't looking, has already made and eaten peanut butter and jelly sushi.

Although many people are most familiar with the hand-formed sushi called nigiri-zushi, sushi comes in many varieties. Rolled sushi (maki-zushi) is made by wrapping a sheet of nori seaweed around the vinegared rice and filling, either with a bamboo mat or simply with the hands. Other types of sushi involve stuffing the rice and filling into a tofu pouch or pressing the ingredients in a special mold.

One important caution: The next few pages tell you everything I have shared with students in my sushi-making classes. But there are some human doings—swimming, for instance—that just can't be entirely communicated in words, or even fully in pictures. You've just got to see it done, experience it yourself. So I urge that before you use this book as a guide to sushi making, you spend a little study (and eating!) time in at least two different Japanese restaurants. And don't sit at a table. Sit at the sushi bar, because working behind it is your master. Watch how the sushi chef deftly forms the little rice mounds with his fingers. See how gracefully and precisely he cuts the vegetables, slices the fish, rolls the paper-thin dry seaweed. See how elegantly and quickly he serves his handiwork on its little wooden or ceramic platter.

Do visit at least two restaurants, because no two chefs work quite the same way. The ambience and serving methods of each place will be different. Seasonings and even absolute freshness may vary. You must watch, compare, eat, and learn. *Then* you will be ready to make full use of this sushi chapter and, indeed, of this whole book.

You will find that making and serving sushi is a special and wonderful kind of fun unlike most other kinds of food making. The reasons for that are two. First, sushi is handmade, and that's satisfying in these days of processed, packaged, machine-made foods. Second, the chef's pleasure in feeding his or her eaters is nearly instantaneous. Only a minute or two need separate the work and gift of your hand from your eater's pleasure. Feedback can be immediate, with no hours-long wait at the pot or the oven. You get smiles, thanks, and happy eaters right away.

Nigiri-zushi takes many years of hard work and discipline to master. An average sushi student trains eight to ten years before he can become a full-fledged chef. His first two years of apprenticeship include menial work such as scrubbing floors, washing utensils, and fanning the hot rice while the chef tosses it with the vinegar mixture. After this stage, he may spend two to three years preparing the fish —which involves skinning, boning, and cleaning—as well as cooking the rice. When the master chef finally promotes him to make sushi before the customers, he will spend another three years under the master's close observation. By then the new chef must be fully aware of the fish, the rice, and the swordplay, as well as how to communicate with customers.

You'll be awed by the speed, ease, and choreographic beauty of the sushi chef's movements and will want to imitate him. For there is a large aesthetic component here. Sushi making is an art, both in the doing and in the actual food served. Physical movements count, and color composition, and above all the freshness and flavor of the foods. Vegetables must be crisp, fish absolutely fresh, fruits firm, rice exactly right; everything a delight to eye, spirit, and tongue.

Home chefs should not expect the same results overnight when trying to make nigiri-zushi. In Japan, not everybody attempts nigiri-zushi; people know they can have the best of it at a sushi bar. If you want the challenge, try it; just keep practicing. And occasionally visit your master at your favorite sushi bar. He makes it look easy. To be truthful, making nigiri-zushi at home isn't all that hard to do. Your first try should at least be edible. Your second might be good to look at. And your third? Hmmm. Unless you goof on the rice (too sticky) or on the choice of fish (not quite fresh), you really can't miss. A clumsy cut won't much diminish the fun of making sushi happen on your own table.

To make and serve sushi, you will need the following:

EQUIPMENT: See Staple Tools for Your Kitchen (page 20) for a description of these tools and utensils.

sharp knife
wooden *shamoji* paddle
fan or magazine
cotton dishcloth for wiping knife and cutting board
bamboo mat (sudare)
large casserole dish or sushi tub

SUSHI RICE (shari): Sushi rice is steamed rice that has been seasoned with sake, salt, and sugar. At the sushi bars sushi rice is called shari, so if you want more rice in your sushi roll ask for more shari. The caliber of a sushi bar is often determined not only by the freshness of the seafood but also by the shari. The texture must be just right, not too soft or hard nor too moist or dry. Many sushi chefs have told me that Americans prefer sweet shari, but shari should not be too sweet or too salty. (Recipe for shari is on page 145.) Use only short-grain white rice for shari as long-grain white rice or short- and long-grain brown rice do not make good shari. One sushi chef, however, told me that he has a health-conscious customer who brings a bowl of steamed brown rice to the restaurant and has him use that in

place of his shari. This sushi chef is an unusually flexible and generous person. You should not expect this to happen in every sushi bar.

NORI SEAWEED: Nori is a dark, green-black, paper-thin, rectangular sheet that measures about 8 by 6½ inches. The whole sheet is
used for wrapping rolled sushi, and half a sheet for cone-shaped
hand-rolled sushi (temaki-zushi). Nori seaweed must be toasted
before use: pass it closely over a gas flame a few times until it
becomes crisp. In toasting, seaweed becomes slightly greener. This
improves taste, aroma, and texture. Both untoasted and toasted types
are sold. If you can find toasted nori seaweed, you can skip this step.
Keep nori seaweed in a plastic bag, free from moisture.

JAPANESE HORSERADISH (wasabi): Wasabi is Japanese horseradish,
hot to the taste and green in color. Only a tiny bit is used at a time,
mixed in a small dish with soy sauce to taste. It is available fresh in
the U.S., but very expensive. You can buy wasabi more economically
in powder form. Wasabi can be very hot and make your eyes tear if
used in excess. Occasionally a sushi chef may put too much wasabi
in the sushi; I think some chefs enjoy seeing women crying over
sushi.

To make wasabi paste from powder, simply dissolve 1 tablespoon
wasabi powder with a few drops of water. Stir until it forms a paste,
adding a drop or two more if the consistency is too dry. Let stand for
5 minutes before using. If using fresh wasabi, rinse the root in cold
water, pat dry, and grate without peeling.

PICKLED GINGER (amazu-shoga): Amazu-shoga is made from fresh shin-shoga ginger. It has a delicious piquant taste, especially when eaten with sushi. It clears the palate between different kinds of sushi so you can savor the individual flavors of each. At the sushi bar pickled ginger is called gari, so be sure to ask for more gari if you run out.

It is difficult to find fresh shin-shoga at the store, so you'll probably want to buy your ginger already pickled. If you do come across fresh shin-shoga you can pickle it yourself (page 229). It's available fresh during midsummer and early fall in some Japanese and Chinese grocery stores. You can tell it by its pale yellow skin blushed with pink.

SOY SAUCE: Soy sauce at the sushi bars is called murasaki, which means purple. Ask for murasaki when you need soy sauce.

SERVING SUSHI

With the sushi serve miso or suimono soup. Salads and appetizers of braised or vinegared foods are popular.

Hot sake, beer, or tea generally accompanies sushi. Tea is usually served at meal's end. When you ask for it, ask for a-ga-ri, which is the term used for tea in sushi bars.

Some sushi eaters at the sushi bar prefer to begin their meal with sashimi, then switch to sushi, especially if they are drinking beer or sake, so as not to fill up with too much rice. For dessert, serve slices of fresh fruit or ice cream.

Everybody has a different appetite for sushi. Sushi can be a snack, lunch, or dinner. Portions should vary accordingly. When you plan to invite people for a sushi party, keep the following guidelines in mind as an average serving for one person. If you wish to combine several types of sushi, adjust the serving size of each accordingly.

Suggested Servings for One Hungry Person

Rolled sushi (hoso-maki-zushi): 2 rolls, 10 to 12 pieces,
  1 inch thick *or*
Large rolled sushi (futo-maki-zushi): 1 roll, 5 or 6 pieces,
  about ¾ inch thick *or*
Hand-molded sushi (nigiri-zushi): 10 to 15 pieces *or*
Pressed sushi (oshi-zushi): 5 to 7 pieces,
  1½ by 2 by 1½ inches each *or*
Hand-rolled sushi (temaki-zushi): 8 to 12 pieces *or*
Stuffed sushi (inari-zushi): 3 or 4 pieces *or*
Stuffed sushi (chakin-zushi): 3 or 4 pieces

BASIC SUSHI RICE
(SHARI)

All the dishes in this chapter use the following basic sushi rice recipe. It yields approximately 6 cups of sushi rice.

Please read these instructions carefully. Your sushi rice may end up lumpy and sticky if you overlook three seemingly unimportant steps. First, when making sushi rice be sure your cooked rice is *steaming hot* as you sprinkle it with the vinegar mixture. Second, toss the rice gently, with a damp *wooden* spoon, being careful not to mash it. Finally, it is critically important that as you sprinkle on the vinegar mixture, a little at a time, you *fan* the rice (with a magazine or a fan) to cool it and to disperse the vapors of the vinegar. These things are all quick and easy to do—and easy to overlook. But they are part of the sushi rhythm and essential for success. If you have a helper it's nice to involve him or her in the work, fanning while you toss the rice.

The sushi vinegar mixture should be adapted to please your palate. Use a teaspoon of sugar according to your taste. An additional half teaspoon of salt will alter the taste without making it too salty. Seasoned rice vinegar is available in Japanese markets, but I recommend that you prepare your own freshly, as the ready-made vinegar contains artificial ingredients.

2½ cups short-grain white rice
1 strip konbu seaweed, about 2 inches long
2¾ cups water
2 tablespoons sake

SUSHI VINEGAR MIXTURE
¼ cup rice vinegar
3 tablespoons sugar
1½ teaspoons salt

Wash rice in water by swishing and swirling it with your hands or a wooden spoon in a large bowl. Drain off the cloudy water. This washing removes powdery surface film from the rice. Repeat several times. Drain. Let stand 1 hour.

Clean konbu seaweed with a damp paper towel. Make a few slits into the seaweed with a sharp knife; this allows its juices to come out.

Combine rice, konbu seaweed, measured water, and sake in a heavy pot. Cover and bring to a boil over high heat. Once the rice has reached a boil, remove the seaweed with a fork or chopsticks, re-cover, and reduce heat to low. Cook without uncovering for 12 more minutes. Remove from heat and let stand, uncovered, for 10 minutes.

Spread the rice in a large, shallow, rectangular pan or on a baking sheet about 9 by 12 inches. Sprinkle on the sushi vinegar mixture, a little at a time, while fanning the rice with a magazine or fan. This keeps the rice from getting sticky. Remember to use a damp wooden spoon to toss the rice. Be careful not to mash the grains.

Cover the rice with a well-wrung damp cloth and store in a cool place until it is ready for use. Do not refrigerate. Sushi rice keeps for only a day.

SUSHI ROLLED IN NORI

(HOSO-MAKI-ZUSHI)
4 SERVINGS

This sushi roll is for beginners who want to practice rolling sushi with the bamboo mat (sudare). Once you've mastered the technique, you can choose any of the fillings listed on page 151.

½ pound raw tuna (maguro) fillet, and/or 1 small ripe avocado, and/or 1 kirby cucumber, and/or ½ European cucumber, peeled
2 sheets nori seaweed, toasted
4 cups Basic Sushi Rice (page 145)
1 tablespoon wasabi paste (page 142)
soy sauce (optional)
4 tablespoons pickled ginger (amazu-shoga)

To make tuna sushi roll, cut the fillet into a rectangle approximately 6 by 2 by 1 inch. With a sharp knife, slice the fillet lengthwise into quarters to make long strips. Keep refrigerated, wrapped in plastic, until ready to use.

Peel avocado and slice in half lengthwise. Slice each half into pieces ⅜ inch thick. Keep refrigerated until ready for use.

Slice cucumber into thin julienne strips, 4 to 5 inches long.

To Assemble the Sushi Roll

Cut toasted nori seaweed sheets in half crosswise and set them on a dry plate.

Prepare a bowl of vinegared water, combining ¼ cup water with 1 tablespoon vinegar. This water is used to moisten your hands while rolling the sushi so the rice won't stick to your hands.

Place the halved sheet of nori seaweed, shiny side down, on a bamboo mat, with the long edge toward you. Moisten your hands with the vinegared water and spread about a cup of sushi rice over the seaweed evenly, about ⅛ to ¼ inch thick to the edges of seaweed on both sides and bottom edge and within ½ inch of the top.

Across the center of the rice bed dab a thin line of wasabi paste, about ¼ teaspoon. If you do not like your sushi "hot," omit it entirely.

Lengthwise across the center of the rice bed place one quarter of the tuna, avocado, and/or cucumber. Holding the filling down with your fingers, lift up the mat with your thumbs and roll it over until the seaweed and rice form a cylindrical tube. Press the bamboo-covered roll firmly to compress the roll enough to cut easily.

Use the remaining ingredients to make 3 more rolls of sushi. The rolls can be kept in a cool place up to 6 hours unrefrigerated. Do not refrigerate, or the rice will get hard and dry.

To serve, wipe a sharp knife with a well-wrung damp cloth. Place a roll lengthwise on a cutting board and slice in half, crosswise. Cut each half into thirds.

Repeat with the remaining 3 rolls. Serve with soy sauce or plain, with pickled ginger on the side.

NOTE: Any fillings suggested on page 151 may be used for rolled sushi.

SERVE WITH String Bean Sesame Toss
Miso Soup with Wakame
Seaweed and Tofu
Vinegared Crab

  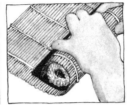 

CALIFORNIA ROLL
4 SERVINGS

Born in California, popularized by sushi chefs throughout the U.S., this sushi has also reached the shores of Japan, becoming a favorite with all sushi lovers. Its special filling of avocado, crab roe, sesame seeds, and cucumber make this roll beautiful and tasty.

4 crab sticks (steamed fish cake with crab
    flavor) or ¼ pound cooked crab,
    shredded
1 small ripe avocado
½ European cucumber
2 sheets nori seaweed, toasted
4 cups Basic Sushi Rice (page 145)
1 tablespoon wasabi paste
2 tablespoons crab roe

Slice crab sticks in half.

Peel avocado and slice into ⅜-inch-thick pieces. Keep refrigerated until ready to use.

Slice cucumber into julienne strips, 4 to 5 inches long.

To assemble the sushi roll, follow instructions for Futo-maki-Zushi.

You should have neat rows of crab, avocado, cucumber, and crab roe fillings laying across the bed of rice. Don't forget to sprinkle with sesame seeds before you roll.

You can have the rice side out by doing a reverse roll. On a bamboo mat lay a well-wrung piece of cloth approximately the same size as the mat. Take a handful of sushi rice and spread it over the mat. Lay a sheet of nori seaweed on top of the rice. Then lay the fillings as you would for regular California roll and roll it carefully, pressing with your hands to mold the rice into a roll. Gently remove the bamboo mat, peeling off the cloth at the same time. Cut the roll as you would a regular sushi roll.

FUTO-MAKI-ZUSHI

(GIANT SUSHI ROLL)

4 SERVINGS

This recipe is a variation of hoso-maki-zushi that incorporates five fillings. The rolling technique is basically the same as for hoso-maki-zushi, but since it incorporates more fillings, a whole sheet of nori seaweed is used. You may use any of the sushi fillings introduced in the other rolled sushi recipes.

½ *Heavenly Omelette (page 111)*
¼ *pound cooked crab meat or 4 crab sticks*
    (crab-flavored fish cakes)
¼ *bunch fresh spinach (about ⅓ pound)*
1 *medium carrot*

SEASONED MUSHROOMS

6 *small dried shiitake mushrooms*
½ *cup water*
2 *tablespoons mirin*
1 *tablespoon sake*
2 *tablespoons soy sauce*

3 *sheets nori seaweed, toasted*
6 *cups Basic Sushi Rice (page 145)*
1 *tablespoon wasabi paste*
2 *tablespoons roasted sesame seeds*
4 *tablespoons pickled ginger (amazu-shoga)*

Make an egg omelette and cool completely. (You will need only half the omelette; save the other half for snacks or breakfast.) Cut lengthwise into long strips measuring approximately ½ by ½ by 7 inches. If they come out short, you can use 2 strips of omelette of equal thickness across the sheet of seaweed.

Shred the crab and use about 2 tablespoons for each roll. If you use crab sticks, split each stick in half and use both halves, end to end, per sushi roll.

Wash the spinach very thoroughly to remove any grit. Boil water in a saucepan with a dash of salt. Add the spinach and boil for 1 minute. Drain. Rinse under cold water and, bunching the ends together, squeeze to remove water. Trim off the roots. Use 1 clump (or 2, if small) of cooked spinach per sushi roll, placed lengthwise across the bed of rice.

Peel the carrot and cut into matchsticks. In a small saucepan, bring water to a boil; add the carrot and cook for 2 minutes. Drain and cool.

Soften shiitake mushrooms in water for 30 minutes or longer. Reserve ⅓ cup shiitake liquid. Discard stems and slice thinly, into ¼-inch-thick strips.

In a small saucepan, combine reserved shiitake liquid, measured water, mirin, sake, and soy sauce and bring to a boil over medium heat. Add mushrooms and continue simmering over low heat until the liquid has been absorbed by the mushrooms. Cool. You will use one third of the mushroom strips for each sushi roll, laying the strips neatly across the bed of rice.

To Assemble Sushi Roll
Prepare a bowl of vinegared water, combining ¼ cup water with 1 tablespoon rice vinegar. This water is used to moisten your hands while rolling the sushi so that the rice won't stick to your hands.

Place a full sheet of nori seaweed, shiny side down, on a dry bamboo mat with the short edge of the seaweed toward you. Moisten your hands with the vinegared water and spread about 2 cups sushi rice over the seaweed evenly—about ⅛ to ¼ inch thick—to the edges of the seaweed on both sides and bottom edge, and within 1 inch of top.

Across the width of the rice bed dab a thin line of wasabi paste, about ¼ teaspoon or more. If you do not like your sushi "hot," omit it entirely.

About 2 inches from the edge closest to you, place a row of the omelette strips across the rice. Follow with rows of crab, spinach, carrot, and mushrooms, topped with roasted sesame seeds. You should have five neat rows of fillings lying across the bed of rice.

Pressing the fillings down with your fingers, lift up the edge of the mat nearest you with your thumbs and roll the mat over until you form a cylindrical tube. Press the mat-covered roll to compress it slightly. Use the remaining ingredients to make 2 more rolls of sushi.

To serve, wipe a sharp knife with a well-wrung damp cloth. Place a roll lengthwise on a cutting board and slice into 4 or 5 pieces. Repeat with the remaining rolls.

Allow several slices for each serving, and serve with soy sauce, or plain, with pickled ginger on the side.

The rolls can be kept in a cool place up to 6 hours, unrefrigerated.

SERVE WITH Basic Miso Soup
Watercress Ohi-tashi
Shrimp Lemon Boats

HAND-MOLDED SUSHI

(NIGIRI-ZUSHI)

APPROXIMATELY 4 DOZEN BITE-SIZE SUSHI
5 TO 7 SERVINGS AS APPETIZER, 4 SERVINGS AS DINNER

Unlike rolled sushi, in which a bamboo mat gives the food its cylindrical form, hand-molded sushi (nigiri-zushi) is entirely the work of human hands. It is your *touch,* like that of a sculptor, that gives the sushi its final form: a hand-patted oval mound of rice topped with a precise slice of pure seafood or vegetable. Once more I must urge you to observe how a professional sushi chef does this elegant work at his sushi bar. When I teach a class in nigiri-zushi making I tell my students that I am a novice at this art, although I have been eating and making sushi for some time. No one will expect you to be an instant master, but you can and should insist on using only the freshest ingredients.

4 cups Basic Sushi Rice (page 145)
1 sheet nori seaweed, toasted
¼ pound each fish fillets, such as fresh tuna,
    yellowtail, red snapper, and flounder,
    or octopus and smoked salmon (1½
    pounds seafood fillets in all)
½ Heavenly Omelette (page 111)
2 tablespoons wasabi paste
¼ cup pickled ginger (amazu-shoga)
    soy sauce

Prepare sushi rice half an hour to 1 hour before you plan to serve it. Cover with a damp cloth to retain moisture. Do not refrigerate.

Cut the nori seaweed into ribbon strips about 3 inches long to strap around each piece of sushi if you wish. Cut fillets into ¼-inch slices, cutting across the grain. Do not saw the fish, or it will be rough in texture and unappealing. Cut with one even stroke, drawing the knife toward you smoothly. Keep in the refrigerator if you wish to make the toppings ahead of time —but not for more than 1 hour.

Prepare the omelette and cut it into ¼-inch slices. (The omelette may be made a day ahead.)

To assemble the sushi, arrange the toppings on a large platter. Set the cooked sushi rice on another platter or in a bowl. In another small bowl, combine ¼ cup water and 1 teaspoon rice vinegar for moistening your palms and fingers; this prevents the rice balls from sticking to your hands as you mold the rice. Put the wasabi paste in another small bowl. In another bowl place the strips of nori seaweed.

Now you are ready to do the elegant handwork.

Dip your right hand in the vinegar solution and rub your hands together to dampen them lightly. Scoop up about 1½ tablespoons vinegared rice with your right hand and shape it into an oval. With your left hand, pick up the topping of your choice. Still holding the rice in the palm of your right hand, dip your right index finger in the wasabi paste and spread a small amount on the topping in your left hand. Now gently press the rice onto the topping with your right index finger, using your left thumb to shape the ends. Turn the sushi over, topping side up, and shape further using the thumb and index finger. Set completed sushi on the serving platter and continue in this fashion until you use up the toppings.

Serve with ginger and soy sauce. Sushi can be prepared an hour ahead of time and stored in a cool place, but do not refrigerate.

SERVE WITH Shrimp Lemon Boats
Basic Miso Soup

Almost any kind of vegetable or seafood works well, and some people enjoy small bits of meat or fruit in their sushi. Your choices will depend on the season and on availability. Here are some variations to try:

VEGETARIAN FILLINGS: carrot, cucumber, seasoned gourd strips, daikon radish sprouts (kai-ware), avocado, spinach, seasoned shiitake mushrooms, egg omelette, roasted sesame seeds, salted plum, fermented soybeans, boiled spinach, boiled okra, boiled green beans, mozzarella, Monterey Jack, Camembert, Brie, kiwi, shiso leaves, pickled burdock, boiled asparagus, pickled daikon radish, seasoned tofu pouches (age).

SEAFOOD: tuna (maguro), yellowtail (hamachi), giant clam (miru-gai), abalone (awabi), shrimp (ebi), sea urchin (uni), round clam (aoyagi), salmon roe (ikura), squid (ika), flounder (hirame), herring (kohada), scallop (hotate-gai), mackerel (saba), sea eel (anago), vinegared mackerel (shime-saba), octopus (tako), smoked salmon (shake), red snapper (tai), crab (kani), fatty tuna (toro), medium-fat tuna (chu-toro), cod roe (tarako), sweet shrimp (ama-ebi), oyster (kaki), Spanish mackerel (aji), seaweed with herring roe (kazunoko-konbu).

SHRIMP SUSHI
(EBI-NO-NIGIRI-ZUSHI)
4 SERVINGS

This is another hand-molded sushi. Cooked shrimp are easier to work with than raw fish fillets, and particularly encouraging for a beginner. I always begin my nigiri-zushi class with shrimp, before I get into the other toppings. The mound of vinegared rice should be molded to fit the shrimp; with practice your hands will make the shape that works best. Be it square, rectangle, round, or oval, what is important is the consistency of shapes. Be sure to put a dab of wasabi paste on the underside of each shrimp if you like your sushi hot.

2 to 2½ cups Basic Sushi Rice (page 145)
12 medium raw shrimp
1 tablespoon wasabi paste
¼ cup pickled ginger (amazu-shoga)
  soy sauce

Prepare sushi rice half an hour to 1 hour before you plan to serve it. Cover with a damp cloth to retain moisture. Do not refrigerate. Prepare your topping as close to serving time as possible.

To prepare shrimp, skewer the underside of each shrimp with a toothpick to prevent shrinkage while cooking. Bring salted water to a simmer in a medium saucepan, add raw shrimp, and simmer for 2 minutes. Drain and rinse under cold water. Peel, remove toothpick, and devein, leaving the tail on for decoration. Spread the shrimp open by making an incision on the underside about three quarters of the way through. Flatten the shrimp with a knife.

To assemble sushi, put the shrimp on a platter. Set the cooked sushi rice on another platter or in a bowl. In another small bowl, combine ¼ cup of water and 1 teaspoon rice vinegar, which you will use to moisten your palms and fingers; this prevents the rice from sticking to your hands. Put the wasabi paste in a small bowl.

Now you are ready to play sushi chef.

Dip your right hand in the vinegar solution and rub your hands together. Scoop up about 1½ tablespoons vinegared rice with your right hand and shape it into an oval. Pick up the tail end of the shrimp with your left hand. Still holding the rice in the palm of your right hand, dip your right index finger in the wasabi paste and spread a small pinch on the shrimp. Place the rice on the shrimp and press down gently with your right index finger, using your left thumb to shape the ends. Turn the sushi over, topping side up, and shape further using the thumb and index finger. Set completed sushi on the serving platter and continue with the next piece of sushi.

Serve with ginger and soy sauce. You can make shrimp sushi an hour ahead of time and store in a cool place. Do not refrigerate.

SERVE WITH Octopus Lemon Boats
  Miso Soup with Enoki
  Mushrooms
  Sushi Rolled in Nori

CRAB SUSHI LOAF
(KANI-NO-OSHI-ZUSHI)
4 SERVINGS

Pressed or molded sushi originated in the Osaka area. It is made by layering rice and other ingredients in a wooden mold called oshi-waku, and is a particularly easy way to make sushi. Here, crab and parsley are wonderful together. Oshi-waku molds are available in Japanese hardware stores, or use a rectangular casserole dish instead.

4 cups Basic Sushi Rice (page 145)
2 tablespoons minced parsley
½ pound cooked crab, shredded
   square casserole dish, 8 by 8 inches
1 lemon
   soy sauce

Rinse the casserole dish with water and dry with a towel.

Toss warm sushi rice with chopped parsley.

Spread shredded crab in the casserole dish. Try to lay it in neat, even rows, as flat as possible.

Spread sushi rice on top of the crab.

Press the rice down evenly with moist fingers. Cover with plastic wrap and place a book on top to press rice. Let stand 30 minutes.

Slice the lemon crosswise, about ⅛ inch thick. Slice each piece into quarters.

Insert a knife around the periphery of the casserole dish. Turn out sushi loaf onto a clean, slightly damp cutting board. With a sharp knife, cut the loaf into bite-size rectangles. Decorate the top of each rectangle with 2 pieces of sliced lemon. Let the points of the lemon slices touch each other to make a butterfly shape.

Serve with soy sauce.

SUSHI HAND ROLLS

(TEMAKI-ZUSHI)

4 SERVINGS

This sushi is hand-rolled to a conical or cylindrical roll without the help of a bamboo mat. It can be made easily at home, and your guests can participate. I call this "party sushi." Students in my sushi classes find this recipe easy and fun because all the fillings are served on one large platter, with another bowl full of sushi rice. Each guest gets a stack of nori seaweed and a plate. The fillings, rice, soy sauce, wasabi paste, and pickled ginger are passed around by your guests so they can create their own unique roll of sushi.

6 cups Basic Sushi Rice (page 145)
16 sheets nori seaweed, toasted, halved
    lengthwise
3 tablespoons wasabi paste
  soy sauce
  pickled ginger (amazu-shoga)

FILLINGS

Much depends on availability, freshness, your budget, and the preparation time involved. A party tray for four people would include at least 10 of the following:

1 European or 3 kirby cucumbers, cut into
    ¼ by 4-inch sticks
1 ripe avocado, cut into eighths
8 to 12 shiso leaves
½ pound tuna (maguro), cut into slices
    ¼ by 4 inches
½ pound cooked crab meat, shredded, or 4
    "sea legs" (crab sticks)

2 kiwis, sliced
2 ounces salmon or crab roe
2 ounces mozzarella cheese sticks
1 Heavenly Omelette (page 111), sliced
4 to 8 pitted salted plums (ume-boshi)
4 to 8 cooked medium shrimp
4 ounces pickled daikon radish (takuan)
4 ounces sea urchin roe
¼ pound smoked salmon, thinly sliced and
    cut into strips
2 ounces fermented soybeans (natto)
4 quail eggs
1 bunch daikon radish sprouts
  bonito flakes
  parsley sprigs
  roasted sesame seeds

Arrange as many of these fillings as you like on a large platter, to make a colorful rose window. Use small chrysanthemum flowers and baby lemons and their leaves to decorate the plate. Store in the refrigerator until just before serving, and prepare as close to serving time as possible. Here are some of the possible combinations:

a teaspoon of salmon roe and a shiso leaf
a piece of tuna and a cucumber stick
2 ounces crab and a slice of avocado,
    sprinkled with sesame seeds
2 or 3 slices of kiwi and a cucumber stick
a cheese stick and a slice of avocado
a slice of omelette and a piece of cucumber
a pitted salted plum and a shredded shiso
    leaf
a cooked shrimp and a cucumber stick
a daikon radish stick sprinkled with sesame
    seeds
sea urchin and a shiso leaf
a strip of smoked salmon and a shiso leaf
2 ounces cooked crab sprinkled with chopped
    parsley and a squeeze of lemon juice
1 tablespoon fermented soybeans splashed
    with soy sauce and sprinkled with
    chopped green onion (green part only)
1 teaspoon salmon roe and a raw quail egg
    radish sprouts and a dusting of bonito
    flakes
2 or 3 slices kiwi and Brie cheese

To Assemble Temaki-Zushi
Each roll is made of half a toasted seaweed sheet. If smaller rolls are preferred, cut the seaweed sheets into quarters. The roll should contain about 2 tablespoons sushi rice, or enough to grasp with one hand. With a spoon or chopsticks, scoop up the rice and lay it on the sheet of nori. Spread with hands, chopsticks, or a spoon. Dab on a little wasabi paste. Then lay 2 or 3 fillings on top of the bed of rice. Wrap the seaweed sheet with its contents into a roll. Dip it in soy sauce. And eat! Freshen your palate with a few bites of pickled ginger and a sip of beverage. Then on to your next handmade taste adventure.

SCATTERED SUSHI

(CHIRASHI-ZUSHI)
4 SERVINGS

This is a sushi dish popularly served by home cooks. It is not rolled or hand-molded. Some of the seafood and vegetable ingredients are simply chopped up and tossed with the vinegared rice. The dish looks much like a pilaf. Sculptured carrots make a beautiful garnish.

4 cups Basic Sushi Rice (page 145)
Seasoned Mushrooms (page 148)
8 pieces of 6-inch-long dried gourd strips
    (kampyo)
1 teaspoon salt
⅔ cup water
2 tablespoons soy sauce
3 tablespoons sugar
½ pound green beans, ends removed
3 thin Egg Pancakes (page 158)
1 medium carrot
1 sheet nori seaweed, toasted
½ pound cooked bay shrimp, peeled
3 teaspoons roasted white sesame seeds
4 teaspoons pickled ginger (amazu-shoga)
    (optional)

Make the sushi rice and seasoned mushrooms; let cool.

To prepare seasoned gourd, rinse gourd strips under cold water. Plunge into a bowl of water with the salt and knead the gourd for 1 minute. Drain. In a small saucepan, combine measured water, soy sauce, and sugar and bring to a boil. Add gourd strips and simmer until most of the liquid has been absorbed and strips become tender and sweet, about 20 minutes. Cool. Chop gourd and mushrooms into ¼-inch pieces and set aside.

In a medium saucepan, boil green beans until tender but crisp, about 3 minutes. Rinse under cold water and slice into julienne strips, about 1½ inches long. Set aside.

Make the egg pancakes. Slice each pancake into ¼-inch-thick strips, 1½ inches long. Set aside.

Peel the carrot and slice it crosswise into ³⁄₁₆-inch-thick pieces, then make sculptured plum flowers (page 15). In a small saucepan, bring water to a boil. Add a dash of salt and the carrot. Turn heat to low and simmer for 2 minutes. Drain. Set aside.

Slice the sheet of toasted nori seaweed into ⅛-inch-thick strips about 1½ inches long. Set aside.

While sushi rice is still warm, incorporate the chopped mushrooms and gourd into the rice and toss gently with a wooden paddle.

Divide the mixed sushi into 4 portions and serve each portion on an attractive dinner plate.

Decorate top of each bed of mixed sushi rice with a quarter of the bay shrimp, julienned green beans, egg strips, toasted seaweed strips, sculptured carrots, and sesame seeds. You may either sprinkle each topping randomly over the bed of rice or lay them in rows to make colorful stripes.

Top with pickled ginger.

NOTE: This sushi is best eaten the day it is prepared. It may be steamed and served the following day, but the flavor is less good. Do not refrigerate.

SERVE WITH Asparagus Celebration
Snow-Covered Mountain
Salad
Snake Eye Suimono

STUFFED TOFU SUSHI
(INARI-ZUSHI)
6 TO 8 SERVINGS

What do you do with leftover sushi rice? It can be stuffed into fried, seasoned tofu pillows (age or usu-age) and served for lunch. Inari-zushi need not be made with leftovers; it's so tasty you may want to prepare fresh sushi rice just for this dish. Serve with a salad, suimono soup, and fruit for dessert. Children like the handiness of this dish.

4 cups Basic Sushi Rice (page 145) or
    Chirashi-zushi (page 156)
12 fried tofu pouches (abura-age or usu-age)
3 tablespoons sake
4 tablespoons soy sauce
2 tablespoons mirin
2 tablespoons sugar
1½ cups dashi

GARNISH
¼ cup pickled ginger
1 tablespoon roasted white sesame seeds

Make little slits in the tofu pouches. Soak them in hot water to remove excess oil. Squeeze out the water.

In a medium saucepan, combine the seasonings, tofu pouches, and dashi and simmer with the lid on for about 8 minutes. Remove from heat. Let the pouches soak to absorb the liquid, about 10 minutes.

Squeeze liquid out of each pouch. Gently stuff it with sushi rice, about ⅓ cup each. Do not overstuff, or the pouches will rip. Place them slit side down on a plate. Sprinkle sesame seeds on top of each stuffed pouch. Serve with pickled ginger on the side.

OPTIONAL: Tie each pillow with seasoned gourd (page 156) as you would Egg Sushi Blankets.

SERVE WITH Spinach Sesame Toss
Cauliflower Florets with
    Miso
Vegetable and Chicken
    Miso Soup

EGG SUSHI BLANKETS

(CHAKIN-ZUSHI)

4 SERVINGS

March 3 is "Girl's Day" in Japan. On this day, Japanese dolls are decorated and girls get to dress in silky kimonos and visit with friends and relatives. They have tiny dolls, brought out of storage only for the occasion. One of the special foods served is chakin-zushi, made of egg pancakes with a delicate pastel color; eating them is like opening a present. If you can, decorate your table with a branch of cherry or plum blossoms. The egg pancake recipe, prepared like thin crêpes, may be halved.

EGG PANCAKES

6 eggs

1 teaspoon salt

2 teaspoons sake

2 teaspoons sugar

4 teaspoons vegetable oil

4 cups Scattered Sushi (chirashi-zushi) (page 156)

Combine all pancake ingredients except oil in a medium-size bowl. Beat well.

Lightly grease a nonstick frying pan and place over medium heat. Wipe off excess oil with a paper towel.

Pour in ¼ cup seasoned egg mixture, tilting the pan to spread it evenly. Cook over low heat until the surface of the egg looks cooked, about 20 seconds.

Remove from heat and turn it over onto a cutting board or large plate. Let stand to cool.

Repeat the process seven more times. (You will have 8 egg pancakes.)

Make 8 oval rice balls with the 4 cups scattered sushi rice.

On the center of each egg pancake place 1 rice ball. Wrap first one edge of the pancake over the rice ball, then the other. Fold the side edges over the rice ball (as if you were wrapping a present). Turn the wrapped rice ball seam side down to keep the folds secure. Allow 2 per serving.

OPTIONAL: You may use seasoned gourd strips (see page 156) to tie each sushi blanket. Cut each gourd strip into 12-inch pieces. Wrap the sushi in egg pancake and tie each one like a present with the gourd strip.

SERVE WITH Spring Clam Suimono
Kiwi Delight

SASHIMI

You will need a sharp knife. If you plan to serve sashimi often, you may wish to invest in a sashimi knife (sashimi-bocho), which is designed especially for slicing fish. Japanese hardware stores, Japanese grocery stores, and some of the more classy American department stores carry them. You might ask your favorite sushi chef where you could buy one like his. A large chef's knife, however, will be okay if it is very sharp. Wipe the knife with a damp, well-wrung cotton cloth after you have sliced 4 to 6 pieces of sashimi (in order to keep the knife free of oils and cutting well). Also basic to sashimi is a clean cutting board, which should regularly be rinsed in water and wiped with a clean cloth.

With the basic instruments in hand and a fresh fish of your choice, you are prepared to make sashimi. There are five basic steps.

Step 1: Filleting a Whole Fish

Most Japanese grocery stores and fish markets will fillet fish for sashimi. However, if you catch the fish yourself, or if you buy it fresh at your local fishermen's wharf, you may want to do the filleting yourself. To fillet firm, white-fleshed fish such as sea bream, sea bass, and red snapper, cut off head by sliding the knife under the bone close to the gills. This will require turning the fish over to cut through the spine. Discard the head.

Holding the fish with one hand, separate meat and bones by sliding the knife along the belly, starting at the head end, cutting through the back of the rib cage, and finishing at the tail end. You will have two fillets, one with bones and the other boneless. Set the boneless fillet aside.

To remove the bones from the second fillet, turn the fillet bone side down. With the knife nearly parallel to the cutting board, cut from the head end, sliding the knife as close as possible to the bones. Now you should have two fillets plus the skeleton with some meat on it. The bones can be used to make Fish Bone Soup (page 58).

  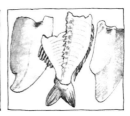

To fillet a flat fish, such as flounder, scale the brown side of the fish. The white side is practically free of scales.

Place the fish tail toward you on a clean cutting board. Make an incision with the knife across the fish right behind the head and another one right above the tail. Following the spine, make an incision from head to tail end. Make incisions along the fins on both sides.

Fillet the fish by sliding the knife as close as possible to the bones and pulling the fillet, as it is cut, away from the bones. Repeat for the other side. You should have four boneless fillets and one skeleton with some flesh.

  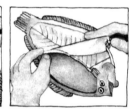 

Step 2: Skinning the Fillets

Before beginning to slice the fish for sashimi, you must remove the skin. Place the fillet skin side down on a clean, slightly damp cutting board, with the tail facing toward you.

Hold the tail end of the fish with one hand and make an incision in the fillet as close as possible to the tail end. When the blade of the knife reaches the skin, pull the skin to the left with one hand while the other hand guides the blade to the right at a slight angle, drawing the knife back and forth and as close to the skin as possible until you reach the other end. Discard skin.

For a delicate fish with soft skin, put fillet skin side down on a clean, slightly damp cutting board, with the head end facing toward you. Hold the fillet with one hand and, with the knife held parallel to the cutting board, let the other hand guide the knife to cut right above the skin, drawing it toward you. Try to slice off skin only. Discard skin.

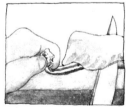 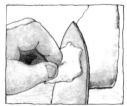

Skinning the fillet   *Trimming the fillet*

Step 3: Trimming the Fillets

Further filleting is necessary for making sashimi slices, after you have filleted and skinned the fish. Only the finest part of the fillet is used for sashimi.

Cut away ribs by sliding the knife at an angle just underneath the bones.

Slice just above the lateral line containing bones by drawing the knife toward you.

Slice off the bone along the lateral line.

Trim bones from the other fillet in the same way.

Step 4: Slicing the Sashimi

You are now ready to make sashimi. There are a number of ways to prepare the fish; mix two or more methods to give your sashimi platter a more interesting appearance.

Basic cut   *Paper thin cut*   *Cube cut*

THE BASIC CUT (hira-zukuri)

This technique can be used on any type of fish. It is a rectangular cut, each slice measuring about ⅜ inch up to ½ inch in thickness.

Place fillet lengthwise on a clean cutting board. The narrow end of the fillet should be toward you. Draw the knife from base to tip in one single motion, slicing through the fillet without much pressure other than the weight of the knife. Slice each piece about ⅜ inch thick. (The firmer the fish, the thinner it can be cut. Soft-fleshed fish such as tuna should be cut rather thick, about ½ inch in thickness.) Occasionally wipe the knife with a well-wrung damp cloth to remove fish oils.

PAPER-THIN CUT (usu-zukuri)

This method is applied to firm fish such as sea bream, flounder, and sea bass.

Place fillet lengthwise on a clean cutting board. The narrow end should face toward you.

Tilt the knife toward the thick part of the fillet and slice as thinly as possible, drawing the knife from base to tip in one single motion. The fillet is cut across the grain. (You may *partially* freeze fillets for easier slicing.)

CUBE CUT (kaku-zukuri)

This method is applied to thick but soft-fleshed tuna and bonito or abalone.

Place fillet vertically on a clean cutting board. Slice off a lengthwise strip ¾ inch wide by drawing the knife toward you in a single motion. Turn the strip 90 degrees and cut straight down at a right angle to achieve ¾-inch cubes.

STRING CUT (ito-zukuri)

This cut is used for very thin fillets of fish such as sillago (kisu) and garfish (sayori). While these fish are rarely seen in American fish markets or Japanese grocery stores, the same technique is applied to slicing squid.

Using the tip of your knife, slice the fillet into thin strips, ⅛ inch thick for squid, 1/16 inch thick for sillago and garfish. Each strip should be about 2½ inches in length.

Step 5: Serving Sashimi

Japanese serve sashimi in odd numbers—3, 5, or 7 pieces. Four is a bad-luck number in Japan ("shi" means 4, and also death). Avoid even portions if you can.

A dish of sashimi should ideally have something from the sea and something from the land. For instance, you may combine sashimi and strips of white radish. A small chrysanthemum flower from your garden can make an excellent garnish. Serve individual small dishes of sashimi, or serve the sashimi on one large dish and let everyone help themselves. Remember the dab of green horseradish, communal soy sauce bottle, and tiny individual dip dishes.

SASHIMI GARNISHES
(ASHI-RAI)

Two types of garnishes accompany sashimi: ken and tsuma. Ken is the garnish that adds nutritional balance and gives the palate a rest before the next bite of sashimi. Common kens are:

SHREDDED DAIKON RADISH: Tangles of daikon radish strips are served like miniature mountains. To achieve such fine strips, use a special Japanese slicing machine that cranks out thin shreds (available in Japanese kitchenware store) or cut in very fine julienne; soak in cold water. Drain and pat dry before use. Allow ¼ cup shredded daikon per serving.

SHREDDED CARROT: Prepare the same way as daikon radish.

SLICED CUCUMBER: Use unwaxed cucumbers, which need no peeling or seeding. Make the slices about ⅛ inch thick, 3 slices per serving.

JULIENNED GREEN ONION: Slice the white part only into julienne strips and soak in cold water for 5 minutes. Drain. Make a miniature mountain using 2 green onions (white part) per serving.

WAKAME SEAWEED (dried or fresh): Wash in running water to remove sand and salt. Soak in water for 20 minutes and then slice into bite-size pieces. Make a small mountain using 2 to 3 tablespoons wakame seaweed per serving.

TSUMA is a garnish that enhances the color and flavor of sashimi. Common tsuma garnishes are sprouts (benitade), baby cucumber with yellow flower (hanatsuki-kyuri), sprigs of sansho plant (kinome), seaweed (suizenji-nori). Some are not readily available in the U.S. Baby chrysanthemum flowers, the yellow ones only (kiku), and beefsteak plant (shisho leaves) are often available in Japanese grocery stores. You can raise your own sprouts, including daikon radish, cucumber, and carrots, all eye-appealing garnishes. Only newborn sprouts and small flowers, a single blossom per serving, are compatible with sashimi. Big flowers are visually overwhelming. Sprouts are beautiful in small bundles of six or eight.

SMOKED SALMON SASHIMI
4 SERVINGS

This is a most simple and effective way to prepare sashimi, using the smoked salmon available in Jewish delicatessens as lox or Nova Scotia salmon. The bite-size pieces are dusted with strained hard-boiled egg yolk to make a colorful dish.

4 ounces smoked salmon
1 hard-boiled egg yolk
4 Chinese pea pods for garnish

Slice salmon into bite-size pieces, about 1½ inches long.

Press hard-boiled egg yolk through a fine strainer to make pollenlike dust.

Briefly blanch pea pods, about 30 seconds, and drain. Slice into julienne strips.

Arrange an odd number of salmon slices on individual serving plates and dust with strained egg yolk. Sprinkle the pea pod strips over the salmon, or bunch them and place them against the fish. Serve chilled.

RED SNAPPER SASHIMI
4 SERVINGS

Called tai in Japanese, red snapper is a felicitous fish, eaten on New Year's, at weddings, on birthdays, etc. Red snapper is readily available fresh and is delicious for sashimi.

1 pound fresh red snapper fillet or 1
    (3-pound) whole fish
1 tablespoon wasabi
    soy sauce
    parsley

To prepare the fillet, clean and cut the fish into 2 boneless fillets, following the method for filleting firm fleshed fish (page 159). Skin the fillet and prepare the fillet

for sashimi. Place the fillet on a clean cutting board and slice through the fillet crosswise about ⅛ inch thick, using the paper-thin cut.

Arrange 3 or 5 slices on a plate and serve with wasabi and soy sauce. Garnish with parsley.

SERVE WITH Spring Rain Shrimp
Asparagus Celebration

FLOUNDER SASHIMI
4 SERVINGS

Flounder is delicate, its meat translucent as glass when sliced thinly. Compared to tuna, flounder is a bit difficult to prepare, but the result is a light, pretty rosette that tastes like eating flavorful air. The maple radish garnish gives the fish a special taste and look.

1 pound flounder fillet or a large whole
    flounder

DIPPING SAUCE
1 tablespoon rice vinegar
1 tablespoon dashi
1 teaspoon mild soy sauce
1 teaspoon sugar

MAPLE RADISH
2 ounces daikon radish
1 dried Japanese chili pepper, seeded

2 tablespoons chopped green onions

Clean and skin the fish and cut into 4 boneless fillets, using the method for flat fish (page 160) or purchase the fillet from the seafood shop. Chill until ready for use, or partially freeze the fillet to make slicing easy.

Place the fillet on the cutting board and slice through it crosswise, about ⅜ inch thick, using the paper-thin cut.

Combine ingredients for dipping sauce.

To make maple radish, peel the radish. Make a hole in one end with a chopstick and with the chopstick push the chili pepper into the hole.

Grate the stuffed daikon radish. You will get blush-colored grated daikon. Wring out the excess daikon water with your hands. (Be sure to wash your hands well to rinse off any hot pepper oil.)

To assemble, arrange slices on a large plate in a rosette pattern. Each fillet should slightly overlap the next.

In the center of the rosette put a mound of chopped green onions and maple radish.

Serve with dipping sauce.

NOTE: The maple radish must be made just before serving to keep its freshness and taste.

SERVE WITH Rice with Peas
String Bean Sesame Toss

TUNA SASHIMI
4 SERVINGS

Tuna is the sashimi most people fall in love with instantly because of its succulent texture and fresh taste. Ready-cut tuna fillets for sashimi are available at Japanese seafood markets and gourmet seafood stores in three basic types: akami —the leanest meat, very red in color; chu-toro—somewhat fatty, dark pink in color; and toro—fatty meat that melts in your mouth like butter (the most expensive). Most novices prefer the akami. A quarter pound of sashimi is enough for 1 appetizer serving or side dish. If you want to serve this dish as an entree, increase each portion to ½ pound or combine the tuna with other fish and serve with soup, salad, and rice.

1 pound tuna sashimi fillet, Hawaiian tuna, if
   available
2 teaspoons wasabi paste
4 shiso leaves (optional)
4 ounces shredded daikon radish
   soy sauce

Place tuna fillet on a dry cutting board. Do not rinse the fillet; water makes sashimi taste soggy. Using the cube cut, slice through the fish on a diagonal, about ¾ inch thick. The sashimi may be served individually or on a large plate to be passed around. Chill until ready to serve. Serve with wasabi, shiso leaves, shredded daikon radish, and soy sauce.

SERVE WITH Icicle Radish with Lemon
Sauce
Four-Mushroom Suimono

SQUID SASHIMI
4 SERVINGS

Squid is delicious as sashimi and easier to prepare than you might expect. Mongo squid, imported from Japan and available frozen at Japanese grocery stores, is the tastiest type for sashimi, but Canadian and local squid can also be eaten as sashimi if very fresh. Sliced thinly into strips, they are as *al dente* as Italian noodles. Rolled with nori seaweed they make a beautiful pinwheel. Thin slices of squid arranged with salmon roe can look like a rose. Serve squid with tuna sashimi for variety.

3 fillets mongo squid, defrosted
1 tablespoon salmon roe
½ sheet toasted nori seaweed
¼ cup shredded daikon radish
4 lemon wedges
1 tablespoon wasabi paste
1 small chrysanthemum flower
  soy sauce

To clean squid, remove eggs, spine, and innards and rinse under cold water. Peel off skin from body and discard. Reserve legs for another use. (The legs may be cooked in boiling water for 2 minutes, chilled, and eaten with soy sauce and lemon juice.)

The fillet of mongo squid is shaped like a triangle. Each triangle fillet should be cut into 4 pieces as follows. First, cut about 1 inch off the top of the fillet and set aside. Next, make the remaining fillet into a square by cutting the small triangles off each side. Set aside in a separate pile.

From the top piece of the fillet, make rose-shaped sashimi by slicing it into thin strips about ¾ inch thick. Lay the pieces end to end, overlapping slightly, to make a strip 5 inches long. Take one end of the strip and roll it to make a pinwheel or rose. Put ½ teaspoon salmon roe in the center. Repeat with remaining top pieces of squid. Arrange the rosettes on a large platter and set aside.

Using the side pieces of the fillet, make noodle-shaped sashimi. Slice each piece into very thin, noodlelike strips with a sharp knife. Arrange in a mound next to the rose-shaped sashimi.

To make the rolled sashimi with nori seaweed, use the square piece that remains after you've sliced off the top and sides. With a sharp knife, score the right side of the fillet about halfway through. Turn the fillet over and lay on it a piece of toasted nori seaweed the size of the fillet. Lift one edge of the fillet and roll it away from you. With a knife, slice the rolled fillet crosswise into pinwheels about ½ inch thick.

Arrange the pinwheels around the rosettes and noodle-shaped sashimi. Garnish the platter with shredded daikon radish, lemon wedges, wasabi, and the chrysanthemum flower.

Serve chilled with soy sauce. You may make this dish an hour ahead of time and keep it chilled in the refrigerator.

SERVE WITH Tuna Sashimi
Autumn Salad

YELLOWTAIL TERIYAKI
4 TO 6 SERVINGS

Teriyaki is a skillet type of Japanese cooking that will be familiar to Americans. It combines soy sauce, sake, and mirin. Some cooks like to add sugar, but I find that the sake and mirin make it sweet enough. The basic teriyaki sauce can be used for many fish and meat dishes and will keep for a week to 10 days in the refrigerator.

sea salt
4 *(6-ounce) yellowtail fillets with skin, ¾ inch thick*

BASIC TERIYAKI SAUCE
⅓ *cup soy sauce*
⅓ *cup sake*
⅓ *cup mirin*

vegetable oil
sliced vinegared ginger (amazu-shoga)
1 *lemon, cut into wedges*

Sprinkle salt over the fillets on both sides. Let stand for 30 minutes.

Combine the sauce ingredients in a saucepan and bring to a boil over medium heat. Let cool.

Lightly grease a heavy skillet (cast iron is best, but heavy aluminum or stainless steel is okay) with vegetable oil, and place fish fillets in the skillet over high heat.

Using a spatula, move fish around gently to keep from sticking or peeling. Let fish cook about 1 minute on each side. Remove from skillet and pour boiling water over fish to remove excess oil and salt.

Wipe the skillet with a paper towel; add the teriyaki sauce, and bring to a boil, then return the fish to the skillet. Tilt the skillet back and forth to make sure the sauce coats the fish evenly. Let cook for about 2 minutes over low heat, or until done. Remove from heat and serve immediately. Pour sauce over the fish as it is served.

Garnish with pickled ginger (amazu-shoga) and lemon wedges.

SERVE WITH Daikon Radish Miso Soup
Burdock Salad with Sesame
Dressing

SQUID TERIYAKI WITH SWEET POTATOES
4 SERVINGS

Do not peel the potatoes; the skin adds color and texture to the dish. The sweetness of the potatoes gives rich flavor to the squid, which is cooked until very tender. Japanese satsuma-imo potatoes are also recommended for this dish and are available in Japanese markets year round.

1 pound sweet potatoes or satsuma-imo
    potatoes
8 to 10 small squid
2 tablespoons vegetable oil
1¼ cups dashi
3 tablespoons sake
1 to 2 tablespoons mirin or sugar
2 tablespoons soy sauce

Wash potatoes well and halve lengthwise. Then cut each half into 4 pieces.

Pull legs off the squid with your fingers, then wash out the innards and pull out the spine under running cold water. Peel off the thin membrane on the surface of the squid. Cut the tips off the legs. Cut the body of each squid into ½-inch rings.

In a medium saucepan, heat oil and sauté sliced sweet potatoes over medium heat for 3 minutes. Add dashi broth and sake and bring to a boil. Combine mirin or sugar and soy sauce. Add squid and let boil again. Remove foam from the surface of the liquid and reduce heat. Let simmer for another 15 minutes, covered.

Serve at room temperature or warm.

FLOUNDER TERIYAKI
4 TO 6 SERVINGS

Any flat fish—sole, halibut, flounder, turbot—is suitable for this recipe. Use the Basic Teriyaki Sauce. Flat fish cooks rapidly because it's so thin.

2 medium flounders, whole
¾ cup dashi
1 cup Basic Teriyaki Sauce, opposite

GARNISH
parsley
grated daikon radish (optional)
lemon wedges (optional)

Clean the fish, leaving head and tail attached. Make crisscross slits on the brown-skin side of the fish, about ¼ inch deep. This speeds up cooking time and allows the rich sauce to penetrate the fish.

Mix together the dashi and teriyaki sauce and pour into a heavy skillet. Bring to a quick boil over high heat.

Place fish in the skillet. If the fish is too large, cut in half on a diagonal; do not overlap the pieces. Cover and cook over high heat for about 5 minutes, then another 5 minutes over medium heat.

Remove from heat and serve on a large platter with parsley to garnish. You may also add grated daikon radish or lemon wedges.

SERVE WITH Watercress Ohi-tashi
        Braised Japanese Potatoes
        and Carrots

SALMON TERIYAKI

4 TO 6 SERVINGS

I've found this slight variation on the Basic Teriyaki Sauce best for salmon steaks. A bit of butter and vinegar are added to enrich the sauce.

sea salt
4 (6-ounce) salmon steaks, about ¾ inch
    thick
2 tablespoons vegetable oil
3 tablespoons butter
3 tablespoons rice vinegar
3 tablespoons mirin
2 tablespoons soy sauce
1 cup chopped green onions
1 lemon, cut into wedges

Salt the salmon steaks on both sides and let stand for 20 minutes.

Heat a heavy skillet over high heat and grease with oil. Cook salmon steaks for 2 minutes on each side over medium heat. Remove fish to a warm plate.

Discard oil in the skillet. Melt butter in the skillet over medium heat and return the salmon to the pan, coating it with butter. Let cook for another 2 minutes, or until done. Remove salmon and serve on individual plates. Save butter sauce in skillet.

To the butter sauce add vinegar, mirin, and soy sauce and simmer over high heat for 1 minute. Pour over the salmon steaks and sprinkle with chopped green onions.

Decorate the plate with lemon wedges.

SERVE WITH Rice with Crab and
        Shiitake Mushrooms
    Snake Eye Suimono

TEMPURA

Here is a style of quick deep-fry cooking the Japanese learned from Portuguese missionaries four hundred years ago. On "Ember Days," when Catholics were not allowed to eat meat, the Portuguese cooked fish fritters and probably ate them with tomato sauce. Japanese ate theirs with a light soy sauce broth and lots of grated daikon radish.

Tempura consists of fresh vegetables and seafood quickly deep fried, usually in an egg batter. Seafood and vegetable tempura are commonly made and served together. In this chapter only the techniques for seafood tempura will be introduced. (See page 131 for a vegetable tempura recipe.)

Serve tempura as hot as you can, right out of the pot. This inevitably means that one person, you, must stay in the kitchen to do all the frying while your guests and family come into the kitchen with their plates to pick up whatever tempura comes out of the pot. Or you may carry the tempura to the dining area. If you have a large kitchen with tables and chairs, entertain your guests there, so you can take breaks and eat with them. Even when not piping hot, tempura tastes delicious if made from fresh ingredients.

Suggested Seafoods

shrimp	red snapper
squid	flounder
sole	scallops
clams	smelt
whitefish	oysters
prawns	nori seaweed

To serve hot tempura in the most delicious and beautiful way, you must be organized. Here is a summary of the steps to follow in preparing tempura:

1. Cut and slice seafood and vegetables. Keep cool.
2. Chill water for batter in the freezer.
3. Prepare dipping broth for tempura.
4. Grate daikon radish and ginger.
5. Make tempura batter.
6. Set the table—rice bowls and bowls for the broth plus chopsticks for each person.
7. Heat oil and begin frying.
8. Serve hot.

The Pot

Use a thick, heavy iron frying pan. (Heavy steel or aluminum is okay, too.) It should have wide sides and plenty of depth to hold oil; shallow and thin frying pans will result in initial high temperature and sudden lowering of temperature when frying.

The Oil

Always use plenty of oil. Being stingy on the oil will result in soggy tempura.

Use approximately 4 cups oil for 4 servings. Don't overcrowd the pot; it should never be more than three quarters to four fifths full, to allow movement of foods while frying.

Vegetable oil is used for tempura—corn, safflower, peanut, etc., but not olive oil. Two parts sesame oil to eight parts other vegetable oil will give a more aromatic, toasty result.

The Temperature

It is crucial to keep the temperature evenly hot. To find the right temperature for frying, drop ½ teaspoonful of batter into the heated oil. If it falls halfway down and sizzles up, it is a little too hot, but still good for frying most seafood and vegetables. If it falls to the bottom and then sizzles to the top right away, it is right for all foods. If the drop stays on the surface, sizzling, the temperature is too high. And if it stays on the bottom, the oil is not yet heated. When making tempura, preheat the oil while you are preparing the ingredients so the oil heats up evenly.

The Batter

The secret of a good tempura is in the batter. You want it to come out light and crispy. Make the batter with *ice-cold* water, fresh eggs, sake, and flour. If the water is ice-cold the batter will be light and less doughy.

If you are going to serve both vegetable and seafood tempura, fry the seafood first and then the vegetables, as the vegetables will give off a lot of moisture and dilute the batter. (Or you may make two separate batches of batter.) Don't let the batter sit next to the heat, and keep the batter bowl afloat in a bowl of water and ice cubes.

Finally, never make too much batter at once; it's better to make a second or third batch later if you run low.

# SEAFOOD TEMPURA
4 SERVINGS

12 *medium to large shrimp or prawns*
4 *small squid*
4 *sea scallops*
8 *string beans*

DIPPING SAUCE

1 *cup dashi*
¼ *cup mild soy sauce*
¼ *cup mirin*
1 *teaspoon sugar (optional)*

BASIC TEMPURA BATTER

1 *cup sifted white flour*
¾ *cup ice-cold water*
1 *tablespoon sake*
1 *egg*
1 *teaspoon cornstarch or rue starch*

white flour
1 *cup grated daikon radish*
1 *tablespoon peeled and grated gingerroot*
lemon wedges (optional)

Wash, devein, and shell shrimp. Make 3 slits horizontally across the underside of each shrimp to keep them from shrinking and curling up while frying.

Wash squid and clean out innards and spine; remove the membrane. Cut into 3 or 4 rings, and dry well with a paper towel, to avoid spattering while cooking.

Cut scallops in half. Cut string beans in half. Refrigerate all tempura ingredients until just before cooking.

In a small saucepan, combine all dipping sauce ingredients and bring to a boil over medium heat. Cook until sugar dissolves, then remove from heat. Keep warm.

Heat the vegetable oil over medium heat.

In a medium bowl, combine all ingredients for the batter. Using a pair of chopsticks or a fork, lightly toss and cut in the ingredients. Do not mix or beat. Don't worry if you find unmixed particles of flour or egg yolk. Set the bowl in a larger bowl filled with ice cubes and water.

In the preheated oil, begin to cook the tempura. Shrimp should be the starter, followed by squid and scallops. (The squid should be dredged in flour before being dipped in the batter, as it tends to resist being coated.) Fry the string beans last, to clear the palate. Drain all the tempura well on paper towels before serving.

Serve the tempura on a plate or bamboo basket lined with a napkin, with small bowls of dipping sauce on the side. Grated daikon radish and ginger may be added to the sauce to taste. Garnish with lemon wedges, if desired.

SERVE WITH Okra and Avocado
Cocktail
Tofu and Wakame
Seaweed Suimono

KAKI-AGE
4 SERVINGS

 Kaki-age is a pancake of chopped seafood and vegetable tempura. Any combination of vegetables and seafood is fun, so you can experiment. This one combines shrimp and mitsuba leaves, but try scallops and onion, shredded carrot and cubes of steamed fish cake, etc.

12 small shrimp
 1 bunch mitsuba leaves
   vegetable oil for deep frying
½ recipe Basic Tempura Batter (page 173)
 3 teaspoons white flour
½ recipe Dipping Sauce (page 173)

Peel and devein shrimp. Cut each shrimp into ¾-inch pieces. Dry with paper towels and set aside.

Wash mitsuba leaves and pat dry with paper towels. Cut into ¾-inch pieces.

Heat the vegetable oil.

Mix batter ingredients. Combine shrimp and mitsuba leaves in a bowl and sprinkle with the measured flour. Divide the shrimp-mitsuba mixture into 4 portions. In a smaller bowl, combine one portion of the shrimp with one quarter of the batter and mix gently to coat. Deep fry over medium heat. Brown on both sides and drain well on paper towel. Serve immediately with heated dipping sauce.

SERVE WITH Octopus Lemon Boats
Bamboo and Wakame
Suimono
Spinach Sesame Toss

SNAPPER TEMPURA WITH ASPARAGUS AND MISO
4 SERVINGS

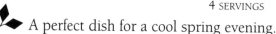 A perfect dish for a cool spring evening.

1½ pounds red snapper fillets
  8 asparagus spears
  4 teaspoons white miso paste
 ¾ cup white flour
  2 eggs, well beaten
  1 cup bread crumbs
    vegetable oil for deep frying
  1 lemon, cut into wedges
    soy sauce

Slice fillets in half. Salt lightly on both sides.

Bring water to a boil in a medium saucepan. Cook the asparagus until it is tender. Slice the stalks into thirds—they should be shorter than the width of the fish fillets.

Dab the middle of each fillet with ½ teaspoon miso paste, or more if the fillet is large. Place 2 or 3 asparagus pieces in the center of the fillet. Roll each fillet and pin together with a wooden toothpick.

Dip each fish roll in flour to coat lightly. Then dip in beaten eggs, and finally in bread crumbs.

Heat oil in a heavy skillet. Deep fry the fish rolls in medium-hot oil until they are golden and crispy. Transfer the fish rolls to a platter, pat with paper towel if oily, and garnish with lemon wedges. Pass a bottle of soy sauce.

SERVE WITH Chilled Tofu with Ginger Sauce
Shrimp Lemon Boats

STUFFED MUSHROOM TEMPURA
4 SERVINGS

Chopped shrimp, sandwiched between two shiitake mushrooms, makes a delicious tempura. This is a fancy appetizer or side dish.

8 dried shiitake mushrooms
5 ounces shrimp
   dash of salt
2 tablespoons chopped green onions

SEASONINGS
½ egg yolk
1 teaspoon sake
½ teaspoon cornstarch or potato starch

3 tablespoons cornstarch or potato starch

BATTER
½ egg yolk
¼ cup cold water
¼ cup sifted white flour

3 tablespoons white flour
   vegetable oil for deep frying
   Dipping Sauce (page 173)

Soften shiitake mushrooms in water for 45 minutes. Squeeze the water out with your hands and pat dry. Remove stems and discard.

Wash shrimp and remove shells. Devein. Chop shrimp into small pieces and add salt. Add chopped green onions and seasonings. Mix well.

Dust inside of 1 mushroom with cornstarch and put a quarter of the shrimp mixture on top. Dust the inside of another mushroom and put it on top of the first mushroom. Continue to make mushroom sandwiches.

Mix the batter ingredients. Dust each sandwich with flour, plunge into batter, and deep fry in heated oil over medium heat till batter turns slightly golden. Serve hot with dipping sauce.

SERVE WITH Bird's Nest Salad
Spicy String Beans

GRILLED SALMON
4 SERVINGS

This is a good, basic fish recipe. The fresh salmon steak is grilled to a delicious crispness while the inner meat remains succulent. Yellowtail, barracuda, red snapper, trout, and sea bass can be prepared this way, too. Serve hot with lemon and/or grated daikon radish.

sea salt
1½ pounds salmon, sliced into 4 steaks
soy sauce
1 lemon, cut into wedges (optional)
1 cup grated daikon radish (optional)

Salt the fish fillets on both sides and let stand for 20 minutes.

Heat coals hot and red in a barbecue pit, or heat your broiler indoors. If you have a Japanese indoor grill, set it on top of the range and heat it until the surface is hot and red. The heat will prevent the fish from sticking to the grill.

Grill the fish skin side down until about 60 percent cooked, about 4 minutes. (Watch the upper side of the fish while grilling. When one side is 60 percent cooked, pinkish bubbles appear from the side.)

Turn the fish over and continue grilling for another 2 minutes, or until fish is thoroughly cooked. Test with a fork; if fish flakes off easily it should be ready.

Serve hot with soy sauce, lemon wedges, and grated daikon radish.

SERVE WITH String Bean Sesame Toss
Egg White Custard with
Shrimp

WRAPPED COD WITH MUSHROOMS
4 SERVINGS

Fresh cod and enoki and shiitake mushrooms are baked in individual foil packets. When you open them, you discover the taste of autumn.

4 (6-ounce) cod fillets
3 tablespoons sake
½ teaspoon salt
4 ounces enoki mushrooms
4 dried or fresh shiitake mushrooms
1 small carrot
4 lemon wedges

Marinate fillets with 2 tablespoons sake and ¼ teaspoon salt for 20 minutes. Preheat the oven to 350 degrees.

Wash enoki mushrooms and remove ends. Soften dried shiitake mushrooms in water for 30 minutes. Remove stems and slice into julienne strips. If using fresh shiitake mushrooms, simply rinse in cold water and pat dry; remove stems and slice into julienne strips.

Peel carrot and slice into julienne strips, about 2½ inches long. Mix carrot and mushrooms with remaining 1 tablespoon sake and ¼ teaspoon salt.

Cut aluminum foil into four 8 by 8-inch sheets. On each sheet lay 1 fillet and a quarter of the mushroom-carrot mixture. Wrap and seal the ends by folding one end over the other. Bake in the oven for 18 minutes, or until fish is thoroughly cooked. Serve wrapped or unwrapped, with lemon.

SERVE WITH Cold-Day Tofu
Braised Konbu Seaweed,
Soybeans, and Konnyaku

STEAMED RED SNAPPER WITH LEMON SLICES
4 SERVINGS

This is a festive fish dish and can be served with tartar sauce or mustard-soy sauce. The head and tail stay on the fish, and the lemon slices resemble bright scales.

1 whole red snapper (about 2 pounds)
1 teaspoon salt
1 tablespoon sake
2 lemons
1 cup fresh peas
soy sauce
3 tablespoons dry Oriental mustard powder
dissolved in 3 tablespoons of water

Clean and gut the fish, leaving head and tail intact; remove scales. On one side of the fish, the side you plan to show on the plate, make diagonal slits to accommodate lemon slices. Make about 8 slits, ½ inch deep.

Rub the salt and sake all over the fish. Place it on a dinner plate. Squeeze the juice of 1 lemon over the entire fish. Let stand for 30 to 45 minutes.

Cut the other lemon into 8 slices. Cut each slice in half. Insert half of the lemon crescents in the slits in the fish skin, reserving the remaining pieces.

Bring water to a boil in a large steamer over high heat. Put the plate holding the fish inside and steam for 20 minutes. While the fish is steaming, cook peas in water and set aside.

When the fish is thoroughly cooked, remove from the steamer. Discard the cooked lemon slices and replace with the reserved slices. Decorate the fish with peas.

Serve immediately with small bowls of soy sauce and mustard for dipping.

SERVE WITH Four-Mushroom Suimono
Snow-Covered Mountain
Salad
Almost-Instant Snow Pea
Pods

STEAMED PERCH WRAPPED IN SOBA NOODLES
4 SERVINGS

This is a very light dish but a wholesome one, consisting of perch, noodles, and vegetables, all steamed in one bowl.

4 (4-ounce) perch or flounder fillets
1½ tablespoons sake
¼ teaspoon salt
½ medium carrot
5 ounces dried soba noodles
1 egg white, beaten
4 ounces enoki mushrooms
¼ pound spinach
1 green onion

BROTH
1⅛ cups dashi
1 teaspoon sake
½ tablespoon mirin
1 tablespoon mild soy sauce

1 cup grated daikon radish

Place fish fillets in a bowl and sprinkle with sake and salt. Let stand for 5 minutes. Meanwhile, bring water to a boil in a steamer. Place the bowl containing the fish and marinade in the steamer and cook for 5 minutes. Remove from heat.

Peel the carrot and slice ¼ inch thick. Trim into flower shapes (page 15).

Bring water to a boil in a saucepan over high heat and add the noodles. When the water boils again, add ⅓ cup cold water and bring back to boil. Cook the noodles *al dente*, about 5 minutes total cooking time. Drain and rinse under cold water until cool enough to handle. Separate the noodles into 4 equal bunches.

Dip each bunch of noodles in beaten egg white, then wrap them around a fillet, tucking the ends underneath. Put each wrapped fillet in an individual heat-resistant bowl.

Trim ends of mushrooms. Wash spinach and bunch up the ends. Cut the spinach into 2½-inch pieces. Chop the green onion and set aside.

Add one quarter of the mushrooms, carrots, and chopped spinach to each bowl and cover with one quarter of the broth.

Bring water to a boil in a large steamer and place the bowls inside. Steam, covered, for 8 minutes.

Serve the fish hot, with chopped green onion and a mound of grated radish.

SERVE WITH Eggplant with Cherry
Blossom Sauce
Snow Peas with Almond
Dressing

HOKKAIDO-STYLE BAKED SOLE
4 SERVINGS

Hokkaido is the far-north island of Japan. Western-style farming is widely practiced on this island, and the people take pride in potatoes and dairy foods. Here is a recipe that breaks the tradition of no dairy foods in Japanese cuisine. The sole is covered with creamy mashed potatoes.

⅓ teaspoon salt
4 (5-ounce) sole fillets
2 tablespoons sake
1 tablespoon soy sauce
1 teaspoon vegetable oil
12 ounces potatoes

SAUCE
2 tablespoons heavy cream
1 egg yolk
⅓ teaspoon salt

vegetable oil
pickled ginger

Salt fillets on both sides and let stand for 30 minutes. Slice each fillet into bite-size pieces, about 2½ inches long.

Preheat the oven to 350 degrees.

Marinate fillets with sake, soy sauce, and oil for 30 minutes. Peel the potatoes and boil until cooked. Mash potatoes while hot and add the sauce ingredients. Mix well.

Oil a shallow baking and serving dish large enough to hold fillets in one layer. Lay the fillets in it side by side.

Bake in the oven for 8 minutes. Remove from the oven, spread the mashed potatoes on top, and slide the dish under the hot broiler for 30 seconds to brown the top. Garnish with pickled ginger and serve at once.

SERVE WITH Carrots with Bonito Flakes
Just Vegetable Suimono

MARINATED COD IN MISO SAUCE
4 SERVINGS

The pungent flavor of miso marinates the fish in this dish. It is unique in flavor, and the miso base keeps for 2 weeks in the refrigerator, so you may use it over and over. Chicken is also delicious marinated in this miso base.

salt
4 cod fillets, with skin (about 1½ pounds)
5 ounces white miso paste
5 tablespoons mirin
parsley

Sprinkle salt on both sides of the fillets. The thick part of the fillet should get extra salting. Let stand at room temperature for 2 hours to firm the meat.

Mix miso and mirin in a bowl until smooth. In a shallow rectangular plastic container with a tight-fitting lid, large enough to hold the fillets in one layer, spread half of the miso mixture. Lay the fillets in it without overlapping them, then spread the remaining miso sauce on top. Close the lid and refrigerate for 2 hours.

Remove fillets from miso sauce, rinse under water, and pat dry.

Broil the fillets until the meat flakes easily with a fork. Allow the top to brown very well. Serve hot, garnished with parsley.

NOTE: For a much milder taste, marinate for 1 hour.

SERVE WITH Kiwi Delight
Fan-Cut Eggplant

ANYTIME STEAMED CHILLED CHICKEN

TERIYAKI OKRA CHICKEN

SEAWEED, CHICKEN, AND VEGETABLES WITH CREAMY MISO

JAPANESE FRIED CHICKEN IN GINGER SAUCE

CHICKEN YAKITORI ON SKEWERS

CHILLED SESAME CHICKEN AND CUCUMBER

SKEWERED CHICKEN LIVERS

C H A P T E R   1 0

MEAT & POULTRY

STEAMED CHICKEN EGG ROLLS

RED WINE STEAKS

SIRLOIN STEAK WITH FRESH DAIKON RADISH

STEAK MISO

SUMMER BEEF CASSEROLE (NIKKO-RO-GASHI)

BEEF AND POTATO CROQUETTES

ROLLED BEEF WITH CHRYSANTHEMUMS (NEGI-MAKI)

JAPANESE BEEF CURRY

JAPANESE PORK ROAST

SWEET AND SOUR PORK

STEAMED BUDDHA'S HANDS

PORK CUTLETS

GINGER PORK

ROLLED PORK WITH ASPARAGUS

CHILLED PORK ROAST

PORK FILLETS MARINATED IN SAKE LEES

TRADITION AND PRICE. These factors, together with concern for a healthy diet, continue to limit the consumption of meat and poultry in Japan. Still, meat and poultry are popular foods and are prepared in especially tasty ways. The family-run butcher shop in Kamakura was just down the street from Grandmother's house, so if we wanted something, we could phone the order in and one of the sons delivered it within minutes—even if it was just a hamburger patty.

Cattle are raised in Japan, and pigs, and rather a lot of chickens. But the land area of the Japanese islands is tiny, compared to its 100-million-plus population, and making extensive use of land for grazing is not economically feasible. Beef is imported from the United States and Australia, but at high cost. Even more expensive is Japanese beef, which is raised in small quantities, mostly in the Kobe area, near Kyoto. Kobe beef is one of Japan's great gourmet luxuries —comparable, in Western cuisine, to the force-fed geese of France, which are stuffed with grain by hand in order to produce especially succulent birds with huge livers for pâté.

Kobe beef are also individually raised, in a special manner. Each animal is fed lots of beer (don't laugh) and is carefully and regularly massaged by hand in order to produce meat that is lean, delicately marbled, and very tender. Kobe beef, therefore, costs several times the price of almost any other good food. It is not a purchase to be casually thrown into one's grocery cart, like apples and rice. Japanese cooks think three times before buying Kobe (or imported) beef. The occasion must be special, the price right.

Meat in Japanese cuisine is served in small portions, only three quarters or even half the customary American serving, and is seasoned interestingly. Meat is often marinated, for both taste and preservation. When preparing any of the recipes that follow, you'll want to cut or slice your meat into bite-size pieces before serving, to make it easier to handle with chopsticks. The food simply tastes better without the metallic taste of knives and forks. Don't hesitate, however, to make Western utensils available to any family member or guests who prefer them.

NOTE: Two beef dishes popular on the menus of Japanese restaurants are sukiyaki and shabu shabu. These and other dishes using beef, pork, and poultry can be found in Chapter 11.

ANYTIME STEAMED CHILLED CHICKEN
4 SERVINGS

 Here is a very light chicken dish that is simple to make and can be prepared ahead of time for appetizer, lunch, or snack. Whenever I have extra fresh chicken in the refrigerator I make this dish. It can easily be transformed into other dishes, such as chicken salad or chicken noodle soup.

1 teaspoon salt
4 chicken thighs (or equal quantity of
    chicken legs or breasts)
3 tablespoons sake
1 green onion
½ European cucumber
2 tablespoons peeled and grated gingerroot
4 tablespoons soy sauce

Heat water in a steamer.

Rub salt on the chicken and put the pieces in a deep soup bowl. Pour sake over them. Place the bowl in a steamer and steam for 20 minutes. Let stand to cool. Refrigerate in the broth, covered, for 3 hours to overnight.

When completely cool, place thighs skin side down on a cutting board. Carefully make an incision in the chicken meat and remove the bone, holding the meat together. Cut the boned thigh into ¼-inch slices.

Cut green onion and cucumber into 2-inch-long julienne strips, and put them in a bowl of ice water to crisp. Put the grated ginger in a small bowl; add soy sauce. Set aside.

Drain the vegetables. Arrange cucumber and green onion strips in mounds and arrange the sliced chicken meat against them decoratively.

Accompany with small individual dishes of soy sauce–ginger mix.

SERVE WITH Fiddlehead Fern Salad
Fan-Cut Eggplant

TERIYAKI OKRA CHICKEN
2 SERVINGS

A simple okra pod can make a chicken look pretty, like a mountain with trees.

3 boneless chicken breasts or 4 boned thighs
2 tablespoons soy sauce
2 tablespoons mirin
2 tablespoons crushed roasted sesame seeds
1 tablespoon vegetable oil
1 tablespoon sesame seed oil
9 to 12 okra pods

Prick the chicken in several places with a fork or knife point to aid marinating and prevent shrinkage while cooking. Marinate the chicken in soy sauce, mirin, and half the sesame seeds.

In a frying pan, heat oil over medium

heat. Sauté each piece of chicken beginning with skin side down. When the skin turns crisp and browned, turn to the other side and reduce heat to low. Sprinkle on the remaining sesame seeds and sesame seed oil and cover. Cook for another 10 minutes, or until the chicken is completely cooked.

While the chicken is cooking, boil okra 2 minutes in salted water. Sprinkle lightly with salt and serve next to chicken. If you plan to eat the meal with chopsticks, slice the chicken into 1-inch pieces. Otherwise, it will be Western knife-and-fork time.

SERVE WITH Moon-Gazing Taro
Potatoes
Basic Miso Soup

SEAWEED, CHICKEN, AND VEGETABLES WITH CREAMY MISO

4 SERVINGS

This is a very light dish, ideal for lunchtime. It is actually a salad, but the chicken gives it more body. Mayonnaise, while not a traditional ingredient in Japanese recipes, has become very popular in Japan, and makes the dipping sauce extra smooth and nice.

½ cup dried wakame seaweed or 1 cup fresh
    wakame seaweed
2 medium carrots
1 cup thinly sliced daikon radish
½ European cucumber or 2 kirby cucumbers
½ pound boneless chicken, cooked and
    shredded (page 184)

DIPPING SAUCE
5 tablespoons mayonnaise
1 tablespoon white miso paste
1 tablespoon rice vinegar

Soften dried wakame seaweed in water for 15 minutes. If using fresh wakame seaweed, soak for 5 to 10 minutes. (Fresh wakame is often salted, so wash off the salt under running water.) Cut the seaweed into 2-inch pieces.

Scrape carrots and daikon radish and cut into matchsticks, 2 inches long.

Cut cucumber into 2-inch matchsticks.

Combine dipping sauce ingredients in a small serving bowl.

Arrange the vegetables on a large platter, with the carrots in the center of the dish. Enhance the bright orange carrots with a semicircle of white daikon radish. The cucumber should be on the opposite side of the platter. The seaweed and chicken can be arranged next to the vegetables.

Refrigerate until you are ready to serve.

SERVE WITH Basic Miso Soup
Panda's Delight

JAPANESE FRIED CHICKEN IN GINGER SAUCE
4 SERVINGS

This is a delicious Japanese version of the all-American favorite dish, fried chicken. Use chopsticks!

2 *pounds chicken thighs, breast, and legs*

MARINADE

2 *tablespoons sesame seed oil*
juice of ½ lemon
4 *tablespoons soy sauce*
2 *tablespoons sake*
1 *teaspoon sugar*
3 *tablespoons chopped green onions*
2 *tablespoons peeled and chopped gingerroot*

cornstarch
vegetable oil
parsley

Bone the chicken and cut into bite-size pieces.

In a large bowl mix together sesame oil, lemon juice, soy sauce, sake, sugar, green onions, and ginger. Add chicken. Marinate 30 minutes to an hour.

Drain off all the sauce by transferring chicken to a strainer. Discard sauce. Dust each piece of chicken with cornstarch.

Heat plenty of oil in a cast-iron skillet or wok over medium heat. Add the chicken pieces and cook until browned. Turn and brown the other side. To cook completely should take about 5 minutes.

Transfer chicken to a plate and blot off excess oil with paper towels. Remove to a serving platter. Garnish with parsley.

SERVE WITH Seaweed and Cucumber
Salad
Rice with Peas

CHICKEN YAKITORI ON SKEWERS
4 SERVINGS

This is everybody's favorite—a shish kebab chicken dish. Grill indoors or on an outdoor barbecue. Alternate pieces of green onion with the chicken for best flavor. Makes a nice party snack or main dish.

2 *pounds boneless chicken*
⅓ *cup soy sauce*
⅓ *cup mirin*
3 *green onions*
Japanese sansho pepper or black pepper
juice of 1 lemon

Preheat the broiler or prepare charcoal.

Cut chicken into 1-inch cubes. Marinate in soy sauce and mirin for 30 minutes.

Cut green onions into 2-inch pieces.

Slide chicken and green onion pieces onto bamboo or metal skewers. Grill or broil, basting and turning often. Total cooking time will be about 10 minutes.

Sprinkle with pepper and lemon juice. Serve right off the grill or, later, at room temperature.

SERVE WITH Fan-Cut Eggplant
Rainbow Salad

CHILLED SESAME CHICKEN AND CUCUMBER
4 SERVINGS

This makes a great appetizer or a light salad-type meal when you want something refreshing. Sake goes especially well with it.

12 ounces boneless chicken (2 large breasts or
    4 small thighs)
4 tablespoons sake
⅔ European cucumber

SWEET AND SOUR SAUCE
1 teaspoon minced garlic
2 teaspoons peeled and grated gingerroot
2 tablespoons chopped green onions
¼ cup sesame seed oil
2 teaspoons chili oil
¼ cup rice vinegar
¼ cup soy sauce
1 teaspoon sugar

Heat water in a large steamer.

In a soup bowl, marinate chicken in sake for 15 minutes. Place the bowl in the steamer and cook for 20 minutes. Let cool completely in the broth, then shred evenly, discarding skin.

Slice cucumber into thin julienne strips, 2 inches long.

Combine sauce ingredients in a small bowl.

Toss shredded chicken and cucumber together. Pour on the sweet and sour sauce.

Chill. Serve well chilled.

SERVE WITH Carrots with Walnut Sauce
Scattered Sushi

SKEWERED CHICKEN LIVERS
4 SERVINGS

As a child I could not stand the bitter taste of liver until I tasted this dish without knowing it was liver. I liked it very much, and still do.

1 pound chicken livers
2 tablespoons sake
2 tablespoons soy sauce
2 tablespoons peeled and grated gingerroot
2 tablespoons vegetable oil
3 large green onions

SAUCE
4 tablespoons mirin
4 tablespoons soy sauce
1 tablespoon sugar

Cut chicken livers in half. Soak in water for 5 minutes to eliminate any odor. Change the water and let stand for another 5 minutes.

Combine sake, soy sauce, and ginger and marinate livers in the mixture for 15 minutes. Discard marinade.

In a medium, heavy-bottomed frying pan, sauté the livers in oil over high heat. Push livers to one corner of the pan, then add the green onions and sauce ingredients, lower heat, and simmer for 5 minutes.

Skewer 2 or 3 pieces chicken livers and green onion alternately on individual bamboo skewers. Serve hot.

SERVE WITH Almost-Instant Snow Peas
Clouds-in-the-Sky Egg
Suimono

STEAMED CHICKEN EGG ROLLS
4 TO 6 SERVINGS

❧ Egg rolls originated in China, where they are usually made with ground pork and garlic. My mother's egg rolls are lighter and less fattening. She uses ground chicken and seasons it with miso paste. The result is a lighter, greaseless egg roll that complements Japanese foods. Egg roll skins are a standard item in any Oriental grocery. If you can't find ground chicken, prepare your own in a meat grinder or food processor.

1 pound ground chicken
1 teaspoon peeled and finely chopped
　　gingerroot
2 tablespoons red or white miso paste
2 tablespoons sake
¼ cup chopped green onions
½ cup chopped cabbage
4 dozen egg roll skins
　　soy sauce
　　parsley

In a medium-size bowl mix together ground chicken, ginger, miso paste, sake, green onions, and cabbage.

Stack about 5 egg roll skins and cut them into ⅛-inch-wide strips. Do the same with the remaining egg roll skins, cutting 5 or 6 skins at a time. (If you stack the skins too high, you cannot achieve a clean-cut edge.) Put the strips in a dry bowl.

Line a steamer with a clean cotton cloth (cheesecloth or a napkin or handkerchief) and bring to boil.

Make chicken balls using about 1 heaping tablespoon seasoned ground chicken for each ball. Wrap each ball with the strips of egg roll skin, covering the entire ball. This will take approximately 4 or 5 strips per ball. You will have 4 dozen balls.

Place balls in the steamer and steam for 10 minutes.

Serve piping hot with soy sauce for dipping. Garnish with parsley.

SERVE WITH Daikon Radish Miso Soup
　　　　　　Pickled Cabbage and
　　　　　　　　Cucumber

RED WINE STEAKS
4 SERVINGS

♣ Red wine together with soy sauce is used for marinating this dish. Use any Western red wine you prefer—Zinfandel is nice. Serve with knife and fork or cut into bite-size pieces.

1½ pounds sirloin steaks, about ½ inch thick
4 tablespoons red wine
5 tablespoons soy sauce
1 cup grated daikon radish

Marinate steaks in wine and soy sauce for 15 minutes. Grill or broil steaks to your preferred doneness.

Grate radish and squeeze out excess water. Put a mound of the radish beside each steak.

SERVE WITH Blushing Pine Nuts
Snow Pea Pods with Hot Mustard

SIRLOIN STEAK WITH FRESH DAIKON RADISH
4 SERVINGS

♣ Steak and a spicy grated daikon radish sauce make a happy marriage of flavors. Have your butcher slice the steak half the usual thickness. Rice or potatoes go perfectly with this steak. There should be a salad to refresh the palate and nutritionally balance the meal.

1½ pounds sirloin steak, in 4 to 6 thin slices

MARINADE
2 tablespoons soy sauce
3 teaspoons sake
2 teaspoons mirin
1½ tablespoons vegetable oil

1 teaspoon vegetable oil
1 cup grated daikon radish
2 tablespoons peeled and grated gingerroot
½ cup chopped green onions
Japanese chili powder (shi-chi-mi togarashi)

Pound the meat with a heavy mallet to tenderize. Combine marinade ingredients and

marinate meat for 15 minutes.

Heat a frying pan or grill medium-hot and grease with oil. Cook the steaks to preferred doneness.

Serve with a bit of grated radish, ginger, and green onion. Sprinkle a dash of Japanese chili powder on top.

You can serve the grilled steak on individual plates with a small mound of the condiments on the side—or, if you wish, have condiments in small dishes to pass around.

SERVE WITH Summer Salad
Brown Rice

STEAK MISO
4 SERVINGS

These are thin steaks marinated in a pungent miso sauce for 2 to 3 days and then grilled to taste. Nice to have on hand for unexpected guests. Make sure you start with fresh meat and let the steaks marinate in your refrigerator. Instruct your butcher to cut your steaks ¼ inch thick—this recipe won't work with thicker steaks.

4 (6-ounce) boneless steaks, each ¼ inch
   thick
  salt
1 cup red miso paste
2 tablespoons sugar
1 tablespoon soy sauce
1 tablespoon mirin
1 tablespoon sake
1 cup grated daikon radish (optional)

Trim fat from meat. Using a meat pounder (or small hammer wrapped in a towel), pound both sides of meat. Lightly salt the meat on both sides. Pat dry with paper towels.

In a small rectangular casserole dish, combine remaining ingredients except daikon radish and mix well.

Reserve half of the miso mixture in a small dish temporarily. Spread the other half evenly in the casserole. Place clean triple layer cheesecloth over the layer of miso paste. Lay the steaks down without overlapping them. Place another piece of triple layer cheesecloth on top of the steaks, and spread the remaining miso paste on it to cover the steaks entirely. Cover the dish tightly with a lid or aluminum foil.

Leave covered in refrigerator for 2 to 3 days. When ready to use, remove the steaks, rinse off the paste, pat dry, and grill to your taste. Since the meat never comes in direct contact with the miso paste, it is tender and fragrant but not too salty. Accompany with grated daikon radish if you wish.

SERVE WITH A Japanese-American
Potato Salad
Almost-Instant Snow Peas

SUMMER BEEF CASSEROLE
(NIKKO-RO-GASHI)
4 SERVINGS

Here's a satisfying meal that is best prepared with the fresh potatoes of early summer. You can make this dish ahead of time and reheat it at the last minute, tossing in the freshly cooked peas for color.

4 medium potatoes
1 large onion
8 ounces thinly sliced (sukiyaki-style) beef
1 tablespoon vegetable oil
¼ cup fresh peas

SAUCE
1½ cups water
2 tablespoons sake
1 tablespoon mirin
2 tablespoons sugar
4 tablespoons soy sauce

Peel potatoes and cut them into 1½-inch cubes. Soak in water.

Cut onion in half, then slice thinly, about ¼ inch thick. Cut beef into bite-size pieces, about 1-inch cubes.

Heat oil in a large heavy skillet and brown beef quickly over high heat, about 2 minutes. Add potatoes and sauté for 3 minutes over medium heat. Add sauce ingredients and reduce heat to a simmer.

Cover skillet and simmer till most of the liquid is absorbed, 7 to 10 minutes.

While the beef is simmering, cook the peas *briefly* in boiling water. They should be firm and bright green.

To serve, uncover the beef and potatoes and toss lightly. Garnish with the freshly cooked peas and serve immediately.

SERVE WITH Basic Miso Soup
Vegetable Tempura

BEEF AND POTATO CROQUETTES
4 TO 6 SERVINGS

This recipe is a favorite in Japan. Served over a bed of crispy chopped cabbage, with lemon wedges, these croquettes make a delicious family dinner.

1 onion
2 tablespoons vegetable oil
12 ounces ground beef
1 teaspoon salt
  pepper
3½ pounds potatoes (4 or 5 medium-size
    potatoes)
  flour
1 egg
2 cups bread crumbs
  vegetable oil
1½ cups chopped or shredded cabbage
  parsley
1 lemon, cut into wedges
  soy sauce

Chop the onion. Heat oil in a medium-size frying pan. Sauté onion over medium-high heat until almost transparent, about 4 or 5 minutes. Add ground beef, salt, and pepper and continue sautéing until beef is cooked, 10 minutes or so.

Peel potatoes and cut into quarters. Boil potatoes till they can be pierced easily with a toothpick. Mash them while hot. Stir in ground beef and onions. Let cool.

Make potato-beef mixture into 8 to 10 patties. Sprinkle flour on both sides of each patty. Pat each patty lightly.

Beat egg in a bowl and dip each patty in the egg. Then roll patty in bread crumbs.

Heat oil to a medium-high temperature in a heavy skillet. Deep fry patties over medium heat until brown on both sides.

Remove from heat and pat dry with paper towels.

Serve hot over a bed of chopped or shredded cabbage. Garnish with parsley and lemon wedges. Provide soy sauce to season at the table.

SERVE WITH Curried Ginger Cucumber
Braised Squash and Okra

ROLLED BEEF WITH CHRYSANTHEMUMS
(NEGI-MAKI)
4 SERVINGS

❧ Sukiyaki beef is used for this dish because it is sliced paper-thin and is easy to roll. Briefly blanched chrysanthemum petals are served on the side in a small mound to give this dish a different look. They are also edible.

MARINADE
1½ tablespoons dashi
1½ tablespoons rice vinegar
1 teaspoon sugar
¼ teaspoon salt
½ teaspoon mild soy sauce

½ cup yellow chrysanthemum petals
1 pound thin slices beef (sliced ⅛ inch thick
    for sukiyaki)
salt
pepper
6 green onions
2 tablespoons vegetable oil
3 tablespoons soy sauce
2 tablespoons sake

To make the chrysanthemum salad, combine marinade ingredients. Blanch flower petals briefly in boiling water for 1 minute. Rinse under running water and squeeze out water. Let stand in marinade for 20 minutes or longer. Keep it in the refrigerator until just before serving.

Season beef with salt and pepper. Cut green onions into thirds and slice in half lengthwise.

Place 2 or 3 green onion pieces in the middle of the meat and roll the meat, tucking the ends underneath. The onions should stick out on both ends.

Heat a lightly oiled frying pan over medium heat. Panfry the beef rolls until all sides are brown and cooked, about 1 to 2 minutes. Add soy sauce and sake and simmer for another minute. Remove from heat.

Serve about a teaspoon-size mound of chrysanthemum salad on the side of the rolled beef.

VARIATION: BEEF ROLLS WITH APPLE-SOY SAUCE. Prepare as above, dipping the plain, pan-fried rolls in a sauce made by combining half a grated onion, 1 peeled and grated pippin apple, ⅓ cup each of sake, mirin, and soy sauce. Bring all the sauce ingredients to a boil, then serve in small bowls.

SERVE WITH Snow-Covered Mountain
    Salad
    Rice with Peas

JAPANESE BEEF CURRY
4 SERVINGS

Curry was introduced to Japan by the British, who learned about this spicy and pungent dish in India. Japanese curry is a bit milder than the Indian version, though still somewhat "hot." Curry may be served over steamed rice or noodles. The Japanese might serve it with pickled vegetables; you may prefer the spicy Indian condiment, fruit chutney. Great dish for sweltering summer days.

1 pound beef for stewing
1 teaspoon salt
  pepper
4½ teaspoons curry powder
4 tablespoons flour
2 tablespoons vegetable oil
4 tablespoons butter
1 onion, chopped
1 garlic clove, minced
1 large carrot, sliced into ¼-inch pieces
1 tomato, chopped
3 medium-size potatoes, peeled and cut
    into 2-inch cubes

CURRY SAUCE
2½ cups beef broth
1 cup water
  salt
1 tablespoon soy sauce
1 tablespoon honey
¼ teaspoon allspice (optional)
¼ teaspoon clove (optional)
1 teaspoon minced gingerroot
1 teaspoon curry powder

Cut meat into 1-inch pieces. Sprinkle with salt, pepper, 1½ teaspoons curry powder, and 3 tablespoons flour. Heat the oil in a heavy skillet and brown the meat over medium-high heat. Remove meat from pan with a slotted spoon and set aside.

Heat butter in the same skillet and fry onion and garlic over low heat until almost transparent. Add remaining 1 tablespoon flour and 1 tablespoon curry powder and stir 2 minutes over low heat. Transfer onion to a large saucepan.

Return meat to pan and add carrot, tomato, and potatoes. Sauté for 3 minutes. Add the sauce ingredients and simmer for 30 minutes.

Serve the curry over hot rice or noodles. Leftovers freeze well.

JAPANESE PORK ROAST
2 TO 4 SERVINGS

❦ This pork roast is tied with string as you would tie Western-style roast pork or beef, but it never enters your oven, and its flavor is different, special. The pork is cooked slowly in a saucepan, together with sake, soy sauce, and ginger, resulting in a tender, slightly sweet, and spicy dish. Leftovers can be enjoyed hot, as cold cuts, in salads, in soups, and in sandwiches.

2 pounds boneless pork loin roast
4 tablespoons sake
6 tablespoons soy sauce
3 tablespoons oil

COOKING SAUCE
⅓ cup sake
⅓ cup soy sauce
3 tablespoons sugar
3 cups water

1 green onion, chopped
2 tablespoons peeled and chopped gingerroot
3 tablespoons dried Oriental mustard
*   powder, mixed with 3 teaspoons water*

Tie the meat with string and marinate in sake and soy sauce for 20 minutes, turning it occasionally. Remove from marinade and pat dry with paper towels.

In a frying pan, heat oil and brown the meat over high heat. This firms up the meat and retains the good flavors.

Transfer meat to a large saucepan and pour in the cooking sauce ingredients. Add the green onion and ginger, cover the pan, and cook over high heat until it boils. Reduce heat to a simmer and let sauce flavor the pork slowly, for about 40 minutes, or until the meat juices run clear when pierced with a skewer.

When the sauce begins to get thick, remove meat and let the sauce reduce over medium-high heat. This takes about 5 to 8 minutes. Return meat to the saucepan and roll to coat the meat with the sauce. This gives the meat a shiny glaze.

Remove strings and slice the roast thinly. It can be served immediately or allowed to cool completely before serving. Arrange the slices on a platter and decorate with fresh radish or green onions cut decoratively. Accompany with Japanese (or American) mustard.

SERVE WITH Broiled Eggplant with
    Ginger
    Braised Hijiki Seaweed
        with Mushrooms and
        Carrots

SWEET AND SOUR PORK

4 SERVINGS

This is a dish that has become synonymous with Chinese food in America. Sweet and sour pork is also popular in Japan. Whenever Japanese borrow a recipe from another culture, some variations occur in the way spices and sauces are used. Usually, the taste becomes milder and less oily, to suit the Japanese palate (and perhaps yours).

1 pound pork loin
1 tablespoon soy sauce
1 tablespoon ginger juice (see page 64)
1 egg, beaten
  cornstarch
  oil
1 cup sliced bamboo shoots
2 medium carrots
1 green onion
4 shiitake mushrooms
6 snow pea pods

SAUCE
¾ cup chicken broth or dashi
2 teaspoons soy sauce
1 teaspoon salt
2 to 3 tablespoons sugar
4 teaspoons ketchup
6 tablespoons rice vinegar
1 tablespoon cornstarch
3 tablespoons water

Cut pork into ¾-inch cubes. Marinate in soy sauce and ginger juice about 10 minutes. Combine beaten egg and cornstarch in a bowl and coat meat lightly with the mixture.

Over medium heat, fry the marinated pork in an oiled heavy cast-iron skillet or wok until lightly golden. Remove from oil and set aside. Clean skillet or wok.

Cut carrots randomly (see page 15). (If you buy whole bamboo shoots, use the same cut as for the carrots.) Cut green onion on a diagonal into about 5 pieces. Soften the dried mushrooms in water for 20 minutes and remove stems.

Lightly boil snow pea pods and carrots in salted water for 2 minutes. Rinse under cold water.

In the iron skillet or wok you used to fry the meat, bring to a boil over high heat the broth, soy sauce, salt, sugar, ketchup, and vinegar. Add all the vegetables except the green onions and let simmer for 5 minutes. Then add the meat and green onions and toss the ingredients together.

Combine cornstarch and water and mix into the sauce. Cook for 1 minute, until sauce becomes shiny and slightly thick. Remove from heat.

Serve in a large bowl or platter while piping hot, with steamed rice.

SERVE WITH Squid with Ginger
Steamed Chicken Egg Rolls

STEAMED BUDDHA'S HANDS
4 SERVINGS

The hand-shaped Chinese cabbage leaves, when stuffed with ground pork, are traditionally said to resemble the graceful hands of Buddha. This dish is steamed, light and healthful.

8 large Chinese cabbage leaves
8 ounces ground pork
1½ teaspoons peeled and grated gingerroot
½ teaspoon salt
1 tablespoon sake
1 egg
1 tablespoon cornstarch
1 tablespoon soy sauce
1 teaspoon cornstarch mixed with
    1 teaspoon water
¼ cup fresh peas

Separate the cabbage leaves and remove the soft, leafy portion; only the firm, white part is used. Slit each leaf lengthwise at ¼-inch intervals to within ¾ inch of the top and bottom. Boil the leaves in a large pot of water for 1 minute. Drain.

Combine ground pork with ginger, salt, sake, and egg.

Sprinkle cornstarch on cooked cabbage leaves. Spread pork mixture across each leaf and fold the leaf over to enclose the filling. The folded stuffed cabbage will remind you of hands.

Heat water in a steamer. Arrange stuffed cabbage leaves on a plate, seam side down, and place them in the hot steamer for 15 minutes. Reserve the broth in the steamer for the sauce.

Combine reserved broth with water to measure 1 cup and bring to a boil in a saucepan. Add soy sauce and cornstarch paste and return to a boil; remove from heat.

Cook the peas briefly in boiling water, just until tender.

Arrange steamed Buddha's hands on individual plates. Sprinkle with cooked peas and pour the hot sauce over the cabbage. Serve hot with steamed rice.

PORK CUTLETS
(TON-KATSU)
4 SERVINGS

There are restaurants in Japan that specialize only in pork cutlets—that's how popular this dish is there. In all seasons you will see and smell the crisp and aromatic pork cutlets in butcher shops, department stores, and the kitchens of Japanese homes. The ingredients for this classic dish are available at any market in the U.S. It's just plain pork coated with bread crumbs and fried in fresh vegetable oil. Serve over a bed of shredded cabbage and garnish with lemon wedges. In many stores a tonkatsu sauce made especially for pork dishes is available. I'd suggest you try it on this wonderful dish.

4 lean boneless pork chops or loin fillets
  salt
  pepper
2 cups shredded cabbage
¼ cup flour
1 egg
¾ cup bread crumbs
  vegetable oil
1 lemon, cut into wedges
  soy sauce
  tonkatsu sauce

Trim excess fat from meat. Wipe off moisture with paper towel. Sprinkle meat on
both sides with salt and pepper.

Shred cabbage finely and let soak in
chilled water for 1 or 2 minutes. Drain and
refrigerate.

Coat each piece of meat with flour and
tap each side with your hands to remove

any excess. Break the egg into a bowl and
beat lightly with chopsticks. Place bread
crumbs in another bowl. Dip each piece of
meat first into the egg, then bread crumbs;
try to get an even coating of bread crumbs
on each piece.

In a large cast-iron skillet or wok heat
oil to 375 degrees. Test the temperature by
dropping a few bread crumbs into the oil.
If the crumbs sizzle up instantly, but do
not burn, the temperature is right for
frying.

Deep fry the cutlets until both sides are
golden brown, about 3 to 4 minutes on
each side.

Cut each cutlet into 1-inch slices. Serve
over a bed of shredded cabbage. Garnish
with lemon wedges. Serve soy sauce and
tonkatsu sauce on the side.

GINGER PORK
4 SERVINGS

Get yourself a fresh piece of gingerroot and good fresh meat to make this
delightful meal. Serve with string beans sautéed lightly in oil.

3 tablespoons sake
5 tablespoons soy sauce
4 tablespoons peeled and grated gingerroot
1½ pounds pork loin fillets (4 to 6 slices,
    each ¼ inch thick)
2 tablespoons vegetable oil
  flour

In a medium-size bowl, combine sake, soy
sauce, and grated ginger. Add meat and
marinate 5 to 6 minutes. Pat meat dry with
paper towels.

In a medium-size frying pan, heat oil
while you dust meat lightly with flour.
Sauté the meat over medium heat until
both sides are golden. Do not cook all 6
slices at once; do it in two batches, keeping the first batch warm and covered so all
can be served hot.

ROLLED PORK WITH ASPARAGUS
4 SERVINGS

With wafer-thin pork loin fillets, you can make a beautiful early-summer statement. This works as an appetizer, too.

1 pound wafer-thin boneless pork loin

MARINADE
3½ tablespoons soy sauce
1 tablespoon sugar
1 tablespoon sake
2 tablespoons mirin

8 asparagus spears
   flour
1½ tablespoons vegetable oil

Marinate pork in the soy sauce mixture for 20 minutes.

In the meantime, cook asparagus until tender-crisp, about 4 minutes, in boiling water. Drain and cut in half.

Pat the pork dry with paper towels and lay 2 pieces of asparagus in the center of each fillet. Sprinkle with a little flour, and roll each fillet, tucking the ends underneath. Asparagus should protrude from both ends.

In a frying pan, heat the oil and panfry the rolled meat over medium heat until browned on all sides, about 3 minutes.

Serve hot or at room temperature.

SERVE WITH Snow-Covered Mountain
Salad
Just Vegetable Suimono

CHILLED PORK ROAST
4 TO 6 SERVINGS

Without going to much trouble you can make this fancy summer pork dish to entertain guests. Chill the meat until you're ready to serve it. It can be eaten hot, but traditionally is chilled.

1 teaspoon salt
2 pounds pork roast
2 green onions, sliced into 4 to 6 pieces
3 tablespoons peeled and grated gingerroot
1 large tomato
½ lemon
1 cup shredded lettuce
3 tablespoons dry mustard
   soy sauce

Rub salt on roast. Then wrap it tightly with string as you would roast beef.

In a large saucepan, cover pork with water. Add sliced green onion and ginger.

Simmer 40 minutes. Let stand to cool.

Slice tomato thinly. Cut lemon into 4 pieces.

Untie pork and cut into ½-inch slices. Arrange neatly on a platter and decorate with lettuce, tomato, and lemon.

Mix mustard with an equal amount of water to make mustard sauce. Serve mustard sauce and soy sauce in small side dishes.

SERVE WITH Clam Miso Soup
Kiwi Delight
Asparagus with Bonito
Flakes

PORK FILLETS MARINATED IN SAKE LEES
4 SERVINGS

Sake lees (sake-kasu) is a by-product of sake, a white sweet paste that is used not only as a marinating paste but also for soups. You can find fresh sake lees in most Japanese food stores, as sake is produced in California. Sake lees is perishable, so refrigeration is a must. It is aromatic, nutritious, and tasty.

1 pound sake lees (sake-kasu)
⅓ cup sake
2 tablespoons red or white miso paste
2 tablespoons sugar or mirin
8 pork loin fillets, ¼ inch thick (about 4
    ounces each)
  salt

Chop sake lees and mix with sake to soften. You may either mix the paste vigorously with your hands or process it in a blender. Add miso paste and sugar, and continue mixing until smooth.

Trim fat from meat. Using a meat pounder, pound both sides. Lightly salt on both sides and pat dry with paper towels.

In a small rectangular casserole dish, spread half the seasoned sake lees paste. Place damp, clean double layer cheesecloth over the layer of paste. Lay the fillets down without overlapping them. Place another piece of cheesecloth on top of the fillets and spread the remaining paste to cover the fillets entirely. Cover the dish tightly with foil and refrigerate.

Leave covered in the refrigerator for 3 days. When ready to use, remove the fillets, rinse off the paste, and pat dry. (You should not keep the meat in the paste for longer than 5 days, or it will become too salty and potent.) Grill or broil the fillets until cooked all the way through. Cut each into ½-inch slices and arrange on a plate. Serve hot.

VARIATION: Lamb, chicken, and fish such as cod, halibut, and salmon can be marinated in the same fashion. The paste keeps well in the refrigerator for 2 weeks. Mix well before reusing.

SERVE WITH Okra Plum Salad
              Healthy Roots

TEPPAN-YAKI

SUKIYAKI

SHABU SHABU

C H A P T E R 1 1
HEARTY ONE-POT DINNERS

CHRYSANTHEMUM NABE

CHICKEN MIZUTAKI

VEGETARIAN NABE

SEA AND MOUNTAIN NABE

WINTER NABE

NABE BROTH RICE DISH (O-JI-YA)

UDON-SUKI

WHEN THE WIND IS COLD and your cat curls up by the fireplace, what do you feel like eating? A steaming bowl of homemade soup? Bouillabaisse? A savory stew? The Japanese feel the same. Nabe-mono, which means "something in the pot," is a hearty soup eaten especially during cold weather. The cooking pot is brought right to the table and meat, seafood, and vegetables cook before your eyes, so it's a convivial dining situation and the chef reigns. Everybody helps themselves, while the host continues to add more ingredients to the pot, so the food is always hot and freshly cooked.

Sukiyaki is perhaps the most familiar of all nabe-mono among Westerners. It is a hot pot full of thinly sliced beef, tofu, and vegetables, all simmered in a soy sauce broth. Japanese dip the sukiyaki ingredients into a bowl of beaten raw egg before carrying them to the mouth. The egg gives the simmered foods a delicious flavor.

The variety of nabe-mono is infinite. Any fresh meat, seafood, vegetables, and tofu can be a candidate for one of these warming soups. You can experiment with just about any other ingredients—fresh or dried mushrooms, sweet rice cakes (mochi), all types of firm fish, lobster, water chestnuts, snow pea pods, noodles—so long as they are fresh and flavorful and the flavors mix harmoniously. Use your imagination and create! Since vegetables tend to hold a lot of water, especially Chinese cabbage, they are used to control the amount of broth in one-pot dinners. If the pot needs more liquid, add Chinese cabbage and a little water or sake. If the broth becomes too abundant, do not add any cabbage for a while. Since nabe-mono is not exactly a soup, the ingredients that you add to the pot should not be entirely immersed; cover two thirds of the way, and turn them while simmering.

To begin nabe-mono cooking, you first prepare the broth. It can be based on seafood, meat, or vegetables, or a mixture of all these. The solid ingredients are cut into manageable pieces that will cook quickly, and arranged attractively on a large platter. Freshness is crucial for a good nabe. From this point on the nabe can be made completely at the table. Using a portable heating element, the broth is brought to a boil. (You may preheat the broth in a saucepan over your kitchen stove and then transfer it to the clay pot or electric skillet on the dining table if you wish.) The solid ingredients are dropped into the simmering pot one by one, then covered while they cook. Timing is extremely important; do *not* overcook. Sake, mirin, salt, pepper, soy sauce, miso paste, and some sugar also play important roles in seasoning many of the dishes.

Condiments are served with the simmered ingredients. With sukiyaki, a raw beaten egg is traditional; with other nabe-mono, grated daikon radish, chopped green onions, lemon juice, Japanese dried chili pepper, and sauces may be offered.

To serve nabe-mono, give each diner a bowl and a pair of chopsticks, as well as a ceramic spoon to scoop up the delicious soup. All help themselves from the pot. When the pot is empty, except for the rich broth, the cook adds more fresh ingredients. You should have enough prepared ingredients to replenish the pot two or three times. After the solid food has all been cooked and eaten, the delicious broth should be served as well.

As in all Japanese cuisine, a key to making nabe-mono attractive and tasty is its presentation. The materials for nabe-mono should be arranged beautifully on a large platter. Don't mix the ingredients; keep each in its own neat pile. Arrange squares of tofu in the center, for instance, ringing it with cabbage on one side and sliced beef on the other, and so on. The more ingredients you have to serve, the more beautiful the platter. When putting the ingredients into the pot or skillet, do not disturb the painting that you created on the platter. Gently transfer the same configuration into the pot and let it simmer gently.

To serve nabe-mono in your home, you don't need exotic utensils. You can buy clay pots, cast-iron sukiyaki pans, and portable gas-burner sets at Japanese hardware stores or gourmet shops, but an electric skillet will do the job very well.

If you do want to invest in a clay pot or sukiyaki pan, here are the ways they should be treated:

CLAY POT (dow-nabe): A new clay pot should be washed well and submerged in water for 30 minutes (these steps help remove the clay odor). Then pour water into the pot and simmer for 1 hour. Remove from heat and drain. Dry completely. Once the clay pot undergoes this process, it is ready for use in nabe-mono. Place the pot on top of the heat source. Do not put the pot over high heat, or it may crack. If it cracks slightly it usually can be salvaged by simmering some o-ji-ya (page 215) in it. While the special rice dish cooks, it also acts as a sealer. These clay pots are available in three sizes: small (1 to 2 servings), medium (2 to 4 servings), and large (3 to 6 servings).

CAST-IRON SUKIYAKI PAN (sukiyaki-nabe): Choose a pan that is thick and heavy-bottomed. Such design provides for even heat, and food is less likely to burn than in thin pans. A new sukiyaki pan should be well washed with water, then treated as follows: First, simmer some water in the pot for 45 minutes, drain, and dry. Next, add a few tablespoons of oil and stir fry some vegetables, such as cabbage or carrot leaves, over medium heat. Discard the vegetables, clean the pan, and dry thoroughly over medium heat. Grease lightly with oil before storing.

To prepare a one-pot meal at the table, you will need a portable heat source. Electric hot plates work well, as do the Japanese braziers designed especially for nabe-mono. These resemble a small, self-contained gas burner on a stove range, and utilize propane gas in small, disposable cartridges. They are safe and easy to handle, and a single cartridge lasts up to an hour. Serious nabe-mono lovers will find this an indispensable appliance.

The small burners used for chafing dishes or fondue pots will not work for nabe-mono, as they do not get hot enough to bring the broth to a boil. You may, however, preheat the pot and broth in the kitchen and bring it to the table to serve, using a small burner to keep the pot hot.

TEPPAN-YAKI
4 SERVINGS

You may have been introduced to this nabe through Benihana restaurants, where chefs toss and slice the meat artistically on a large grill. Since you do not have such a large grill at home, an electric skillet or griddle will do the job. Or make a barbecue with the same ingredients. This recipe works for both summer and winter.

2 onions
2 bell peppers
2 Japanese eggplants
12 mushrooms
1 large ear of corn, fresh or frozen
2 zucchini
3 green onions
2 pounds thinly sliced lamb, beef sirloin, or
    pork loin
  vegetable oil

SAUCE
1 grated pippin apple, peeled and cored
1 garlic clove
1 teaspoon peeled and grated gingerroot
½ onion, grated
⅔ cup soy sauce
¼ cup vegetable oil
1 teaspoon sesame oil
1 tablespoon sesame seeds

Peel the onions and slice them into ¼-inch rings. Slice green peppers into 8 sections and remove seeds and membranes. Cut eggplants in half and cut each half into quarters lengthwise. Clean mushrooms and cut each in half. Cook the corn in boiling water for 3 or 4 minutes and cut into 4 pieces. Cut zucchini into ¼-inch slices. Slice green onions diagonally into thirds. Arrange all vegetables on a platter.

Have your butcher slice the meat very thin, ⅛ inch thick. Arrange on a separate plate.

Combine all ingredients for the sauce and mix well.

Heat a skillet or barbecue pit, oil the surface with vegetable oil, and begin grilling. The meat takes approximately 2 minutes to cook on each side. The vegetables should be allowed to brown lightly; they can be flipped and turned several times to brown. The meat should be turned just once.

Let each guest pick up the cooked foods straight off the grill, or first transfer the cooked foods to a large platter and then let guests help themselves. Accompany each serving with ¼ cup sauce. Each bite should be dunked in the sauce before being carried to the mouth.

Serve with hot rice.

SUKIYAKI
4 SERVINGS

Perhaps the most internationally known nabe dinner, sukiyaki is a flavorful beef-based dish. Since beef is a precious and expensive food in Japan, sukiyaki dinners are a real occasion. The beef is sliced paper-thin and cooked in a sweet soy sauce broth with tofu and vegetables. As a condiment, a raw beaten egg, into which each mouthful of beef, tofu, and vegetables is dunked before being eaten, accompanies the dish. The raw egg dip is optional, but it gives the dish a special rich flavor. If you like your sauce sweeter, add more sugar or honey. You may sprinkle a few teaspoons of sweeteners directly into the skillet. If you like it saltier, add more soy sauce. If you like the taste milder, add water or dashi but not too much, as it will make the vegetables and meat soggy.

2 pounds beef sirloin, sliced paper-thin

6 green onions

12 ounces chrysanthemum leaves (shungiku)

2 (8-ounce) cakes grilled tofu or 1 (19-ounce) cake firm tofu

8 ounces shirataki noodles

8 dried shiitake mushrooms

8 ounces bamboo shoots

4 eggs

2 ounces beef suet (or a bit of oil)

1 cup water or dashi

SAUCE

⅔ cup soy sauce

⅔ cup mirin

⅓ to ½ cup sugar or honey

The beef should be sliced thinly. Ask your butcher to partially freeze it and slice it for you, about ⅛ inch thick. If the pieces are large, cut them in half.

Cut green onions diagonally in half. Wash chrysanthemum leaves well to remove sand and cut them in half. Cut the tofu into 1½-inch cubes.

Blanch shirataki noodles in hot water for 1 minute and cut in half.

Soak dried shiitake mushrooms in water to soften for 30 minutes. Remove stems and slice mushrooms in half. Slice bamboo shoots into quarters if they are whole. Arrange all the foods decoratively on a large platter.

Bring the sauce ingredients to a boil in a saucepan. Set aside.

Break an egg into each of 4 small dishes and stir once or twice with chopsticks or a fork. Place a serving dish and dish of egg at each diner's place.

Heat a dry skillet over medium-high heat, then add the beef suet, moving it around the skillet until it is well coated.

Add a quarter portion of the beef, let it cook halfway, and pour in a quarter of the sauce. Cook for 2 minutes over medium heat.

At this point guests may help themselves to the beef slices with chopsticks, dunking them in the beaten egg.

As they are enjoying the beef, add roughly one quarter of the tofu, green onions, shirataki noodles, mushrooms, chrysanthemum leaves, and bamboo shoots to the skillet. Add a little more sauce and let it simmer for a couple of minutes. Add more meat while the guests serve themselves tofu and vegetables. Keep alternating.

Pour in ½ cup or so of water or dashi if the sauce is becoming too reduced and syrupy. The water prevents the foods from becoming too salty or sweet, and restores the proper consistency to the sauce.

Rice and pickled foods are traditionally served with this nabe.

SHABU SHABU
4 SERVINGS

Shabu shabu literally means swish-and-swash, and this is exactly how the nabe is prepared. Held between a pair of chopsticks, the meat is swished through hot, seasoned broth and cooks instantly—as quick as you can say the words shabu shabu—because the meat is sliced paper-thin. The leftover broth becomes a soup for the finale. You may add udon noodles if you wish; serve them with the broth as a hearty soup. If you do not have any seaweed for the broth, start the hot pot with any chicken or meat broth.

2 pounds beef sirloin, sliced paper-thin
½ pound Chinese cabbage
4 to 8 large shiitake mushrooms
8 ounces bamboo shoots
10 green onions
1 bunch spinach (about 12 ounces)
2 cakes firm tofu
1½ pounds cooked udon noodles or 1 pound dried udon noodles (optional)

LEMON DIPPING SAUCE

8 tablespoons lemon juice
4 tablespoons soy sauce
4 tablespoons dashi
⅓ teaspoon salt

SESAME DIPPING SAUCE

4 tablespoons sesame seed paste (atari-goma or tahini)
2 to 3 teaspoons sugar
2 tablespoons red or white miso paste
2 tablespoons soy sauce
2 tablespoons sake
6 tablespoons rice vinegar
1 tablespoon mirin
dash of seven-spice mixture (shichimi-togarashi) (optional)

4-inch piece konbu seaweed
½ cup chopped green onions (optional)

Ask your butcher to partially freeze the meat and slice it for you, about ¹⁄₁₆ inch thick. Each slice should be bite-size. Arrange the uncooked slices of meat on a large platter and refrigerate.

Cut cabbage leaves into 3 parts. Remove stems from mushrooms and cut in half. Cut bamboo shoots in half if large. Green onions should be cut diagonally into 2-inch pieces. Cut spinach in half. Arrange all the vegetables decoratively on another large platter. Refrigerate until ready to use.

Cut tofu cakes into 1½-inch cubes. Arrange on the same platter as the meat and refrigerate until ready to use. If using dried noodles, cook the noodles until they begin to look translucent. Drain and rinse under cold water. Arrange on a large plate and refrigerate until ready to use.

Combine the ingredients for the two dipping sauces; blend well and set aside.

To make the nabe, bring all the uncooked ingredients to the table. Plug in your electric skillet or hot pot and fill it about two thirds full with water. Drop in the konbu seaweed. Bring to a boil and remove the seaweed *immediately*. Reduce heat to a slow, gentle boil.

Each person should have a pair of chopsticks, a bowl, and a small dish of each dipping sauce. Each person picks up a slice of meat, dips it in the hot broth, and swishes it through until it is cooked, then dips it in one of the dipping sauces and eats.

Meanwhile, put the vegetables and tofu cubes in the hot broth and allow them to cook for 3 to 5 minutes over medium to high heat. Remove surface film with a spoon. Let everyone continue to pick morsels from the pot while you replenish it.

When all the meat and vegetables are gone, the broth that remains is served. If desired, add the cooked noodles and chopped green onions to the broth and cook for 1 or 2 minutes. If there is too little broth left in the pot, add ½ to 1 cup water with 1 tablespoon each soy sauce and sake and a dash of salt. Taste the broth and adjust seasonings. Serve the broth and noodles in separate individual serving bowls.

SERVE WITH Shrimp Lemon Boats
Gingered Vanilla Ice Cream

CHRYSANTHEMUM NABE
4 SERVINGS

The visual attraction of this nabe is the blooming chrysanthemum flower made of egg that floats in the middle of the pot. The Chinese cabbage in the pot represents the leaves of the flower, the pork the earth.

1 recipe Egg Pancakes (page 158)
1 pound pork loin, partially frozen (or presliced paper-thin)
½ large Chinese cabbage (12 ounces)
4 cups chicken broth or dashi
2 tablespoons sake
1 teaspoon salt
4 lemon wedges
  pepper
  soy sauce

Slice the egg pancakes thinly.

Slice the pork thinly, then cut slices into 2-inch pieces.

Separate Chinese cabbage leaves and trim ends. Cut each leaf crosswise, about 2 inches thick. Arrange on a large platter with the pork. In the middle of the platter, arrange egg pancake strips into a petaled mound that resembles a chrysanthemum flower.

In the nabe dish or pot, bring 3 cups broth, sake, and salt to a boil and quickly reduce heat to medium.

Carefully transfer cabbage and pork from the platter to the hot pot. Place the chrysanthemum flower on top of the pork and cabbage, and simmer until the pork is cooked, about 5 to 7 minutes. Do not put all the cabbage and pork in the pot at once; save some for a second round. Replenish broth if necessary.

Let diners help themselves to a serving of pork and cabbage with some of its wonderful broth. Sprinkle with squeezes of lemon, pepper, and soy sauce before eating. Serve with rice.

CHICKEN MIZUTAKI
4 SERVINGS

Fresh chicken makes an especially delicious broth. I go to a live poultry place in Los Angeles' Chinatown to buy whole chickens. You will never want to buy another frozen chicken once you have spoiled yourself with truly fresh chicken. Make a trip to your local fresh poultry market; you will taste the difference in this delicious nabe.

1½ pounds chicken thighs and drumsticks
    (with bones), or breasts
  6-inch piece konbu seaweed
 7 cups water
 1 teaspoon salt
 1 carrot
12 ounces spinach
½ Chinese cabbage
 1 (8-ounce) cake firm or grilled tofu
 6 to 8 lemon wedges
  soy sauce
 1 cup grated daikon radish
¾ cup chopped green onions

Rinse chicken in boiling water to remove odor. Wipe konbu seaweed gently with moist paper towel to remove surface dust.

Place the measured water in a medium saucepan over high heat, along with the seaweed, chicken, and salt. When it reaches a boil, immediately remove the seaweed and reduce to a simmer. Continue to simmer for 1 hour. Remove the chicken to a large platter, saving the broth for the pot.

Peel the carrot and slice thinly, about ¼ inch crosswise. If you have a Japanese veg-etable cutter, cut out the carrot into floral shapes. Arrange the carrot next to the chicken.

Wash spinach and cabbage and cut across into 2½-inch pieces. Arrange on the platter next to the chicken and carrot.

Slice the tofu into 2-inch cubes and arrange next to the chicken, carrot, and spinach.

Now you are ready to bring the ingredients to the table. Heat 3 cups of the reserved broth in a pot or electric skillet until it boils; reduce heat to medium. Add the chicken and vegetables and simmer, covered, for 5 minutes. Do not put all the ingredients in the pot at once; save some for replenishment.

Each diner is given a serving bowl and a pair of chopsticks. They each pick the foods directly from the pot into the serving bowl, then add squeezes of lemon, soy sauce, about 2 tablespoons grated daikon radish, and green onions to make a sauce.

Serve rice with this nabe.

SERVE WITH Rosy Enoki Mushrooms
            Steamed Chestnut Cake

VEGETARIAN NABE
4 SERVINGS

It is healthy to make an occasional meal solely of vegetables. My choice for an all-vegetable meal is one that combines vegetables from the mountain, the garden, and the vegetable stand. Here they are served with a miso-sesame sauce.

THE SAUCE

3 tablespoons roasted black or white sesame
    seeds
3 tablespoons red or white miso
3 tablespoons sake
3 tablespoons mirin
1 teaspoon grated lemon peel

3 green onions
4 to 6 dried shiitake mushrooms
¾ pound spinach or chrysanthemum leaves
    (shungiku)
8 ounces bamboo shoots
1 (19-ounce) cake firm tofu
2 large zucchini
1 cake konnyaku
4 to 6 deep-fried tofu pouches (usu-age)
6 Chinese cabbage leaves
4 small turnips
1 large carrot
5 cups dashi broth
3 tablespoons sake
1 teaspoon salt

To make the sauce, grind the roasted sesame seeds completely until they are paste-like in texture. You may use an electric blender to grind the sesame seeds (in that case, double the amount).

In a small saucepan, combine the miso, sake, and mirin and stir well over low heat for 3 minutes. Cool. Toss the sauce with the ground sesame seed paste; add grated lemon peel. Set aside.

Slice green onions diagonally into 2-inch pieces. Soak the mushrooms in water for 30 minutes to soften. Save the broth for the nabe. Wash the spinach well, discard roots, and cut in half. Slice the bamboo shoots into 3-inch pieces. Cut the tofu cake into 2-inch squares. Slice the zucchini ¼ inch thick. Blanch the konnyaku for 2 minutes, drain, and rinse under cold water. Slice the tofu pouches in half. Cut the Chinese cabbage leaves *crosswise* in thirds. Drain and then cut into 1-inch cubes. Arrange these vegetables neatly on a large platter.

Peel turnips and carrot and slice into ¼-inch pieces, crosswise. If you have a Japanese vegetable cutter, make into floral shapes. Invigorate the platter with these decoratively cut vegetables.

To make the dish, pour 3 cups dashi broth and the sake into an electric skillet or a clay pot heated on a tabletop cooking unit. Add salt, stir well, and bring to a boil. Put the vegetables in one by one and let them cook, covered, for 4 minutes. Cook only what is to be eaten right away. Replenish the pot with more food and dashi.

Let each diner scoop up the vegetables into individual serving bowls, dipping with the sauce for a pungent flavor.

SERVE WITH Blushing Pine Nuts
           Orange Agar-agar

SEA AND MOUNTAIN NABE

4 SERVINGS

Here is a one-pot dinner that takes you to the sea and to the mountains. Mushrooms, spinach, Chinese cabbage, chicken, and tofu represent the mountains. Crab, fish, and shrimp represent the riches of the sea. In the middle of this beautiful scenery floats a konbu seaweed boat carrying miso sauce.

MISO SAUCE

5 tablespoons sesame seeds
1 teaspoon sugar
2 tablespoons sake
2 tablespoons mirin
4 tablespoons white miso paste

1 sheet konbu seaweed, about 6 inches long
1 pound crab legs, fresh or frozen
4 jumbo shrimp
8 ounces fish fillets (flounder, red snapper, cod, perch)
12 ounces spinach
1 cake konnyaku
8 ounces Chinese cabbage
1 cake firm tofu
3 green onions
4 ounces fresh mushrooms (forest, enoki, shimeji)
8 ounces boneless chicken thighs
6 cups dashi
3 tablespoons mirin
3 tablespoons soy sauce
1 teaspoon salt
2 tablespoons sake

Buy roasted sesame seeds or roast them in a dry frying pan until fragrant but not burned. Grind the sesame seeds in a Japanese mortar or in a blender at high speed. Add sugar, sake, mirin, and miso and mix well.

Soak the seaweed in water for 10 to 30 minutes, until tender. Reserve soaking liquid for the broth. Place the miso sauce on top of the seaweed, as if the seaweed were a boat carrying the sauce. Since the seaweed boat is flat, the miso sauce will naturally get dissolved with the broth when placed in the pot, making the broth tastier.

To prepare the pot, begin with the seafood. Shell the crab leg and cut into 4 or 5 pieces. Arrange on a large platter. Next rinse and devein the shrimp and place them on the platter. Cut the fish into 2-inch morsels and place the pieces next to the shrimp. The food from the sea should occupy only half of the platter.

Next, assemble the mountain foods. Boil the spinach in lightly salted water for 1 minute. Drain it and cut into 2-inch pieces. Bundle the spinach together neatly and arrange on the opposite side of the platter.

Rinse konnyaku in hot water. Cut konnayaku into ¾-inch squares.

Cut the cabbage into 2-inch pieces, discarding the hard white cores. Cut the tofu carefully into 2-inch squares. Slice green onions on the diagonal into 2-inch pieces.

If purchased in dried form, soak the mushrooms in water for 15 to 30 minutes until they soften. Reserve liquid for the hot pot broth.

Cut chicken into 2-inch pieces. Arrange all the mountain ingredients on the platter next to the seafood.

In an electric skillet or clay pot heated on a tabletop cooking unit, combine about 3 cups dashi broth with ½ cup each of the mushroom and seaweed broths. Add the remaining ingredients. Bring to a boil, then reduce heat to medium so liquid boils gently.

Transfer the sea and mountain foods to the pot piece by piece. Remember to put in first ingredients that require long cooking time, such as chicken and fish. Add the cabbage and tofu last, as they only need about 2 to 3 minutes of cooking. This timing takes practice—your second and third nabes will be better and better. Place the seaweed boat in the center of the pot. Simmer, covered, over medium heat for 5 minutes.

Let all help themselves to the ingredients and replenish the pot with more sea and mountain foods and broth. Eat the simmering food with the pungent sauce afloat the konbu seaweed boat. All help themselves to the sauce by scooping up some with chopsticks and dabbing it on the sea and mountain foods.

Serve the nabe with rice and pickled foods.

SERVE WITH Roe Roe Roe Your Boat
Green Tea Fruit Pudding

WINTER NABE
4 SERVINGS

For a cold day, here is a hearty one-pot dinner that will be a delicious variation on your grandmother's chunky soup. Simmer the vegetables and meat in the broth first and eat them with grated daikon radish, lemon juice, chopped green onions, and soy sauce. With the leftover broth, make a rice dish with the recipe that follows.

6 to 8 dried shiitake mushrooms
12 ounces fresh spinach or dandelion leaves
2 green onions
1 (8-ounce) cake deep-fried or grilled tofu
8 Chinese cabbage leaves
1 medium carrot
1½ pounds lean boneless pork loin
4 cups warm water

CONDIMENTS
soy sauce
1 cup grated daikon radish
1 cup chopped green onions
4 lemon wedges

Soften shiitake mushrooms in water for 30 minutes. Reserve liquid for the broth.

Wash spinach or dandelion leaves and rip off the roots. Cut the leaves in half.

Cut the green onions into 2-inch pieces. Slice the tofu into 2-inch squares. Wash the Chinese cabbage, cut out the tough cores, and cut the leaves into thirds. Peel and slice carrot into ½-inch pieces crosswise. (If you have a Japanese decorative vegetable cutter you may cut out floral shapes.)

Partially freeze the pork to make slicing easy and neat. Slice it into paper-thin pieces, about 2½ inches long. (Japanese grocery shops sell pork thinly sliced as well, or you can ask your butcher to slice it for you.)

Arrange all the ingredients on a large platter and bring it to the table. On the table set up a cooking pot or electric skillet and add the warm water. Heat until the water boils, then turn it down to a simmer and add the meat and vegetable pieces, one by one. Don't overfill the pot. Cover and let the meat and vegetables simmer for 4 minutes; skim the surface occasionally.

When the dish is ready, all help themselves to the ingredients with their chopsticks. Have soy sauce and grated radish (about 2 tablespoons per person) in individual serving bowls so they can dunk their vegetables and meat before eating. Sprinkle on chopped green onions and a squeeze of lemon juice if you wish.

When the pot starts to empty, replenish with more food and about 1 cup water or mushroom broth, if necessary, and continue simmering.

NABE BROTH RICE DISH
(O-JI-YA)
4 SERVINGS

The broth left over in the nabe pot may be seasoned with salt and eaten as is. Or you can use it to make a delicious rice dish that will give your guests even more enjoyment.

3 cups nabe-mono broth
2 cups cooked short-grain white rice
1 egg
¼ teaspoon salt
1 tablespoon soy sauce
½ cup chopped green onions

When all the solid nabe ingredients have been eaten, remove all but 3 cups broth from the pot (or add more mushroom soaking liquid and/or water if needed), add the rice, and allow it to cook for 3 minutes over low heat, covered. Remove the lid, beat the egg, and mix it into the rice briefly. Season with salt and soy sauce. Sprinkle with chopped green onions and serve immediately in individual rice bowls. Delicious with pickled foods.

Udon-Suki
4 SERVINGS

The ingredients for this nabe are similar to other nabe dinners: fresh seafood, chicken, and vegetables. It is the noodles and the garnish that make this nabe unique. The garnish is made of daikon radish grated with Japanese dried red chili peppers, not only to give it a reddish color like the color of a maple leaf, but also to give it bite. This garnish is called momiji-oroshi, which means "grated maple leaf."

1 to 1½ pounds dried udon noodles
1½ pounds boneless chicken thighs
8 fresh cherrystone clams
1 (19-ounce) cake firm tofu
12 ounces spinach
8 ounces Chinese cabbage
1 carrot
4 dried shiitake mushrooms

GARNISH
1 medium daikon radish (about 2 pounds)
3 Japanese dried chili peppers

STOCK
7 cups dashi
3 tablespoons mirin
3 tablespoons mild soy sauce
1 teaspoon salt

1 lemon, cut into wedges
   soy sauce

Cook udon noodles following instructions on page 81. Drain and set aside.

Cut the chicken into bite-size pieces. Let the clams soak in salted water for at least 20 minutes to rid them of sand. The clams prefer a dark, quiet place, like the bottom of the ocean, so be accommodating if you want them to clear all the sand from their shells. Arrange chicken and clams on a large platter.

Cut the tofu into 2-inch cubes and arrange on a plate. Trim the ends of the spinach and Chinese cabbage and cut in half. Arrange on the plate next to the chicken, tofu, and clams.

Peel the carrot and cut crosswise, about
¼ inch thick. Soak mushrooms in water
for 30 minutes to soften. Remove stems.
Arrange carrot and mushrooms next to the
chicken and place the cooled cooked noodles next to them.

To prepare the grated maple leaf, peel
the daikon radish and cut in half crosswise
to make grating easy. Make two holes in
one end of each piece of radish with a
chopstick. Remove seeds of the chili peppers and insert the peppers into the radish
with a chopstick. Then grate the radish
into a bowl. Wring out daikon liquid with
your hands and put the maple radish in a
clean bowl. (Be sure to wash your hands
well.) The maple radish will keep for 1
day.

Bring the stock ingredients to a boil in a
small medium saucepan. Transfer the
warm stock to your cooking pot. If you
have a clay pot, set it on a gas burner or
hot plate with an asbestos or metal mesh
mat in between to avoid direct heat; if you
are using an electric skillet, set the heat to
high. Bring the stock to a boil and add all
of the meat and seafood. Let it cook for 3
to 4 minutes over medium heat. Add the
mushrooms, carrot, and tofu and cook for
2 minutes, covered. Add the cabbage and
the spinach at the end, because they

release a lot of liquid and can make the
broth watery. Finally, add the noodles.
The cooked morsels have enriched the
broth and will make the noodles tastier.

Each diner should have a pair of chopsticks and a bowl. Let them pick the morsels directly out of the pot and into their
bowls. The dish is garnished with grated
maple leaf and seasoned with squeezes of
lemon and soy sauce.

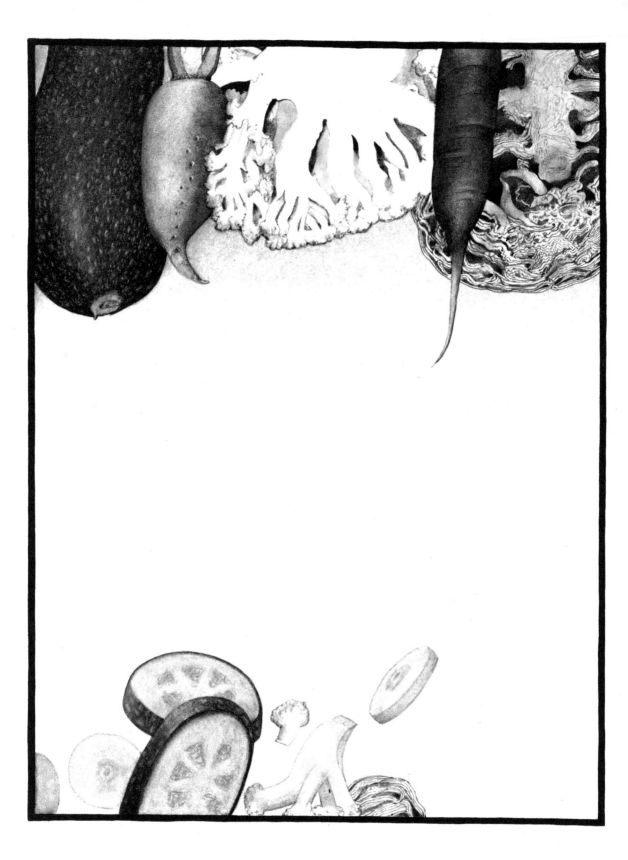

CHINESE CABBAGE PICKLES (HAKUSAI-NO-SHIO-ZUKE)

ASSORTED SWEET AND SOUR PICKLED VEGETABLES

TENDER APRICOT AND CABBAGE PICKLES

C H A P T E R   1 2

"NEW AROMAS" (PICKLES)

RICE BRAN PICKLES (NUKA-MISO-ZUKE)

DAIKON RADISH PICKLES

PICKLED CABBAGE AND CUCUMBER

PICKLED GINGER (AMAZU-SHOGA)

PICKLED AND MARINATED VEGETABLES

SOME AMERICANS LIKE THEIR SALAD BEFORE THE MEAL, some afterward. In Japanese cuisine, salads are served both before and after. Before the meal they function to clear the palate for goodies to come. At meal's end they provide a final bold taste and aid digestion.

Starting salads, like those in Chapter 5, called suno-mono, are commonly green, often vinegared, and served in small portions. After the main course a final salad appears. It is also served in small portions, often with rice and miso soup, and is typically a pickled dish called oshinko, which literally means "new aromas."

Japanese pickled vegetables are flavored with salt, miso paste, rice bran, vinegar, red chili pepper, and other seasonings. American-style dill-flavored brine and peppercorns are not used, so oshinko are characteristically a bit more subtle and delicate than Western pickled foods.

Popular vegetables for pickling are carrots, cabbage, zucchini, green pepper, Chinese cabbage, daikon radish, broccoli, and, of course, cucumbers (which everyone knows make pickles). Actually, almost any vegetable can be pickled, and many fruits, such as green plums (ume) and watermelon rind, are also good candidates for the tasty pickling process.

The Japanese have created a variety of pickles, and certain districts, Nara and Kyoto particularly, are famous for their specialty, pickled vegetables, which are shipped and sold not only all over Japan but throughout the world.

Warning: It's possible to get addicted to Japanese pickles. The variety of shapes, colors, and tastes can be so inviting that you might want to try them all, and keep eating. Many Japanese overindulge themselves in pickles, the way many Americans gorge on chocolate. They eat whole meals of pickles! One result is high blood pressure—from too much salt—in a significant part of the population. Eaten in small quantities, oshinko are a healthy delicious food, not for gorging but for taste, beauty, and end-of-the-meal digestion. So enjoy, but in moderation.

Commercially prepared "pickles" are available in great variety. The most popular are nara-zuke (a zucchini-like vegetable called uri); sakura-zuke (daikon radish pickled with cherry blossom leaves—pinkish in color and quite beautiful); shiba-zuke (pickled eggplant); amazu-shoga (pickled gingerroot); beni-shoga (pickled ginger with red coloring); takuwan (daikon radish, yellow in color); and everybody's all-time favorite, ume-boshi (pickled plums), considered medicinal—many Japanese eat them daily.

Japanese homemakers like to keep several kinds of pickles in the refrigerator and serve a variety every day. Pickles that can be made overnight together with pickles that are preserved for several months make an interesting and tasty combination.

EQUIPMENT

In the old days every Japanese household had a large pickling tub of wood or clay, with a large stone to press the contents down. Today most households use a smaller plastic tub that fits in the fridge. Its lid has a built-in adjustable screw that applies pressure to the contents. You can improvise your own pickling tub from a ceramic bowl and some kind of weight, such as a big stone or book. Pickles made in the traditional way in a large tub of wood or clay seem tastier, but for practical purposes a makeshift pickling tub is just fine.

PICKLES YOU CAN BUY

Pickled vegetables are regional delicacies that come in a great variety. Here is a list of some you can buy in American-Japanese grocery stores—and in some American supermarkets.

PICKLED CUCUMBERS (Kyuri-no-shio-zuke): Fresh cucumbers pickled in brine with Japanese chili peppers and seaweed. They keep, refrigerated, for a week. To serve, rinse in water and slice into ¼-inch pieces.

PICKLED CHINESE RADISH (Daikon-no-shio-zuke): Fresh Chinese radish pickled in the same manner as above. Rinse in water and slice into ¼-inch pieces.

NARA PICKLES (Nara-zuke): Nara is an ancient city near Kyoto where all types of pickles are enjoyed. Nara pickles are eggplants and squash (uri) pickled in a tangy, malty, yeast paste. They are aromatic and crunchy. Available in vacuum-sealed plastic bags, they keep in the refrigerator for 3 weeks after the seal has been opened. Rinse them in water and cut into thin slices.

YELLOW RADISH PICKLES (Takuan): These are made of Chinese radish (daikon) and have a distinct gold color. The yellow color is derived from the gardenia pods that are used in the pickling medium. They come in vacuum-sealed plastic bags. Keeps in refrigerator for a month after the seal has been opened. Rinse them in water and cut into half-moons ¼ inch thick, or slice into thin strips. Garnish with sesame seeds.

SHIBA PICKLES (Shiba-zuke): Eggplant, ginger, cucumber, and myoga (a spicy vegetable), native to Kyoto. They are purple in color from the beefsteak leaves (shiso) used in pickling. They are sold in vacuum-sealed plastic bags. Keep in refrigerator for 3 weeks after the seal has been broken. Slice into ¼-inch pieces.

PICKLED PLUMS (Ume-boshi): Unripe and ripe plums are pickled in salt and shiso leaves. They are considered medicinal, as they contain lots of enzymes, vitamins, and minerals. They will keep for several years in a cool, dry place.

PICKLED GINGER (Amazu-shoga): Americans may be familiar with ginger because it accompanies sushi in restaurants. It is available at Japanese markets, and many of the commercial brands are of U.S. origin. The pink color is natural and beautiful. The flavor is sweet and sour. It is most often served with sushi, broiled fish, and poultry. There is another type of pickled ginger, called beni-shoga, which is red. It is beautiful but the color is unnatural; I never use it for that reason.

CHINESE CABBAGE PICKLES

(HAKUSAI-NO-SHIO-ZUKE)

4 SERVINGS

This is one of the most popular pickles in Japan. It can easily be prepared at home with a pickling device. If you have a terrace or yard, put the cabbage out in the sun for several hours. This is not essential for the recipe, but it sweetens the cabbage.

½ *small Chinese cabbage*
¼ *cup sea salt*
1 *strip konbu seaweed, 10 inches long*
2 *red Japanese dried chili peppers*
¼ *lemon peel, slivered*

sesame seeds (optional)
soy sauce

Wash the cabbage and discard outer leaves. If you can, put cabbage out in the sun for 4 hours. Rinse briefly under running water.

Slice cabbage into quarters. Put a cabbage wedge in the bottom of the pickling device and generously sprinkle salt over it. Break the strip of konbu seaweed into 6 pieces and add 2 pieces. Slice chili peppers into thirds and put 2 pieces on top of the first wedge. Layer another wedge on top of the first at a right angle to it, and continue to layer salt, chili peppers, seaweed, and cabbage. Sprinkle the lemon peel slivers on top.

Secure the screw of the pickling device and turn as far as possible to apply maximum pressure. Let stand in the refrigerator or a cool place. In 6 hours the moisture in the cabbage should be released and enable the cabbage to pickle in its own brine. After 6 hours, loosen the pressure slightly and let stand for another 8 hours in the refrigerator or a cool place.

To serve, take the pickled cabbage out of the container. Rinse under water. Chop coarsely or slice into strips. Sprinkle with sesame seeds if you wish. Slice the konbu seaweed thinly and sprinkle on top of the cabbage. Serve with soy sauce.

Keeps in the refrigerator for 1 week.

ASSORTED SWEET AND SOUR PICKLED VEGETABLES
4 SERVINGS

These pickled vegetables will last in the brine for a month. You may continue to add more vegetables for pickling. A glass jar of these makes a beautiful present for the holidays.

2 cups of any assortment of raw vegetables:
   cabbage, carrots, daikon radish,
   cauliflower, broccoli, zucchini

PICKLING SOLUTION
1 cup rice vinegar
6 ounces mirin
4 tablespoons sugar
½ tablespoon salt

Cut the vegetables into bite-size pieces. Put them in a glass jar that will just hold them without crowding.

Combine vinegar, mirin, sugar, and salt and mix well. Pour over the vegetables. Fasten the lid securely and shake gently to mix contents. Refrigerate.

Allow vegetables to pickle for at least 4 days, or as long as a month.

To serve, drain off pickling solution and serve a few pieces in small individual dishes.

TENDER APRICOT AND CABBAGE PICKLES
4 SERVINGS

Very little salt is used to make this dish. The natural sweet and sour flavor of the apricots and the spicy touch of ginger make the cabbage come alive.

8 dried apricots
8 ounces cabbage leaves
1 teaspoon salt
1 tablespoon peeled and minced gingerroot .

Slice apricots thinly.

Remove the hard core of cabbage leaves and blanch the soft leaves in boiling water for 1 minute. Drain and rinse briefly in cold water. Chop cabbage while still warm; sprinkle with salt.

While cabbage is still warm, combine minced ginger and sliced apricots in a medium bowl. Cover with a weighted plate, or transfer ingredients to a pickling jar and apply pressure. Let stand for at least 6 hours before serving.

Rinse lightly under water. Squeeze out water before serving. Arrange small servings on individual dishes.

Keeps in the refrigerator 3 to 4 days.

RICE BRAN PICKLES

(NUKA-MISO-ZUKE)

4 TO 10 SERVINGS

Any type of firm vegetable can be pickled in a fermented rice bran medium. The result is a tangy, crunchy, and tasty pickle full of enzymes. The vegetable pickles overnight, so once you have the right pickling medium you can have pickles every day. *One crucial task is involved: keeping the rice bran medium alive.* You must stir the medium with your hands or a wooden spoon once a day. The medium has a distinct odor of fermentation. This is often associated with Japanese homemakers, because they're in charge of putting their hands in the pickling tub. Rice bran, the basis of the pickling medium, is available in Japanese grocery stores. You will need a clay jar, enameled pot, or glass bin with a lid. Keep the jar in a dark, cool place—the garage, the basement, or under the kitchen sink.

The rice bran medium has a texture similar to miso paste. Preparation takes about 5 days. This step is tedious and time-consuming, but once you have trained the medium you can keep it for years.

RICE BRAN MEDIUM (NUKA-MISO)

1 pound sea salt

3 cups water

4 pounds rice bran (nuka)

1 pound cabbage, carrot tops, or daikon
     radish leaves, approximately

8 ounces gingerroot, peeled and cut randomly

1 strip konbu seaweed, dried, cut
     into 2-inch pieces

10 ounces Japanese dried chili
     peppers (togarashi)

3 garlic cloves, peeled

2 slices of chopped bread (day-old is okay),
     white or wheat
     rind of 1 lemon

½ cup beer (leftover is fine)

Put salt and measured water in a large pot and bring to a boil over medium heat for 1 minute. Let cool.

With your hands or a wooden spoon, mix together the remaining ingredients.

The texture should be smooth, like miso paste, but softer.

Transfer the rice bran medium to a pickling container—a 3- to 4-quart lidded clay jar, enameled pot, or glass container. Add ¼ pound cabbage, carrot leaves, or daikon leaves. The leaves should be covered completely with the rice bran medium. Let stand overnight.

Next day, discard the vegetables. Add another ¼ pound vegetables, then mix the medium well with your hands to allow air movement. Let stand overnight.

Repeat the above process for the next 3 or 4 days to train the medium. Do not eat these vegetables; they are used only to train the medium.

You will be ready to pickle vegetables on the fifth day. You may keep peeled garlic cloves in the medium all the time to keep the bugs away. Replace with fresh cloves every month.

Treating the Rice Medium

Mix the medium with your hands or a wooden spoon once or twice a day to activate the enzymes in it.

Replenish the medium with rice bran and any type of bread, and adjust thickness of the medium with beer as well as salt, every week. To replenish, make a mixture of 10 parts bran or bread to 1 part salt. Adjust thickness with beer. The texture should be slightly softer than miso paste.

If you plan to take a trip and won't be able to care for the rice bran medium daily, put the entire jar in a plastic bag and refrigerate. It will keep for a month.

If you see water or mold form on the surface of the rice bran medium, simply scrape or scoop it off and continue usage; it's fine.

Always store in a cool, dark place.

Making the Pickles

Vegetables should remain in the pickling medium for 12 to 24 hours. The longer they stay in the medium, the tangier and saltier they become. You should not keep the vegetables in the medium any longer than 2 days. Pickled vegetables may be stored in the refrigerator, tightly covered, for a couple of days. Any of these vegeta-bles are good candidates for pickling, and should be prepared as described below.

Vegetables to Pickle

cucumber: Unwaxed pickling cucumbers are recommended. They may be pickled whole, or in 1/4-inch to 1/2-inch slices.

daikon radish, carrot, turnip: Peel and cut into 3-inch pieces.

cauliflower: Cut a whole cauliflower head into 4 pieces and pickle.

cabbage, Chinese cabbage: Use only hard stems that you would otherwise discard.

Japanese kabocha squash: Peel and cut into 1 1/2-inch pieces.

Japanese eggplant: If large, make 2 or 3 slits in the flesh before pickling. Small ones can be pickled as is. Large American eggplants are not recommended for pickling. If you wish to enhance the color of the eggplant, put a rusty nail in the pickling tub. The iron in the nail makes the eggplant prettier and healthier.

Serving the Pickles

Remove the pickles from the rice medium and rinse under running water. Pat dry with paper towels. Slice each pickled vegetable into 1/4-inch-thick pieces and arrange on a plate.

DAIKON RADISH PICKLES
4 SERVINGS

Serve this in the place of cole slaw with fried chicken.

1 pound daikon radish
1 tablespoon salt

PICKLING SOLUTION

5 tablespoons rice vinegar
2 tablespoons sugar
3 tablespoons water
1 teaspoon salt

1 dried red Japanese chili pepper

Peel the radish. Cut in half lengthwise and slice each half thinly into ⅛-inch crescents. Place in a medium bowl. Generously sprinkle salt over the sliced radish and mix well with your hands until it becomes limp. Cover with a plate that will fit inside the bowl and press with a weight over the radish for 4 hours (or put the radish in the pickling device and apply pressure for same time).

Rinse the radish under cold water. Squeeze out water.

Mix vinegar, sugar, measured water, and salt in a small pot and bring to a boil. Remove from heat and pour over the pressed radish.

Keeps in the refrigerator for 1 week.

To serve, place small portions in individual bowls. Cut the chili pepper crosswise into thin slices to garnish the radish.

PICKLED CABBAGE AND CUCUMBER
4 SERVINGS

The pastel green of cabbage, jade green of cucumber, and forest green of shiso leaves will make you appreciate the subtlety of the colors, not to mention flavors, that nature provides us with. The shiso leaves add a minty taste and are high in vitamin A. For best flavor, serve this the day after it is made.

3 large savoy cabbage leaves
3 teaspoons salt
4 shiso leaves
2 kirby cucumbers
½ teaspoon ground sansho pepper
1 tablespoon peeled and chopped gingerroot

soy sauce
1 teaspoon sesame seeds (optional)

Shred the cabbage leaves and place in a bowl. Sprinkle generously with salt; mix well with your hands until water is released and the leaves turn limp. Squeeze out excess water with your hands. Slice the cucumbers thinly and repeat salting process.

Chop shiso leaves. Mix cucumbers, cabbage, shiso leaves, pepper, and ginger together in a bowl and cover with a weighted plate for 30 minutes (or put vegetables in a pickling device and apply pressure for the same time). Remove weight and store in refrigerator overnight, covered tightly.

Rinse the vegetables under running water to remove the salt; squeeze out excess water. Serve small portions with soy sauce on the side. Sprinkle with sesame seeds if you wish.

PICKLED GINGER
(AMAZU-SHOGA)
4 TO 8 SERVINGS

This is the ginger that is served with sushi. Made fresh, it is a special pleasure.

½ *pound fresh gingerroot (shin-shoga)*
2 *teaspoons salt*

MARINADE
1 *cup rice vinegar*
¼ *cup water*
3 *tablespoons sugar*

Wipe ginger with a clean damp cloth. Peel and sprinkle with salt. Let stand, covered, for 1 day.

Combine ingredients for the marinade in a glass pickling jar. Mix well until sugar is dissolved. Add the ginger, cover, and let stand for a week.

To serve, slice root thinly, about ⅛ inch thick, along the grain.

The pickled ginger will keep in the refrigerator for 4 months and will turn quite pink.

AGAR-AGAR FRUIT COCKTAIL (AN-MITSU)

GREEN TEA FRUIT PUDDING

WATERMELON SORBET

GINGERED VANILLA ICE CREAM

C H A P T E R   1 3

DESSERTS

GREEN TEA ICE CREAM

GREEN TEA LAYER CAKE

SWEETENED CHESTNUTS

MUSHI-GASHI (STEAMED FRUITCAKE)

ORANGE AGAR-AGAR

CHUNKY AZUKI BEAN PASTE I (TSU-BU-SHI-AN)
(PRESSURE-COOKER METHOD)

CHUNKY AZUKI BEAN PASTE II (TSU-BU-SHI-AN)

JAPANESE PANCAKES WITH AZUKI BEAN PASTE FILLING (DORA-YAKI)

OHAGI

KINAKO-NO-OHAGI

STEAMED CHESTNUT CAKE

TOFU APPLE CAKE

CREAM PUFFS

IN AMERICAN CUISINE, desserts are usually served at the end of a meal. In Japan they are more often served as a snack or to visit friends at teatime. Often the conclusion of a Japanese meal will be something fruity—a wedge of watermelon, fresh berries sprinkled with powdered sugar, cherries, tangerines, and peaches. Also often served after meals these days are small Japanese tea cakes. Western cakes are more commonly served between meals.

The one ingredient that most distinguishes Japanese pastries from Western pastries is anko. It tastes something like carob or chocolate, but lighter, not fatty. Anko is a delicious sweetened azuki bean paste, red in color, used for an infinite variety of dessert treats. Up until recently its delights were not much known in the West.

In puréed form anko is called coshi-an. In chunky solid form it is tsu-bu-shi-an. At home we often made zensai, a chunky sweet soup made with the puréed beans and served with toasted mochi (rice patties) on cold winter days. Anko can also be rolled into small balls and used as fillings for a rice dessert called ohagi, which looks something like a macaroon. Anko can be made into a gelatin dessert using agar-agar, or mixed with vanilla ice cream. You can even eat it straight with a spoon if you wish. Anko must be the most versatile sweet in the world. Some Americans love anko at once. For others it is an acquired taste. Once you develop the taste, you will be hooked for life. Anko is nutritiously high in protein, keeps well in the refrigerator for 2 weeks, and is lower in calories than chocolate—more good reasons to develop a fondness for these sweetened beans.

When I lived with Grandmother in Kamakura, we were one of the few families who owned an oven. It was from our kitchen that the neighbors first experienced the unfamiliar smells of vanilla and butter, and the aroma of sweet cakes baking.

These days ovens are more common in Japan, but the baking of sweets in the home is still unusual. My grandmother has a sweet tooth. Though her cuisine in general is classically Japanese, her desserts somehow are international. Besides traditional Japanese desserts, she also bakes such wonders as good old American chocolate cake and fruitcakes. Our family and friends love them.

Just as Grandmother influenced me, so she shaped the taste of my younger sister Fuyuko, who loves pastries and cakes most of all. When she was twenty, Fuyuko convinced our parents to let her go to France. There she apprenticed herself for seven years to the craft of pastry making, on the staff of the master chef and famous cookbook author Le Nôtre. Fuyuko is now a full-fledged pastry chef in Tokyo.

But I know a bit about Japanese desserts. And I won't resist giving you Grandmother's recipes for steamed chestnut cake and cream puffs, which are now very popular in Japan.

AGAR-AGAR FRUIT COCKTAIL
(AN-MITSU)
4 SERVINGS

As a girl, after playing a hard game of volleyball I looked forward to going to a Japanese-style café where delicious snacks were served. An-mitsu was my favorite, and I could easily have two servings and still go home hungry for dinner. It is still my favorite dessert.

1 stick agar-agar
1⅞ cups water

SYRUP
¾ cup brown or white sugar
5 tablespoons water
1 tablespoon honey

1 cup diced fresh pineapple
1 banana, sliced
1 cup hulled and sliced strawberries
1 cup peeled and sliced peaches
1 cup seedless grapes
1 cup Chunky Azuki Bean Paste I or II
    (pages 240–241) (optional)
    vanilla ice cream, Green Tea Ice Cream,
    or Gingered Vanilla Ice Cream (page
    236) (optional)

Wash agar-agar stick. Break into pieces and let soak in measured water for 45 minutes.

Transfer soaked agar-agar and water to a saucepan and simmer until agar-agar is completely dissolved. Strain liquid through a sieve into a small (1-quart) square casserole dish at room temperature to set. Chill. Cut into ½-inch squares.

Combine the syrup ingredients in a saucepan and bring to a boil. Cool and then chill.

Serve a quarter portion of agar-agar cubes in 4 small deep bowls. Top each bowl with fresh fruit. Pour 2 tablespoons syrup over fruit and agar-agar squares. Scoop a little bean paste and ice cream on top of each fruit cocktail and serve immediately.

GREEN TEA FRUIT PUDDING
4 SERVINGS

This dessert is made with matcha, the powdered tea used in the tea ceremony. It is enjoyable for its fragrance and unique patrician flavor.

1 tablespoon plain powdered gelatin
6 tablespoons warm water
1½ cups plus 2 tablespoons milk
2 large eggs
5 tablespoons sugar

⅔ cup heavy cream
2 teaspoons matcha tea powder
2 tablespoons water
10 strawberries or 20 raspberries

Dissolve powdered gelatin in the warm water. In a separate bowl, mix the 2 tablespoons milk, eggs, and sugar and beat well. Combine the softened gelatin with the egg mixture. Heat the remaining 1½ cups milk until warm and stir it gently into the gelatin mixture.

In another bowl whip the cream until stiff, then add the gelatin-milk mixture. Continue whipping.

Transfer half the mixture to another bowl.

Dissolve the powdered tea with 2 tablespoons water and add it to half the pudding batter. Pour into an aluminum or copper mold and let it harden in the refrigerator for 1 hour. Pour the rest of the plain mixture on top of the green tea mixture. Refrigerate until the mixture hardens, about 2 hours.

Turn the mold onto a plate. Decorate with berries.

Keeps in the refrigerator for a week.

WATERMELON SORBET
4 TO 6 SERVINGS

In the summertime, Grandmother would get us a nice, heavy watermelon, around which she tied a rope so she could drop it deep in our backyard well to chill. When she was ready to serve the watermelon, she played a game called "crack-the-melon." All the children were blindfolded and given sticks to swing at the melon, like a piñata. The lucky one who cracked the melon got the biggest piece.

Watermelon makes a beautiful red sorbet that tastes heavenly. Serve it after any type of Japanese meal, especially sushi; it clears the palate. Choose a watermelon that, when tapped, makes as nice a sound as a drum—it will be red and sweet inside. This recipe can be made with or without an ice-cream machine.

5 cups watermelon (or 2 cups watermelon juice)
2 tablespoons lemon juice
1 cup water
½ cup sugar
1 tablespoon unflavored gelatin, dissolved in 1 tablespoon water
1 egg white

Remove seeds from watermelon with fork, then purée the fruit in a blender to make 2 cups juice. Add lemon juice.

In a medium saucepan combine measured water and sugar and bring to a boil.

Dissolve gelatin in water and gently add to the boiling liquid. Reduce heat and simmer for 1 minute, then remove from heat. Cool completely.

Mix watermelon purée and sugar-water mixture and pour into an ice-cream machine. Freeze according to instructions. If you don't have an ice-cream machine, place the purée in the freezer for 30 minutes. Break into chunks and purée in a blender or food processor briefly until smooth. Return to freezer until completely frozen.

GINGERED VANILLA ICE CREAM
4 TO 6 SERVINGS

Although I have never seen gingered vanilla ice cream in Japan, it appears to be a common and popular dessert in Japanese-American restaurants. It is a dessert that will clear your palate with its pleasant spicy flavor.

2 cups heavy cream
2 cups light cream
1 cup sugar
1½ teaspoons vanilla extract
  pinch of salt
4 tablespoons finely diced candied ginger

Pour the 2 creams directly into the canister of an ice-cream machine. Add sugar,

vanilla, salt, and diced candied ginger; stir with a wooden spoon until the sugar dissolves. Freeze according to manufacturer's instructions.

Serve in small portions, decorated with additional candied ginger, if desired. Keeps for 1 to 2 weeks in the freezer.

GREEN TEA ICE CREAM
4 TO 6 SERVINGS

Fragrant and rich, green tea ice cream makes a nice finale to a Japanese meal. Serve with berries or peaches if you wish. You'll need an electric or manual ice-cream freezer for this treat.

1½ tablespoons cornstarch
  3 cups milk
  1 cup sugar
  2 eggs
    pinch of salt
  ¾ cup evaporated milk
  ½ pint heavy cream
  3 teaspoons matcha tea powder dissolved in
    4 tablespoons hot water

In a saucepan, mix cornstarch with 1 cup milk until smooth and thick. Add the remaining 2 cups milk and cook over low

heat until creamy and smooth, mixing constantly with a wooden spoon to avoid lumps.

Blend sugar, eggs, salt, and evaporated milk with an electric mixer. Add hot milk mixture and beat well. Add cream and dissolved green tea powder. Cool mixture. Pour into the canister of an ice-cream freezer and freeze according to manufacturer's instructions.

GREEN TEA LAYER CAKE

4 TO 6 SERVINGS

This is a traditional sponge cake, but the frosting is a minty green and it's decorated with berries.

5 eggs, separated
½ cup sugar
1 teaspoon vanilla extract
¾ cup sifted flour
4 tablespoons (½ stick) butter

FROSTING
1 cup heavy cream
4 to 6 tablespoons sugar
1 teaspoon vanilla extract
1 tablespoon matcha tea powder dissolved in
  2 tablespoons warm water

2 cups sliced strawberries or 1 cup
  raspberries

Preheat the oven to 350 degrees.

To make sponge cake, beat egg whites in a bowl with a mixer until stiff peaks form. Add sugar and continue beating for 2 minutes. Add vanilla and egg yolks. Then gently fold in flour and toss gently. Melt butter and pour into the batter; mix lightly.

Pour cake mixture into a 9-inch cake mold and bake for 30 minutes. Test cake with a toothpick to see if it comes out clean. Cool completely on a rack, then turn out onto a plate.

To make the frosting, whip the cream and sugar until stiff peaks form. Add the vanilla and dissolved green tea.

Slice sponge cake in half. Spread green tea frosting on the bottom half and add a layer of sliced berries. Replace the top half of the sponge cake and spread top and sides with remaining frosting. Decorate with berries.

SWEETENED CHESTNUTS
4 SERVINGS

If you like *marrons glacés,* the sweetened chestnuts of France, you will like the Japanese ones as well, which are equally tasty and easier to make. While they do require several days to prepare, the process is really quite simple. Sweetened chestnuts may be eaten plain, served with ice cream, or used as fillings for ohagi. Eaten alone, they go especially well with tea, as the two tastes are complementary.

1 pound raw chestnuts
1½ cups sugar
2 cups water

Peeling chestnuts can be a chore, but here is the simple way to do it: Soak chestnuts in warm water for 2 hours, or overnight, to tenderize the skin. Cut off the bottom first, then the shell. Pare the inner skin away.

To make the syrup, combine sugar and measured water in a medium saucepan and bring to a boil over medium heat. Reduce heat and simmer until the liquid becomes syrupy, about 25 minutes.

In a medium pot, combine chestnuts and water to cover and bring to a boil over high heat. Reduce heat and simmer for 20 minutes. Remove from heat, drain, and rinse under cold water.

Combine the chestnuts and syrup and simmer over low heat for 15 minutes, covered. Cool to room temperature and let stand overnight in the refrigerator.

Repeat the simmering process on the second day to thicken the syrup even further. Again, let cool and stand overnight in the refrigerator.

The sweetened chestnuts will be ready to serve the next day and will keep 1 month in the refrigerator.

MUSHI-GASHI
(STEAMED FRUITCAKE)
4 SERVINGS

The Japanese do not have a long tradition of baking cakes; most sweets are steamed. So, while many Japanese kitchens today are equipped with ovens, steamed cakes are still the favorite.

⅔ cup sifted rice flour (jo-shin-ko)
1 teaspoon baking powder
4 eggs, separated
½ cup sugar
½ cup chopped dried fruit (raisins, apricots, etc.)
1 teaspoon vanilla extract

Sift flour and baking powder into a bowl. In another bowl, beat egg whites until stiff peaks form. Add sugar and fold well till mixture begins to shine. Beat the egg yolks and gently stir into egg whites.

Fold flour mixture into egg mixture gently; *do not beat or stir.* Cut in and toss the batter to keep egg whites from collapsing. Add the chopped dried fruit and vanilla and toss gently.

Bring water to a boil in a steamer. Line a 3-cup enameled bowl with damp cheesecloth, or oil it evenly. Pour in the batter and place the bowl in the steamer; steam for 20 minutes. Test cake with a toothpick to see if it comes out clean. Remove the bowl from the steamer and turn onto a plate.

Cut into wedges and serve hot or at room temperature.

VARIATION: Melt 1 ounce sweet chocolate. Transfer a third of the batter to a separate bowl and mix with the melted chocolate. Pour the plain batter into the enameled bowl, then gently pour the chocolate batter on top and swirl with a fork to achieve a marbled effect. Steam as indicated above.

ORANGE AGAR-AGAR
4 TO 6 SERVINGS

This orange dessert is molded in an empty orange shell. When you serve it, simply cut the orange into wedges; inside will be orange-flavored agar-agar sweetened lightly with sugar or honey. Your guests will say "Ahh!" twice—first when they see the dessert, then when they taste it.

   2 sticks agar-agar
   5 medium navel oranges
1½ cups water
 ½ cup sugar or honey
   maraschino cherries (optional)

Break the agar-agar sticks into small pieces and soak in water for 30 minutes. Slice the top off each orange, about 1 inch from top. Scoop out the orange pulp carefully without breaking the shell. Squeeze the orange pulp to make 1½ cups orange juice.

Squeeze the water from the agar-agar. Put measured water in a pot with the well-wrung agar-agar and simmer for 15 minutes. When agar-agar begins to dissolve,

add the sugar or honey. Simmer another 5 minutes, then remove from heat. Strain through a sieve to filter out any undissolved agar-agar particles.

Slice a small piece off the bottom of each orange shell, about ¼ inch from bottom, so that it stands upright.

Combine the orange juice with the agar-agar mixture and pour into the orange shells. Carefully put them in the refrigerator and chill until set, 2 hours or overnight.

To serve, cut each orange into quarters. Place 4 or 5 quarters on each serving dish. Decorate with maraschino cherries if you wish.

CHUNKY AZUKI BEAN PASTE I
(TSU-BU-SHI-AN)
APPROXIMATELY 3 CUPS

Consider azuki bean paste the chocolate of the Orient. The easiest and fastest way to make the bean paste is with a pressure cooker. My grandmother persuaded me to invest in one, and I have never felt more efficient in the kitchen, especially when making ohagi desserts, than when using this handy appliance. This recipe must be started the day before it is to be used.

1½ cups dried azuki beans
  1 cup sugar
   pinch of salt

One day before cooking, wash azuki beans under water. Soak overnight in water to cover.

The next day, drain, and add 3 cups water to the beans. Pour beans and water into pressure cooker.

Bring water to a boil. Drain beans and return to the pot with 3 more cups water.

Close the cover of the pressure cooker securely and place the pressure regulator on the vent pipe. Cook over medium heat for 15 minutes with the pressure regulator rocking gently. Turn off heat and let the pressure drop of its own accord (about 10 minutes).

Open the cover, add sugar and salt, and simmer for 20 minutes, mixing frequently with a wooden spoon, until the liquid is mostly absorbed. The beans should be semicrushed and have an oatmeallike texture. Remove from heat and cool completely.

The bean paste is now ready to use as fillings and toppings. It will keep for 2 weeks, well covered, in the refrigerator.

CHUNKY AZUKI BEAN PASTE II
(TSU-BU-SHI-AN)
APPROXIMATELY 3 CUPS

This recipe can be made without a pressure cooker. Its texture is somewhat softer than that of Chunky Azuki Bean Paste I. I soak the beans in hot water and keep them in a large (5-cup) Thermos overnight to soften.

1½ cups dried azuki beans
1½ cups sugar
   pinch of salt or baking soda

Wash azuki beans under water. Soak in hot water to cover for 1 hour; discard the water. Resoak overnight in hot (not boiling) water to cover in a large Thermos or insulated container. If you do not have a Thermos, simply soak overnight in hot water.

Drain and add 3 cups water to the beans. Pour beans and water into a large pot.

Bring water to a boil and cook for 7 minutes. Drain the beans and return to the pot with 3 more cups water.

Reduce heat to medium and cook the beans for approximately 1 hour, until they are soft. To test readiness, remove a bean with a spoon, cool for a few seconds, then crush it with your fingers. If it crushes easily, it is ready.

Add sugar and salt and continue to cook over medium heat for 5 minutes.

Remove from heat and drain beans, reserving the liquid. Return bean liquid to the cooking pot and simmer over medium heat for 15 minutes, or until liquid becomes syrupy. Add the beans to the syrup and simmer for 15 to 20 minutes longer, mixing frequently with a wooden spoon until liquid is mostly absorbed. The beans should be semicrushed and have a smooth but slightly lumpy texture. Remove from heat and cool completely.

The bean paste is now ready to use as fillings and toppings. It will keep in the refrigerator for a week, well covered.

JAPANESE PANCAKES WITH AZUKI BEAN PASTE FILLING
(DORA-YAKI)
4 SERVINGS

In Japan as in France, pancakes are enjoyed for dessert. These are made just the way you make good old flapjacks, but instead of stacking them up high and covering them with butter and maple syrup, you make a sandwich using 2 small pancakes filled with sweet azuki bean paste.

1 cup flour
3 tablespoons sugar
2 teaspoons baking powder
   pinch of salt
¾ cup milk
3 tablespoons vegetable oil
1 egg
½ teaspoon vanilla extract
¾ cup Chunky Azuki Bean Paste I or II,
   preceding

To make pancake batter, sift flour, sugar, baking powder, and salt into a bowl. Make a small well in the flour mixture and pour in milk, oil, egg, and vanilla. Toss with a fork for 2 minutes until smooth. Do not overmix.

Heat a heavy cast-iron skillet over medium heat. Grease the surface of the skillet lightly. Make 8 pancakes, measuring approximately 3 inches in diameter.

To assemble, spread about 2 tablespoons azuki bean paste on a pancake, then top with a second.

Eat hot or at room temperature. The pancakes will keep in the refrigerator for 3 to 4 days; fill just before serving. (You can heat the filled pancakes in the oven if you like them hot.) They are eaten with fingers.

OHAGI
10 BALLS

Ohagi is a sweet tea cake eaten all year round, especially in fall, when the weather begins to get nippy and one craves something sweet. Ohagi is stuffed azuki bean balls, filled with sweet rice. It is a delicious snack and dessert that goes well with green tea, and some Japanese people eat 1 or 2 pieces for breakfast like a Danish pastry. If you have a sweet tooth you may be tempted to do the same.

SWEET RICE FILLING
1 cup sweet rice (mochi-gome)
⅓ cup sugar
1 cup water

3 cups Chunky Azuki Bean Paste I or II (pages 240–241)

Wash sweet rice under water. Soak overnight in water to cover. Drain.

Lay a moistened, well-wrung cheese or cotton cloth in a hot steamer. Pour rice over the cloth and cover steamer. Steam over medium heat for 45 minutes. Remove from heat.

In medium-size pot add sugar and measured water and bring to a boil. When the sugar is dissolved in water, add the steamed sweet rice and bring to a boil for 2 minutes. Remove from heat and cool completely. The sweet rice absorbs the sugar water and will expand in volume.

The sweet rice filling is now ready to use for Ohagi.

When the sweet rice filling is cold, form it into 10 balls. Each should be about 2½ inches in diameter.

With the bean paste, make same number of balls, slightly larger than the sweet rice balls.

Take 1 bean paste ball, flatten it with your fingers, place a sweet rice filling ball on top, and envelop it with the bean paste dough. Seal the bottom by pinching. Repeat for remaining sweet rice and bean paste balls.

Keeps for 2 days in the refrigerator.

VARIATION: OHAGI STUFFED WITH CHESTNUTS. If desired, a Sweetened Chestnut (page 238) may be pressed into the center of each sweet rice ball before you wrap it with the azuki paste. The flavors blend beautifully.

KINAKO-NO-OHAGI
10 BALLS

This is an inside-out variation of ohagi, in which the chunky azuki bean paste becomes the filling of the sweet rice balls. The sweet rice balls are coated with roasted soy flour, which is yellow in color, toasty and tasty in flavor.

approximately 3 cups sweet rice filling (the amount will depend on the size of your ohagi), opposite
2 cups Chunky Azuki Bean Paste I or II (pages 240–241)
1 cup soy flour (kinako)

Make 10 balls of the sweet rice filling, as you would meatballs. Each should be about 2½ inches in diameter.

Make the same number of bean paste balls, slightly smaller than the sweet rice balls.

Take 1 rice ball, flatten it with your fingers, place a bean paste ball on top, and envelop it with the rice dough. Seal the bottom by pinching.

Coat each ohagi with soy flour. Pat lightly.

Keeps for 2 days in the refrigerator.

STEAMED CHESTNUT CAKE
6 SERVINGS

Chestnuts bring fall to the table. Served as a dessert, this confection is light and goes well with green tea or coffee.

⅓ cup butter
½ cup sugar
5 tablespoons milk
1 teaspoon vanilla extract
3 eggs, separated
1½ cups dry white bread crumbs
8 ounces sweetened chestnuts, homemade (page 238) or canned

Line a small pound cake mold with wax paper. Heat water in a steamer.

Beat together butter and sugar till fluffy.

Add milk, vanilla, and egg yolks and mix well; toss in bread crumbs.

Drain the chestnuts and chop coarsely. Add to the batter.

Beat egg whites until stiff peaks form and fold them into the batter.

Pour batter into the mold and cook in the hot steamer for 40 minutes. Remove and cool completely.

To serve, cut the cake into 2½-inch squares.

TOFU APPLE CAKE
4 SERVINGS

Everyone who tastes this easy-to-make cake wonders what makes it so delicious and moist. Is it zucchini or carrot? I tell them it's tofu. They open their eyes wide and treat themselves to another slice. It disappears very fast.

2 cups sifted white flour
1½ teaspoons baking soda
1 egg
½ cup vegetable oil
¾ cup brown sugar
1½ teaspoons cinnamon
½ teaspoon salt
1 teaspoon vanilla extract
1 8-ounce cake firm tofu, mashed
½ cup chopped walnuts
1 cup peeled and chopped pippin apple
   (about 1 large apple)
½ cup raisins

Preheat the oven to 350 degrees.

Sift together flour and baking soda and set aside.

In a bowl, combine egg, oil, sugar, cinnamon, salt, and vanilla. Beat with a mixer until smooth. Add tofu and mix until just blended. Fold in flour mixture and toss gently. Add walnuts, apple, and raisins.

Pour cake mixture into a 9-inch cake pan and bake for 30 minutes, until a toothpick inserted in the center comes out clean. Cool completely on a rack, then turn onto a plate.

Serve the cake warm or at room temperature.

CREAM PUFFS
6 PUFFS

Cream puffs are my favorite dessert. Grandmother's always puff up high and big and look like swans. When I tried making them as a child, mine were usually small and rarely puffy. But now I know the trick: *The batter must be well beaten and no resting is allowed before flour and eggs are added.* The filling in Japanese cream puffs is not plain custard; Grandmother always adds whipped cream to make the confection creamier and tastier.

2½ tablespoons butter
⅓ cup water
⅓ cup sifted white flour
3 eggs

FILLING
2 tablespoons sifted white flour
⅓ cup sugar
3 egg yolks
1 cup milk
1 teaspoon vanilla extract
1 tablespoon butter
½ cup heavy cream

Preheat the oven to 400 degrees.

In a medium saucepan combine butter and measured water. Bring to a boil over medium heat, then add the flour all at once. Mix vigorously over medium heat with a wooden spoon. When thoroughly mixed, remove from heat.

Add eggs to the batter one at a time while continuing the vigorous mixing. Each additional egg will smooth the batter. To test thickness, drop the batter off the spoon from a foot above the bowl. If batter drops slowly, leaving a tail behind, it is perfect. If it drops into the bowl in one heavy lump, it is too heavy and needs another egg. The batter is now ready for baking.

Spoon 6 mounds of batter on a greased baking sheet. Each mound should be about 2 tablespoons and should be round and smooth. Bake at 375 degrees for 12 minutes. To prevent puffs from collapsing, do not open the oven while baking. Reduce the oven to 250 degrees and bake for another 2 minutes. Remove from the oven and cool on racks.

To prepare filling, mix together flour, sugar, and egg yolks in a medium pan. Add milk and simmer over low heat, stirring constantly. The mixture will start to thicken in about 5 minutes. Add vanilla and remove from heat. Melt butter and stir it in. Cool completely.

Beat cream until stiff and fold into the custard mixture. Refrigerate until ready to use.

To assemble cream puffs, slice off the top of each puff and remove inner dough to make a hollow cup. Fill each puff with cream. Replace the lid of each puff.

Cream puffs *must* be kept in the refrigerator until ready to serve. Filled, the puffs will keep for 2 to 3 days.

MATCHA (POWDERED TEA)

SENCHA (HIGHEST-QUALITY TEA)

GYOKURO ("JEWEL DEW")

BANCHA

HOJI-CHA (ROASTED TEA)

C H A P T E R 1 4

CELESTIAL BEVERAGES: TEA & SPIRITS

TEA OF LUCK

GINGER TEA

PLUM TEA

SHIITAKE-CHA (MUSHROOM TEA)

MUGI-CHA (ROASTED BARLEY TEA)

PERSIMMON TEA

SAKE ON THE ROCKS

SAKE SCREWDRIVER

SAKE AND GINGER ALE

HOMEMADE PLUM WINE

The first cup moistens my lips and throat.
The second cup breaks my loneliness.
The third cup searches my barren entrails
and finds therein five thousand volumes
of old ideographs.
The fourth cup raises a slight perspiration—
all the wrongs of life
pass out through my pores.

At the fifth cup I am purified.
The sixth cup calls me to realms of the Immortals.
The seventh cup—ah, but I can take no more!
I only feel the breath of cool wind
that rises up my sleeves.

Where are the islands of Immortality?
Let me ride away to them
on this sweet breeze.

Lu T'ung
eighth century

PEOPLE OF THE FAR EAST HAVE ENJOYED TEA SINCE ANCIENT TIMES. It was appreciated not only as an aromatic and soothing drink but also for its hygienic value—as a tonic, even to cure illness.

Tea came to Japan in the eighth century, introduced by Chinese traders. (The same word, *cha,* is used to describe tea in China, Japan, and India.) By the twelfth century it was in general use, made popular by Zen monks who drank tea to combat drowsiness during meditation. Later they developed tea drinking into an aesthetic and philosophical ritual that evolved into the tea ceremony.

Many modern Japanese like my grandmother (who is a Tea Master) perform the tea ceremony weekly or even daily. It purifies the body, delights the aesthetic sense, and lifts the spirit. It is an austere though pleasurable meeting of friends and family.

The tea ceremony is normally performed in a special room with tatami mats, an altarlike platform displaying a single scroll painting (changed to suit the seasons), and a vase of specially arranged fresh, preferably wild, flowers. Near the doorway is a stone basin of fresh water, in which guests wash their hands before entering. The tea master and guests gather in a prescribed formal way, engage in polite stylized conversation, and one by one drink from a single beautiful bowl (often a fine, signed antique from a well-known potter).

The tea ceremony may take 2 to 4 hours. On special occasions, small servings of seasonal meals (known as Kaiseki cuisine) are served to increase the guests' appetite for tea. Both the tea master and guests take time to appreciate not only the manner in which the tea is served but the atmosphere that was carefully prepared by the tea master. Since all steps to make, serve, and drink tea are done in a ritual manner, the tea ceremony takes time and patience, especially for a person not accustomed to sitting for long hours on a tatami mat.

As a child, I used to participate in Grandmother's tea ceremony toward the end—when the dessert was served. I had just enough perseverance to sit properly through the dessert period. I also loved the azuki bean tea cakes that Grandmother kept for this occasion.

Because of its complexity, and the hours required, the tea ceremony is probably not feasible for general Western practice. But perhaps you will want to incorporate aspects of the ceremony into your own life, or into the ways you prepare and serve meals.*

The essence of the tea ceremony, according to Grandmother, is to become "nothing," to forget worries and tensions even if momentarily. This act of becoming "nothing" and performing a simple act like making tea purifies the soul. Whether you choose to make tea, write a poem, bake a cake, or play with your child, you can reach a level where this free spirit can be felt. The tea ceremony teaches respect for food, for human labor, for practice of the arts, and for the spiritual unity of all people.

The tea ceremony is of course not the only way to take tea. Even in Japan, most tea drinking is done simply for pleasure, digestion, and sociability—without formal ceremony. There are more than thirty kinds of Japanese tea.

THE VARIETIES OF TEA

Most varieties of Japanese tea are steeped or steamed (the exception is the special powdered tea used in the tea ceremony, which is whipped with hot water before serving). Freshly picked green leaves are steeped in very hot (not boiling) water, which produces tea that

---

* For a complete description of the tea ceremony and its history you might want to refer to *The Book of Tea* by Kakuzo Okakura (New York: Dover Publications, 1964).

is jade green in color. This is different from many Ceylon, India, and China teas, which, before preparation, are allowed to ferment till they become copper-colored, brown, or black. Such fermented teas are often less delicate and more robust than Japanese teas, and contain more caffeine. (If you miss the coffeelike lift of caffeine, and a fine aromatic taste, try black lapsang souchong tea, from China.) Japanese teas are served without sugar or milk. The tea alone is full of flavor.

Testing and tasting a variety of teas is fun. You can become a connoisseur. Many Japanese markets in the United States stock rare Japanese teas, although they can be quite expensive.

Note: The vitamin C content of two cups of most of these teas is higher than that of a whole green pepper or a bunch of spinach. Japanese tea is also thought by some to work as a cancer preventive as well as a cholesterol and high-blood-pressure reducer. Whether or not this is the case, the leisurely ritual of tea drinking, in any of its many forms, is a relaxing, restorative experience sure to have many benefits.

Important: Tea leaves marry water. The best tea is made with mountain water—fresh natural water that is alive and clear. If you live in a city, such water is hard to get. Try bottled spring water (noncarbonated) for best results.

According to Chinese poet Lu Wu, who wrote the *Ch'a Ching (Holy Scripture of Tea),* there are three states of boiling water. The first boil is when the little bubbles, like the eyes of a fish, swim on the surface; the second boil is when the bubbles are crystal beads rolling in a fountain; the third boil is when the billows surge wildly in the kettle. When you reach the final point, turn the heat off and let the hot water stand for 1 minute. Do not be impatient.

MATCHA

(POWDERED TEA)

4 SERVINGS

Matcha is a special tea used in the tea ceremony. The powdered tea is made from leaves ground to a fine powder in a stone mill and whipped to a frothy green liquid. The taste of whipped tea is slightly bitter, but invigorating, and mellow on the tongue. The whisk, as well as matcha itself, is sold at Japanese stores in most large American cities. Have a bean cake or something sweet to accompany the bitter mellow tea. To serve, a tea bowl would be ideal, but if you do not have one, whip the powdered tea in an ordinary bowl and transfer it to the tea cups gently, so as not to lose the froth on top.

2 cups water
8 teaspoons matcha tea powder

Bring measured water to a boil. Meanwhile, warm the tea bowl or cups with hot water. Discard the water and add 2 teaspoons matcha to each bowl.

Add ½ cup boiling water to each tea bowl or cup. With a bamboo whisk, whip the powder into the hot water until it becomes a frothy jade liquid. Serve while warm and bubbly.

SENCHA

(HIGHEST-QUALITY TEA)

4 SERVINGS

Sencha is tea of the highest quality, appreciated not so much as a thirst quencher as for its fragrance. It is served in small pots called kyusu and drunk mal or special family occasions. According to tradition, tea leaves used for sencha are to be picked on the day following the eighty-eighth night after the first buds appear. These leaves are small, young, and tender.

1 cup water
2 teaspoons sencha tea leaves

Bring measured water to a boil, let it stand for 1 or 2 minutes, and pour into a pot, preferably a small one made of porcelain or clay. Gently add the sencha tea leaves. Let stand for 1 minute. During the wait, let your soul rest; haste will make bad tea. Preheat the tea cups with hot water and discard the water.

To serve, pour the tea bit by bit from one cup to another, so everyone gets an equal amount, of equal strength. Pour off any hot water left in the teapot after you have finished serving, leaving the leaves behind. (When you let leftover tea sit in tea leaves, you will get bitter tea the second time around.) On formal occasions, sencha tea leaves are thrown out after a single use, as it is a drink enjoyed for its aroma. However, at home a second serving can be obtained from the same tea leaves, although the tea will be less aromatic. The second time around, pour on boiling water.

GYOKURO
("JEWEL DEW")
4 SERVINGS

Gyokuro, which translates as "jewel dew," is the king of steeped teas. Young baby tea buds of ancient bushes are grown with utmost care. When the buds appear in early spring, they are covered and shielded from the sun's rays. This produces small quantities of young and tender leaves. They yield an irresistible aromatic tea—rare and expensive. It is consumed in very small portions, mainly for flavor. Like matcha, it is slightly bitter but mellow. A small pot is ideal for this tea, preferably one made of clay or porcelain. You can find tiny cups in Oriental stores.

1 cup hot water
4 teaspoons gyokuro tea leaves

As with sencha tea, measured water used for gyokuro tea should be boiled and then cooled by letting it stand for 1 or 2 minutes.

Put the tea leaves in the pot, then gently add the hot water. Let stand for 1½ minutes. Pour small amounts into 3 or 4 tiny cups, pouring off any tea remaining in the pot. Add fresh hot water for the next serving. Enjoy the first round for sweetness; the second for its bitterness; and the third for the subtle earthy flavor.

BANCHA
4 SERVINGS

Bancha is made from tea picked sometime later than the eighty-eighth day of growth. The leaves are larger and more mature. Bancha is a good basic tea to be drunk at home and restaurants. It is steeped the way most Western and Chinese teas are prepared. The more mature the tea, the more twigs and stems it will contain. However, a few twigs and stems at the bottom of your cup are considered attractive and interesting—tea is for the eye as well as the palate. If a twig or stem is seen afloat in the tea cup in a vertical position, which is rare, it is considered a sign of good luck coming your way.

2 cups hot water
2 to 3 tablespoons bancha tea leaves

Bring measured water to a boil. Put tea leaves in a medium-size porcelain or clay pot and gently pour hot water over them. Let stand for 2 minutes to allow tea leaves to open up before serving. Pour into individual cups.

Also try genmai-cha, or rice tea, a mixture of bancha tea and popped or roasted rice. It has a smoky, nutty flavor.

HOJI-CHA
(ROASTED TEA)
4 SERVINGS

Hoji-cha or "roasted tea" is bancha that has been roasted to a tawny brown color. It has a smoky taste and aroma, and less caffeine than other teas. It is popular among the elderly and children as a thirst quencher. You can dry-roast your own hoji-cha by putting bancha leaves in a nonstick pan over medium heat and roasting until they are fragrant and nutlike, about 2 minutes.

2 cups hot water
2 tablespoons bancha tea leaves

Roast regular bancha tea leaves in a dry nonstick frying pan over medium heat for 2 minutes. Prepare as for Bancha tea.

TEA OF LUCK
4 SERVINGS

This is tea for celebrated occasions such as New Year's Day. Konbu seaweed and small salted plums are placed in a tea cup and sencha tea is poured over them. The result is a fragrant savory tea.

1 konbu seaweed strip
4 small salted plums (ume-boshi)
2 8-ounce cups Sencha (page 252)

Soften the konbu in water for 20 minutes.

Cut into 8 strips ¼ inch by 3 inches long and tie each in a knot. Put 2 seaweed knots in each cup, along with 1 salted plum. Pour sencha gently over the ingredients. Serve warm.

GINGER TEA

Ginger tea is drunk for its medicinal properties and its fragrance. A small pinch of ginger in Japanese green tea—sencha or bancha—warms the body and is said to help with colds, fevers, and dizziness. If possible, use tender pink gingerroot (shin-shoga), available in the summertime.

Simply drop ½ teaspoon grated fresh gingerroot into prepared tea and drink while warm.

PLUM TEA

Bancha tea goes with salty foods like pickled vegetables and salted plums (ume-boshi). In rural Japanese homes, people gather around foot warmers during the long winter and drink tea while nibbling on pickles. Pickled plums or salted plums help with colds and coughs and ease sore shoulders and stress.

Simply pour bancha tea over 1 salted plum in a tea cup. The plum may be eaten with chopsticks.

SHIITAKE-CHA
(MUSHROOM TEA)
4 SERVINGS

 When shiitake mushrooms are cooked with foods, the water that is used to soften the mushrooms is often discarded. It shouldn't be. It is highly nutritious and is believed by some to prevent cancer. Grandmother keeps the soup of the mushrooms in the refrigerator and drinks it as tea every day.

4 or 5 dried shiitake mushrooms (forest
   mushrooms)
3 cups water

Soak the mushrooms in measured water. Use the mushrooms in any recipe that amuses you. Drink the mushroom tea for health and its woodsy fragrance.

MUGI-CHA
(ROASTED BARLEY TEA)
6 TO 8 SERVINGS

This is a boiled tea to be enjoyed chilled during the hot season.

2 quarts water
½ cup roasted barley (mugi-cha)

Bring measured water to a boil. Add the roasted barley and simmer over medium heat for 5 minutes. Strain the liquid into a pitcher, discarding the barley, and refrigerate.

Serve over ice in tall glasses.

PERSIMMON TEA
4 SERVINGS

In the old days in Japan, it was said that when the persimmon fruits ripen to a red color, the doctors turn pale. That's because its fruit and leaves are full of vitamin C. Use the tea leaves in the same manner as you would bancha and sencha. If you like a roasty flavor, you may dry-roast the tea leaves in a nonstick frying pan over low heat for a couple of minutes before preparing your tea.

2 cups water
2 teaspoons persimmon tea leaves

Bring measured water to a boil. Put tea leaves in a medium-size porcelain or clay pot. Gently pour hot water into the pot. Let stand for 30 seconds to allow tea leaves to open up.

Pour into individual cups.

NOTE: If there is a persimmon tree in your backyard or your neighbor's, make your own tea leaves by picking the fresh young leaves in late spring and drying them in the sun.

Wash the freshly picked leaves. Devein and chop thinly. Squeeze gently to remove excess moisture. Put the chopped leaves in a flat basket and let dry in the sun for 3 days. Store in a container with a tight lid.

SAKE

One of the most pleasant surprises of Japanese cuisine is the rice wine known as sake. Water and a variety of teas are the staple beverages of Japanese meals, and beer, whiskey, and fruit wines are also taken on occasion, but sake is the traditional drink. It is pure, mild, clear as water, unexpectedly low in alcohol content, and is made of choice rice and fresh water.

Only the clean cores of the rice grains are used in making sake. These hearts of rice grains are combined with water and allowed to ferment for six to nine months in cedar barrels. Unlike wines made from grapes, sake needs little aging. When the sake is transferred to individual bottles it undergoes a brief heat treatment to stop the fermentation; aging ceases.

In Japan sake is available in several grades, according to fragrance, color, and taste. There are first, second, and third grades, as well as "superior" classes. However, connoisseurs of sake have differing opinions about this grading system. Some say that the second-grade sakes are spiked with pure alcohol, as much as 10 percent by volume. This extra alcohol results in a less fragrant and stronger-tasting drink. Another type of sake is called genshu. This is sake fresh from the barrel, without heat treatment to stop fermentation. Genshu must be drunk as soon as the barrel is opened. It is served on special festive occasions in tiny square cypress boxes, with a bit of salt on the side.

You won't find genshu in your local liquor store; it can't travel in bottles. Second- and third-class sakes are also not available; Japan exports only its top two grades of sake, usually labeled "superior" or "deluxe." Good brands that are available in the West include Kikumasamune (very dry), Shochikubai (neutral), and Sawanotsuru (moderately sweet).

Sake is often thought to be a strong drink like tequila, vodka, and whiskey, which often contains up to 40 percent alcohol. But the alcohol content of sake is only 8 or 9 percent, about the same as a good sherry.

Part of the pleasure of drinking sake is in the manner of its preparation and serving. In Japan this process is an enjoyable social ritual —like decanting, tasting, and offering a toast in the West.

Usually sake is served moderately hot. Heating doesn't reduce the alcohol content but does release the rice fragrance. Small-mouthed little ceramic jugs are used for serving, and are available inexpensively in almost any Oriental shop.

Pour your sake from the bottle into the jug and place it in a pot of simmering water for 3 to 4 minutes. Temperature is arbitrary; taste to see if it's warm enough—or feel the bottom of the jug. (Skin temperature or a bit warmer is about right.) Serve on a small tray with tiny sake cups (or shot glasses). With a good meal, one or two jugs (about 1½ cups) should please an average guest. Be prepared to heat several jugs. Two are roughly equal in alcohol to one restaurant-size glass of red or white wine.

The sake ritual begins with the host. He or she serves sake to each guest, who holds up the cup to make pouring easier. The guest tastes, then reciprocates by serving the host. If there are too many guests to serve, each person can reciprocate the toast with the person next to him or her. As in the West, there may be appreciative comments on the wine's fragrance and taste. Repeated toasts of friendship or love or good luck in business dealings are quite in order. Of course, less formal use of sake is also pleasant. A quickly warmed jug makes a delightful relaxant after sport or work or for an intimate evening tête-à-tête.

Sake comes in half-gallon, 30-ounce, and 25-ounce bottles, attractively labeled and packaged. When making a gift of sake, a half-gallon bottle, however big it may seem, is the appropriate size. The price for a half gallon is surprisingly low—usually under ten dollars.

Once the bottle is opened, sake quickly loses its fragrance, so it should be prepared and served right away. A closed, partially full bottle, however, should keep for up to 6 months in the refrigerator. If you have any heated sake left over, don't drink it; use it in cooking instead. It's an excellent flavor enhancer and tenderizer for stews, stir-fried foods, soups, and even over your steaks. Warning: Do not confuse sweet cooking sake (mirin) with drinking sake. Drinking sake can be used for cooking, but mirin is not intended for drinking.

SAKE ON THE ROCKS
1 SERVING

In a 6-ounce glass, pour 2 ounces sake directly from the bottle over ice cubes. Splash in a little lemon or lime juice and garnish with a slice of lemon or lime.

SAKE SCREWDRIVER
1 SERVING

Pour 1½ ounces sake over ice in an 8-ounce glass. Add 4 to 6 ounces orange juice.

SAKE AND GINGER ALE
1 SERVING

Pour 2 ounces sake over ice in an 8-ounce glass. Fill with 4 to 6 ounces ginger ale.

OTHER JAPANESE SPIRITS

Japanese whiskey and beers are becoming increasingly popular in the West. Suntory whiskeys are available in many liquor stores. Japanese beer, too, is gaining fans all over the United States. Asahi, Sapporo, and Kirin are the major brands, all good, each distinctive. The Japanese also produce good wines, but exportation is limited.

Another potent alcoholic beverage is called shochu. It is similar to vodka or gin in that it is made of potatoes, rice, or millet. Alcoholic content is 25 to 35 percent, generally, but can be as high as 90 proof (45 percent). It is drunk straight, or used as a base to make umeshu, known as plum wine in the West.

Plum wine is delicious over ice. In Japan it is considered a healthy medicinal drink that can be made at home. Making plum wine takes some work, but you and your guests will be rewarded by its delicious taste.

You will need a supply of small *green* ume plums, commonly available in Japanese markets (they are grown in the United States as well as in Japan). The big purple American plums won't do. You also have to find rock crystal sugar, available in Japanese markets and some health food stores.

HOMEMADE PLUM WINE
2 QUARTS

This is Grandmother Ishikawa's super-special recipe for plum wine. My mother learned the recipe and served it often to guests. Now I pass it on to you.

2 pounds unripe green plums (ume)
1¼ pounds rock crystal sugar
2 quarts shochu or gin

Wash plums and remove stems. Dry completely with a towel and put them out in the sun for a couple of hours, turning occasionally for full exposure. Put alternate layers of plums and sugar in a 1-gallon glass jar with a tight-fitting lid. Pour the shochu or gin over the sugar and plums. Seal firmly. Store jar in a dark, cool place, such as under the sink or in the basement, for at least 3 months; longer and the taste will be even better, and a bit stronger.

Serve chilled or over ice.

MENU PLANNING

JAPANESE MENUS CHANGE WITH THE SEASONS, like the colors of leaves in a forest. The freshest in-season foods become the centerpiece. All-year-round foods are served to complement the seasonal foods. Your eaters are kept in touch with the procession of seasons by the savory dishes you bring to your table.

For instance, a dish decorated with cherry blossoms tells us of the arrival of spring. A dish of fresh chestnuts and mushrooms served on top of a colorful autumn leaf, such as maple, can convey a lyrical message of fall.

The basic structure of a Japanese menu is three dishes and a soup, or five dishes and a soup, plus steamed rice and pickled foods.

A variety of dishes are enjoyed for their taste and the manner in which they are prepared. Some Americans might think that the more dishes to serve, the more tedious and time-consuming the work in the kitchen. This is not true. With the exceptions of steamed rice and soup, many Japanese dishes are enjoyed at room temperature, so they can be made ahead of time and served in small portions to feed the family for a whole week. You may serve all dishes at once or one at a time.

Even though I have devoted an entire chapter to appetizers, most dishes in this book can be used as appetizers if served in small portions. In fact, an American having a full-course Japanese dinner may wonder when the main course is going to be served, because all dishes seem equally important. To make a stronger impression with a particular dish, the garnishes may be more elaborate or portions increased. Here are per-person serving guidelines for a three- to five-course meal:

APPETIZER: 2 to 4 ounces meat, seafood, vegetable, or fruit
SASHIMI: 3 to 5 slices of fish
STEAMED, BROILED, GRILLED, BRAISED, AND DEEP-FRIED DISHES: 4 to 6
   ounces meat, seafood, or vegetables
SALAD: 4 to 6 ounces per dish
RICE: ⅔ cup
PICKLED FOODS: 3 to 5 slices of assorted pickles
SOUP: ⅔ cup

If you plan a menu around a hearty one-pot dinner, cooked at the table, you may serve the salad while the pot is heating. Skip the soup, because the hot pot is itself a soup-style food. The rice should be served toward the end, to keep tummies from filling up too soon and spoiling the meal.

Sushi is also in a class by itself. Since it is largely rice and seafood, it alone can be quite satisfying; however, you also may serve a salad and miso or suimono soup.

Here is the order in which dishes are served for a very elaborate, formal meal (you can modify this menu by eliminating dishes and one of the soups for more casual, weeknight fare):

FIRST PART	APPETIZER
	SUIMONO SOUP
	SASHIMI
SECOND PART	BROILED OR GRILLED DISH
	STEAMED DISH
	BRAISED DISH
	DEEP-FRIED DISH
	SALAD
THIRD PART	MISO SOUP
	STEAMED RICE
	PICKLED FOODS
FINALE	BEVERAGES
	DESSERT

GOOD MORNING
(O-ha-yo)

Breakfast is the first meal of the day. It breaks our temporary fast, so it should be well balanced and wholesome. The Japanese wake up to a breakfast of eggs, miso soup, salad, rice, and fruit.

A SIMPLE JAPANESE BREAKFAST

Many modern Japanese prefer toast to rice; my grandmother bakes her own loaf of bread twice a week. She spreads butter on her toast and tops it with a piece of toasted nori seaweed. It's delicious!

Bread with butter and toasted nori seaweed

Tea, coffee, orange juice

A HEARTY MORNING MEAL

A more complicated morning repast.

Scrambled eggs with crab meat

Sliced tomatoes

Basic miso soup

Steamed rice

GOOD AFTERNOON
(Kon-ni-chi-wa)

American lunches often feature two pieces of bread with meat between them—a hot dog, a hamburger, or a sandwich. Japanese lunches are mostly based on rice and may be contained in small lunch boxes called bentoh boxes. These boxes are divided into several compartments, in which steamed rice, vegetables, meat, seafood, and egg are packed in a decorative way. With leftovers from the night before, you can pack a creative lunch box. Here's a simple bentoh box:

Japanese fried chicken in ginger sauce

Heavenly omelette

Sliced cucumbers

Healthy roots

Rice with peas

Fruit

YEAR-ROUND LUNCH

Most people don't want to spend too much time preparing lunch. A
quickly stir-fried Japanese-style chow mein noodle dish is easy. Serve
it piping hot.

Yaki-soba

Celery and carrot salad

Fruit

OMELETTE LUNCH

This is a hot lunch that takes very little preparation. Chicken and
vegetables give the omelette extra flavor and nourishment. Serve over
very hot rice! Deep donburi bowls are preferred, as they keep the
rice hot.

Parent and child

Pickles

Fruit

SPRING LUNCH

Sushi is popularly served for lunch. Inari-zushi is fried tofu pouches
(usu-age) stuffed with vinegared rice. Like pita pocket sandwiches,
they can be eaten with the fingers.

Stuffed tofu sushi

Spring clam suimono

Seaweed and cucumber salad

Kiwi delight

Tea

JAPANESE PIZZA PARTY

Japanese pizzas are free of cheese, tomato, and yeast. Bring an electric grill to the table and make the pizza with your friends or family.

Japanese pizza

Vinegared crab

Beer, sake, or tea

HOT SUMMER DAY LUNCH

Cold somen noodles floating in a bowl of ice cubes are refreshing, and the addition of chilled egg custard and watermelon sorbet make even the warmest summer pleasant.

Hand-wrapped somen noodles
Egg tofu delight
Watermelon sorbet
Iced tea

EVERYDAY SUMMER LUNCH

Curry is typical of India, but also of Japan, especially during summertime.

Japanese beef curry
Rainbow salad
Iced tea

AUTUMN LUNCH

This lunch should be colorful, like the scenery outside your window. You will feel like a painter instead of a cook.

Scattered sushi
Watercress ohi-tashi
Autumn salad
Four-mushroom suimono
Steamed chestnut cake
Tea

COLD WINTER LUNCH

Noodles are popular year-round. While summer noodles swim in ice-cold water, winter noodles are served in a steaming-hot broth. Serve the noodles in a deep donburi bowl.

Kamo-namban
Fruit
Tea

GOOD EVENING
(Kon-ban-wah)

HIBACHI BARBECUE DINNER

You can flavor any barbecue foods with Japanese seasonings. Also, try grilling oval-shaped balls of rice (about ⅔ cup steamed rice for each ball), brushed with soy sauce; grilled rice balls are absolutely heavenly.

Teppan-yaki
Grilled rice balls
Green salad
Watermelon
Gingered vanilla ice cream
Iced tea, beer

BUFFET FOR A LARGE CROWD

You can make all these dishes ahead of time so you can nibble with your guests throughout the evening. If a hot dish is in demand, broil the chicken yakitori on skewers at the last minute and let the tasty aroma travel.

Summer salad
Japanese-American potato salad
Assorted sashimi
Chicken yakitori on skewers
Sushi rolled in nori, California roll
Chilled pork roast
Agar-agar fruit cocktail
Ohagi
Beverages

A FORMAL SEAFOOD DINNER

Get the freshest seafood in season and prepare an elaborate dinner. You may serve the dishes one by one or, except for the appetizer and dessert, all at once.

Octopus lemon boats
(appetizer)
or sashimi

Tofu and wakame seaweed suimono
Grilled salmon
Everything-in-it custard
Braised hijiki seaweed with mushrooms and carrots
Stuffed mushroom tempura
Steamed rice
Pickled foods

Green tea ice cream

A FAMILY DINNER

Croquettes are a favorite family meal, and potato croquettes are by far the most popular. With scrambled tofu, they make a very balanced menu.

Beef and potato croquettes
Asparagus with bonito flakes
Scrambled tofu
Miso soup with enoki mushrooms
Steamed rice
Pickled foods

Fruit
Beverages

TEMPURA DINNER

Use a variety of seafoods and vegetables. Slice all the ingredients ahead of time and make sure you chill the water for the batter in order to get crispy tempura. With tempura, serve a very light salad. As an appetizer, sliced kiwi with a tablespoon of plain yogurt is incredibly refreshing.

Kiwi with plain yogurt

Seafood and vegetable tempura
Vinegared crab
Steamed rice
Pickled foods

Fruit
Beverages

VEGETARIAN DINNER

Meatless menus are in demand these days. It is very easy to find vegetarian recipes in Japanese cuisine because of its meatless culinary tradition. Here is a menu that is different.

Sesame tofu
(appetizer)

Vegetarian "burger"
Everything-in-it custard (made without chicken or seafood)
Rainbow salad
Brown rice
Just vegetable suimono

Green tea layer cake
Beverages

SUKIYAKI

A hearty one-pot dinner warms up the whole body and creates a congenial atmosphere for your diners.

Roe roe roe your boat
(appetizer)

Sukiyaki
Steamed rice
Pickled foods

Green tea fruit pudding
Beverages

A TYPICAL JAPANESE DINNER

My husband lives on this menu.

Tuna sashimi
Vinegared shrimp
(appetizer)

Basic miso soup
Yellowtail teriyaki
Watercress ohi-tashi
Steamed rice
Pickled foods

Green tea ice cream
Beverages

A SPRING DINNER

In the spring sprigs of cherry blossoms are arranged in the home.
Cherry blossoms are served in tea. Foods are blushed with such
spring color. When you plan a spring dinner, keep the colors of
spring in mind and try to create this season in your dishes.

Sesame tofu
(appetizer)

Squid sashimi
Teriyaki okra chicken
Braised Japanese potatoes and carrots
Clam and vegetable custard
Vinegared crab
Rice with peas
Snake eye suimono
Pickled foods

Fruit
Beverages

A SUMMER DINNER

The summer heat can scorch our bodies, so the dinners should be
something cool and refreshing. A salad on top of a bed of crushed ice
is wonderful. Serve the dinner on the patio under the twinkling stars.

Shrimp, okra, and wakame seaweed over crushed ice
(appetizer)

Salmon teriyaki
Carrots with bonito flakes
Steamed rice
Pickled foods

Green tea ice cream
Beverages

A FALL DINNER

The harvest season brings a variety of possibilities to the menu list. This is what I suggest:

Tuna and squid sashimi
(appetizer)

Lotus root with plum sauce
Wrapped cod with mushrooms
Snow peas with almond dressing
Vegetable and chicken miso soup
Steamed rice
Pickled foods

Cream puffs
Beverages

A WINTER DINNER

Shabu shabu is an ideal winter dinner that can be made right at the dinner table. Try to get your butcher to slice the beef paper-thin.

Matsutake mushroom and shrimp surprise
(appetizer)

Shabu shabu

Gingered vanilla ice cream
Beverages

GLOSSARY: A CORNUCOPIA OF JAPANESE FOODS

AGAR-AGAR (kanten): Made of "Ceylon moss," agar-agar seaweed comes in the form of a translucent rectangle. Used like gelatin, it hardens at room temperature, and gives sweets and salads a texture that is firm but not rubbery. Its calcium content is higher than milk's when compared by weight, so it is very healthy. You can find agar-agar in health food stores and Japanese, Korean, and Oriental grocery stores. Sugar, fruit, milk, and essence are added for flavor and color. It is also available powdered or shredded. Keeps indefinitely in a dry place.

ARROWROOT STARCH: SEE KUZU.

AZUKI BEANS (azuki): Azuki beans are served all year round but especially for festive occasions such as birthdays and weddings. The beans are sweetened and made into a paste called anko, which serves as fillings for Japanese desserts. Unsweetened beans can be found in rice dishes as well as vegetable dishes. Azuki beans are available in supermarkets and Japanese grocery stores. Canned azuki paste is available in most Japanese grocery stores. It tends to be very sweet but makes a pleasant instant dessert served plain or with ice cream.

BAMBOO SHOOTS (takenoko): The young shoots of bamboo are dug up in spring and cooked. They are treasured for their crunchy texture and delicate flavor, which complements both meat and vegetables. Water-packed and canned shoots are available in Oriental and American grocery stores. Once bamboo shoots are removed from the package, they keep in the refrigerator for about a week. Canned bamboo should be blanched in water before use to remove the distinct odor of can.

BEAN SPROUTS (moyashi): The Japanese prefer to eat bean sprouts briefly cooked rather than raw (as many Americans prefer). Sprouts are high in protein. Get sprouts that are unbruised and crispy-looking. Daikon radish sprouts are also delicate and delicious.

BONITO FLAKES, DRIED (katsuo-bushi): Katsuo-bushi is a basic ingredient for making dashi broth. Used also for sprinkling over boiled or broiled seafood and vegetables as well as over tofu. It is full of calcium and can be munched on as a snack. Available in vacuum-packed containers, it keeps indefinitely in a dry place.

BURDOCK ROOT (gobo): A family relation of the carrot, gobo is a long brown root vegetable. To serve, it is scrubbed and washed under water and pared or sliced into matchsticks. Overscrubbing the skin will take away its woodsy flavor, so treat it gently, just rinsing the dirt off. The raw vegetable must be soaked in water for 20 minutes or so to remove bitterness. Stir-fried burdock is delicious. It keeps in the refrigerator for about a week. Choose roots that are firm, not limp.

CHESTNUTS (kuri): Readily available in most supermarkets in the fall, chestnuts are tasty accompaniments to vegetable and meat dishes. The Japanese like them roasted, cooked in rice and in desserts. Sweetened chestnuts in heavy syrup are available in Japanese grocery stores. They are expensive but can be used straight out of the jar. They go wonderfully well with vanilla ice cream.

CHILI PEPPER, DRIED (togarashi): These are dried red peppers not unlike Mexican peppers, to be used sparingly in braised dishes. Remove seeds before using. Store in a dry place. They keep indefinitely.

CHINESE CABBAGE (hakusai or nappa): This is a versatile vegetable used in salads, one-pot dinners, and soups and made into pickles. The leaves are loosely packed, compared to savoy cabbage, light green, and quite crispy. Keeps fresh in the refrigerator for about a week. Avoid those with speckles on the leaves; they are past their prime.

CHINESE SNOW PEA PODS (saya-ingen): Bright green pods that are tender and delicate. The pods are eaten along with the peas inside. Look for crisp, dark green pods without bruises.

CHRYSANTHEMUM LEAVES (shungiku): These are not actually from chrysanthemum flowers, but a vegetable that looks much like spinach or dandelion leaves. They are very fragrant. Used in one-pot dinners, such as sukiyaki. They stay fresh in the refrigerator about 4 days.

"CRAB STICKS": See Fish cake, steamed.

CUCUMBER (kyuri): Small, seedless Japanese cucumbers are hard to find in this country, but you may use any of the native varieties instead. There are many types of cucumber; the two most common are the large, dark-green standard cucumbers, which are usually waxed to prevent moisture loss, and the smaller cucumbers called kirbies, which are commonly used for making dill pickles. Also available are European cucumbers which are more expensive, but seedless, bumpless. If you can't get kyuri, these or kirbies are the best substitute. If regular cucumbers are used, they should be peeled and seeded first.

CURRY POWDER (kay-rey): Japanese cuisine is theoretically spiceless, but curry is an exception—a spicy blend of turmeric, cumin, coriander, red peppers, and other aromatics borrowed from Indian cuisine.

DAIKON RADISH (daikon): A big white radish that is used in a multiplicity of ways. It is grated and served as a condiment with tempura and seafoods. Sliced, it can become a central ingredient for miso soup or salad. It is treasured for its medicinal properties—it helps digestion, as it contains lots of enzymes, vitamin C, and pepsin. Daikon is sold fresh all over the U.S. It is also available dried, sliced into strips (kiri-boshi-daikon). To use, kiri-boshi-daikon strips are soaked in water to soften and sautéed with tofu and other vegetables. Pickled daikon radish called takuan is one of the most popular pickled foods in Japan.

DASHI CONCENTRATES (dashi-no-moto): Like bouillon cubes, these concentrates are convenient when you do not have time to make stock from scratch, but are much better-tasting than beef and chicken concentrates. Powdered dashi is available packed like tea bags as well as straight out of a jar. Keeps indefinitely in a dry cool place or in the refrigerator. Liquid dashi concentrate is also available. Once opened, it should keep in the refrigerator for a month. Always be sure to check the label of your dashi concentrate; some contain salt and MSG.

EGGPLANT (nasu): Japanese eggplants are much smaller than American eggplants. They are sweeter and mellower in flavor. Enjoyed as a salad, in soup, and in simmered dishes. They keep about a week in the refrigerator. They are simple to grow in your backyard.

ENOKI MUSHROOMS (enoki-dake): These tiny delicate white mushrooms with long skinny stems are sold in a bunch with roots still attached. Delicious in miso soups and one-pot dinners such as sukiyaki. Available fresh only. Choose unbruised ones that have pretty caps.

FIDDLEHEAD FERN (warabi): The curled young fern tips are delicate messengers of spring. They are served in soups and salads. Also called bracken fern, they are sold in water-packed bags or fresh at produce stands. They keep in the refrigerator for 3 to 4 days.

FISH CAKE, STEAMED (kamaboko): Made of puréed white fish such as cod and shark, kamaboko is steamed and has a texture slightly firmer than that of tofu. Kamaboko comes in a variety of types. Chikuwa is cylindrical in shape and hollow in the center. Regular kamaboko comes on a sheet of cedar board, which makes slicing easy, and may be tinted pink around the edges. Kani-kamaboko is steamed fish cake with artificial crab flavor, known here as "crab sticks" or "sea legs." It is often served in sushi restaurants. Deep-fried kamaboko and kamaboko with mixed seafood, seaweed, and vegetables are also available. Kamaboko is found in the tofu section. Once the package is opened, it lasts for about a week. Delicious as is or cooked in one-pot or noodle dishes.

GINGERROOT (shoga): Available fresh in the U.S., this vegetable, aromatic and spicy, is peeled and sliced thinly or grated. A Japanese grater is useful for grating gingerroot because it is designed to receive the ginger juice, which should not be discarded. Keeps in the refrigerator 1 week. Buy the ones that are firm, with skin that is shiny and not dry. Pickled gingerroot (amazu-shoga) is also available, used as a popular condiment with sushi. Amazu-shoga is made from shin-shoga ginger, a pinkish ginger available late spring through early autumn. Red pickled ginger (beni-shoga) is dyed and not very natural, but the amazu-shoga is pickled ginger in its own natural color.

GINKGO NUTS (gin-nan): Gin-nan are symbols of autumn. These nuts are tasty and served in many Japanese dishes, such as chawanmushi and grilled dishes. They are available fresh or canned. If fresh, you must panfry them, then shell each one to get the meat.

GOURD SHAVINGS, DRIED (kampyo): Fresh gourd is shaved into a long strip and dried in the sun. To use, kampyo is softened in salted water for 1 hour. It is massaged frequently while soaking in water to increase absorption. Kampyo is seasoned with soy sauce, sake, and sugar and used to tie sushi rolls or incorporated into sushi rolls. Available in 1-ounce vacuum-packed containers. Unopened, it keeps indefinitely.

HARUSAME NOODLES (harusame): These translucent, slippery noodles are made of mung beans, rice, or potato starch, and are often called cellophane noodles. Chinese have a slightly different version of cellophane noodles called saifun or maifun noodles and they can be used in the place of harusame noodles if you can't find any. Harusame noodles are used in one-pot dinners (nabes) and salads.

HIJIKI SEAWEED (hijiki): A mass of twiglike seaweed that is jet-black in color. Highly rich in calcium and iron, sold in dried and fresh form. Soak at least 20 minutes in water prior to cooking (will triple in size). Keeps indefinitely in a dry cool place.

KAMABOKO: See Fish cake, steamed.

KIKURAGE MUSHROOMS (kikurage): This is a rubbery-looking mushroom that is curly on the edges. Sold in dry form; you must soak it in water for a minimum of 30 minutes to soften. Delicious in salads and soups.

KINOME (kinome): A very fragrant leaf of the sansho tree, which is related to the pepper tree. The leaves are used in soups, sushi, and salads. It is rarely sold in Japanese grocery stores, but if you can obtain the seeds, they grow very well. To store, wrap kinome in damp newspaper or paper towel and then in plastic. Keeps in the refrigerator for 3 to 4 days.

KONNYAKU (konnyaku): Also called devil's tongue or alimentary paste. A cake made from the devil's tongue plant, which is related to the yam. The cake is firm, grayish, jellylike, and sometimes dotted with black flecks of seaweed. Similar to tofu in shape, the cakes are often found near tofu in Japanese grocery stores, fresh or in cans. Fresh konnyaku comes in water-packed containers. It has a distinct odor, which can easily be removed by blanching for 1 minute. Konnyaku is very bland-tasting and does not absorb seasonings easily, so it must be simmered with other ingredients for a while. Konnyaku is very low in calories and treasured for its reputed ability to clean one's digestive tract. To store, keep konnyaku covered with plastic in the refrigerator. Keeps fresh for about 1 week.

KONBU SEAWEED (konbu): The king of seaweed. Used to make seafood broth, it is a wide, brownish-green kelp of the algae family and high in minerals. You can get it only in dried form. Konbu from the far-north island of Hokkaido is considered the best. Konbu is sold not only in sheet form but as kizami-konbu (slivered konbu), oboro-konbu (shaved konbu), and tororo-konbu (sliced strips of konbu). There is also a tea, kobucha, made of powdered konbu, salt, and sugar, which is mixed with hot water. To use, konbu should not be washed in water. The powdery white surface is part of konbu, which releases flavor when returned to water. To clean konbu, simply wipe gently with a damp paper towel.

KUZU: A lumpy white powder made of arrowroot, it thickens foods in the same way as cornstarch. It is much finer than cornstarch because it is free of odor; it is almost clear when dissolved in water and has no taste of its own, so it will not change the flavor of dishes to which it is added. It is alkaline and neutralizes acidity; some feel it has medicinal properties. Kuzu can be found in Japanese food stores and health food stores and the spice section in supermarkets. It should be sifted before use.

LOTUS ROOT (renkon or hasu): Lotus root is a crispy vegetable with hollow spaces that run through the vegetable like canals. Served in tempura, simmered dishes, and salads. Fresh lotus root is available in Oriental grocery stores and gourmet markets. Choose the ones that are unbruised and firm. When cut, its surface will discolor, so you must soak sliced lotus root in water with 1 or 2 teaspoons rice vinegar to prevent discoloration. Keeps for a week in the refrigerator.

MATSUTAKE MUSHROOMS: The king of Japanese mushrooms, highly aromatic and delicious. Very expensive, like caviar, matsutake are enjoyed in small portions in soups and rice. Curiously, matsutake mushrooms are grown in Seattle, Washington, and exported to Japan in large quantities. They are called pine mushrooms in English, because they grow on the stumps of pine trees. You may get fresh matsutake mushrooms at the Japanese grocery store in the fall.

MIRIN (sweet sake): This rice wine has a syrupy consistency that sweetens and firms food. Use it for cooking, never for drinking. If you cannot find mirin in your market, substitute 1 teaspoon sugar for each tablespoon of mirin. Like regular sake, it is used sparingly.

MISO PASTE (miso): Along with rice and soy sauce, miso paste is one of the most basic foods in Japan. Miso paste is a blend of soybeans, rice mold (koji), and salt, which is matured like wine for approximately three years. While soybeans are the central ingredient, wheat, barley, or rice is often added during the maturation process to give the miso paste texture, aroma, and flavor. Light, white, or yellow miso, called shiro-miso, is relatively sweet and commonly served in the wintertime; dark, red miso, called aka-miso, which is made of barley and soybeans, is saltier than shiro-miso and enjoyed particularly in the summertime. Also light and yellow is Shinshu-miso, which comes from the Shinshu area of Japan. It is a good basic miso paste with a tart flavor. Hatcho-miso is strong and salty, containing chunky soybeans. This type is best suited for soups. There are also variations of red and white miso that are labeled as inaka-miso (country-type miso), akadashi-miso (red miso), saikyo-miso (white miso), Sendai-miso (red miso), etc. You will have to try a variety of miso pastes to appreciate the different types. See Chapter 4 for further discussion of miso.

MITSUBA (mitsuba): A green, three-leaved garnish used in soups and salads. An aromatic vegetable, like strong mint, mitsuba is very delicate. Keeps for 2 or 3 days in the refrigerator, covered with a damp paper towel and wrapped in plastic.

MOCHI: See Rice cakes.

NAMEKO MUSHROOMS (nameko): Tiny round mushrooms coated with a slippery substance. They are flavorful and popular ingredients for miso soup and salads. Available in cans in small portions of 4 ounces. Should be eaten within 3 days after the can is opened.

NOODLES: See Chapter 6 for a complete discussion of types and cooking methods.

NORI SEAWEED (nori): These soft, crispy sheets of black seaweed commonly used to wrap sushi are available in dried form in bundles of large sheets or in small rectangular bite-size pieces. Most nori seaweed comes toasted, but you can make it crispier by waving each sheet over a hot flame for a few seconds. Must stay in airtight container to avoid exposure to moisture. Keeps in a dry place for several months, but tastes best when fresh. In powdered form (often sprinkled over rice or noodles) it is known as ao-nori.

POTATO STARCH (kata-ku-ri-ko): A silky white powder used as thickener, like cornstarch, and to coat foods for braising or deep frying. A variant is kuzu starch (see Kuzu). If potato or kuzu starch is not available, use cornstarch.

RICE (okome): The Japanese prefer the short-grained rice grown abundantly in California. Short-grain rice is stickier than long-grain rice and very moist. Raw rice is washed in water before use; however, overwashing will result in the loss of essential nutrients. Some Japanese prefer to wash it until the water of the rice is practically free of talc. This makes the cooked rice shinier and tastier than unwashed rice. Short-grain rice should soak in water for at least 15 minutes before cooking to achieve high moisture.

RICE CAKES (mochi): Mochi is made by pounding steamed sweet rice and kneading it till it becomes very smooth. To serve, mochi is broiled or boiled and seasoned with soy sauce. Mochi is often wrapped with nori seaweed. It can also be served as a dessert, coated with sugar and soy flour (kinako). To store mochi, wrap in plastic and refrigerate. It also freezes and keeps up to 2 months. Mochi becomes moldy like cheese upon exposure to moisture, but you can remove surface mold simply by scraping it off with a paring knife. When broiled, mochi puffs up like popcorn. It is a fun and tasty treat for children.

RICE VINEGAR (su): Rice vinegar, available in Oriental groceries and most American supermarkets, is milder than cider or distilled vinegar.

SAKE (sake): This smooth rice wine is discussed in detail as a beverage in Chapter 14. Sake is also used sparingly in the preparation of many Japanese dishes. Cooking sake is available, but regular drinking sake is as good or better. Just a dash of sake tenderizes and flavors foods and adds a rich flavor to broths.

SATSUMA POTATOES (satsuma-imo): The most popular of all potatoes in Japan. Its sweetness makes it satisfying for dessert as well as part of the meal. Has red skin and bright yellow meat. A fall food. In the U.S. you may find it in Japanese grocery stores. American yams and sweet potatoes will substitute for satsuma-imo, though they are not as sweet.

SESAME SEED OIL: This is a nutty-flavored oil made from sesame seeds. It is very nutritious and low in cholesterol; it actually helps to reduce cholesterol in the blood. Daily use is highly recommended.

SESAME SEEDS (goma): These are available black or white, raw or roasted, as well as a ground, ready-to-use paste (atari-goma). Gently dry-roast them in a heated frying pan over medium heat for about 30 seconds, or until the seeds start popping. Do not burn the seeds. To grind sesame seeds, use a Japanese mortar and pestle (suri-bachi and suri-goki) and grind until you achieve a pasty texture. If you don't have a mortar and pestle, triple the amount of sesame seeds called for and use a blender to make paste. Salted sesame seeds (gomo-shio) are wonderful sprinkled over white or brown rice. Both black and white salted sesame seeds are available.

SEVEN-SPICE MIXTURE (shichimi-togarashi): A seasoning that consists of red pepper flakes, sesame seeds, poppy seeds, mandarin orange peel, black hemp seeds, mulberry, and nori seaweed flakes. Use an occasional pinch, sprinkled over hot udon noodles, cold soba noodles, soups, and vegetables. This complex mixture may turn out to be your favorite flavor enhancer.

SHIITAKE MUSHROOMS: The most common mushroom in Japanese cooking. Available both fresh and dried. You must soak dry shiitake for at least 20 minutes to regain softness. The soaking liquid is treasured, so do not discard it. It is considered quite medicinal, even, many Japanese think, as a cancer preventive. Daily consumption is recommended by many health-conscious Japanese.

SHIMEJI MUSHROOMS (shimeji): Like enoki mushrooms, they are small and bundled up. Color is slightly brown-gray. Popular in one-pot dinners. They are not as fragrant as enoki mushrooms, but tasty. Get the ones that are unbruised. They keep in the refrigerator for 3 days.

SHIRATAKI NOODLES (shirataki): Like konnyaku, shirataki noodles are made from the devil's tongue plant. Blanch them in hot water to remove distinct odor. Go well in one-pot dinners with meat and vegetables. Shirataki are available fresh in water-packed containers where you find tofu. They are also available canned, but the flavor is not as tasty as that of fresh shirataki. Shirataki keep in the refrigerator for about a week.

SHISO LEAVES (shiso): Very aromatic, these broad, fringed leaves are from the mint family. If you can get seeds, they will grow in your garden like weeds. A common garnish with sushi and sashimi, also with cold somen noodles and tofu. If you cannot find shiso leaves, use parsley or mint.

SOYBEANS, FERMENTED (natto): Some Japanese eat this soft and quite aromatic staple food every day. To the Westerner, the aroma may be too strong at first. Delicious over hot rice with sashimi and sushi. A traditional breakfast meal, natto is very nutritious, full of B vitamins, iron, and lots of protein. It is available fresh in Japanese shops, commonly found near tofu. It keeps in the refrigerator 4 days.

SOY SAUCE (shoyu): Made from soybeans and wheat, soy sauce is the product of fermentation and careful brewing. It is a brown taste enhancer, quite pungent, to be used judiciously. There are three basic types of Japanese soy sauce. The mild version (usu-kuchi-shoyu) is pale amber in color, and its use prevents darkening of delicate foods and soups. Do not confuse this with low-sodium soy sauce; they are not the same. The standard soy sauce (koi-kuchi-shoyu) is darker and less salty than the light type. Tamari sauce is darker still, and quite thick; I seldom use it because it seems too strong. It should be used mainly for marinating. Chinese soy sauce is the saltiest type and is not recommended for Japanese cooking. Unless otherwise specified, recipes call for standard soy sauce.

SQUASH (kabocha): This Japanese variety looks like a small pumpkin but is green in color. The meat is bright yellow and sweet like yam. Kabocha is difficult to cut, as it is very hard, so cut gently, holding it with one hand. Remove seeds and steam or boil.

TARAKO: The roe of the codfish. The tiny, blush-colored eggs come enclosed in their own membrane.

TARO POTATO (sato-imo): A brown, small, hairy potato, mild in flavor and quite slippery when peeled. Should be soaked in water with 1 or 2 teaspoons vinegar to remove slipperiness. Taro potato is available in some U.S. supermarkets and in Oriental grocery stores.

TOFU (tofu): A tender, silky square made from pure soybean curd, tofu is high in protein, minerals, and vitamins. Unlike meat, tofu is extremely low in fats and cholesterol. See Chapter 7 for further discussion of tofu.

TONKATSU SAUCE (tonkatsu sauce): A Japanese Worcestershire-like sauce made of ketchup, Worcestershire sauce, sake, dark soy sauce, and mustard. Used to season deep-fried foods such as fish and croquettes. It is also used to season yakisoba noodles. Keeps in the refrigerator for 6 months.

UME-BOSHI (pickled plums): A salty, pickled fruit considered by many to have medicinal properties. The plums, sold in jars, are often red in color, and will keep indefinitely tightly covered.

WAKAME SEAWEED (wakame): A soft, tasty seaweed served in soups and salads. Buy it in dried form or fresh. The fresh seaweed is often treated with salt, so it must be soaked in water for at least 10 minutes, then rinsed again with fresh water. Fresh wakame keeps for a few months in the refrigerator.

WASABI (wasabi): Grown in clean mountain stream beds, it looks like horseradish but is much smaller in size. Wasabi is only occasionally seen fresh in the U.S. (and at exorbitant prices) but is readily available in Japanese grocery stores in the dried or paste form. Powdered wasabi should be dissolved with a few drops of water until it reaches a pasty consistency. Wasabi paste can be used straight out of the tube. The green pungent paste makes an important accompaniment to sushi and sashimi. Fresh wasabi keeps only for a week in the refrigerator, but powdered wasabi and wasabi paste keep indefinitely.

YAMA-NO-IMO: This is a potato that can be eaten raw. It is slippery and sticky, served grated or sliced. As you grate the potato, it forms bubbles and makes a soupy sauce. The grated potato is delicious straight over sashimi such as tuna, or soba noodles. A small dab of horseradish and soy sauce plus a few strips of nori seaweed are traditional accompaniments to this dish. The skin of this potato is sometimes irritating to sensitive skin, so use rubber gloves to peel, wash, and grate it. Rub vinegar on the surface of the yam to reduce slipperiness while handling. Wash your hands well after treating the potato to prevent skin irritation. Expensive—but unique in taste. Mostly imported from Japan, it comes protected by sawdust. Keeps in the refrigerator, uncovered, for a week.

ACKNOWLEDGMENTS

Heartfelt appreciation to Carol Southern for her moral support and to Pam Krauss for her thorough and remarkable editorial assistance. She also tested many of my recipes. Thanks to my wise literary representative, Roberta Pryor, Etienne Delessert for his imaginative and lyrical illustrations, and to Rita Marshall, who is responsible for the elegant design of the book. Also to Nettie Lipton, Marissa Roth, and Alma Hecht, who helped prepare the manuscript. To Noritoshi Kanai of Mutual Trading Company who provided me with accurate information on Japanese foods. To my whole family, the Kondos, for their support and patience. Finally, thank you to my husband, Sakai, who encouraged me to write and tasted all my recipes, and to Sakae, my son, who is still too young to hold chopsticks but loves my miso soup, tofu custards, and teriyaki fish.

A GEOGRAPHICAL LIST OF SHOPPING SOURCES FOR JAPANESE FOODS

These Oriental and health food stores carry Japanese food products.
An asterisk indicates stores that will fill telephone or mail orders

ALABAMA

Ebino Oriental Foods
323 Air Base Blvd.
Montgomery 36108

Oriental Super Market #1
3480 Springhill Ave.
Mobile 36608

ARIZONA

Hi-Health
4420 North Miller Rd.
Scottsdale 85251

*Oriental Food Center
3920 N.W. Grand Ave.
Phoenix 85019
(602) 841-6215

Tokyo Store
5919 East 22nd St.
Tucson 85365

CALIFORNIA (NORTH)

ABC Fish & Oriental Food
1911 Potrero Way
Sacramento 95822

Alpha Beta Markets
(check your local store)

Asahi Ya
229 East Alpine Ave.
Stockton 95204

Asia Food Market
2000 Judah St.
San Francisco 94122

Dobashi Company
240 E. Jackson St.
San Jose 95112

First Food Market
4454 California St.
San Francisco 94118

Maruiwa Foods Co., Inc.
1737 Post St.
San Francisco 94115

Noris
1119 West Texas
Fairfield 94533

Pacific Food Center
1924 4th St.
San Rafael 94901

Pusan Market
1125 Webster St.
Oakland 94607

Safeway stores
(check your local store)

Tokyo Fish Market
1908 Filmore St.
San Francisco 94115

CALIFORNIA (SOUTH)

Alpha Beta
(check your local store)

Best Food of Torrance
3030 W. Sepulveda Blvd.
Torrance 90505

Daisho Mart
16108 S. Western Ave.
Gardena 90247

East-West Coffee & Tea
1801 Hillhurst Ave.
Los Angeles 90041

Enbun Co.
124 Japanese Village Plaza
Los Angeles 90012

Far East Market
8848 Lankershim Blvd.
Sun Valley 91352

Fujiya Market
601 N. Virgil Ave.
Los Angeles 90004

Higashi Market
9066 Wodman Ave.
Arieta 91331

Kyodo Fish Market
1337 E. Chapman Ave.
Fullerton 92631

Meiji Tofu
16440 S. Western Ave.
Gardena 90247

*Modern Food Market
318 E. Second St.
Los Angeles 90012
(213) 680-9595

Nippon Foods
2935 W. Ball Rd.
Anaheim 92804

*Rafu Bussan, Inc.
326 E. Second St.
Los Angeles 90012
(213) 614-1181
(Dried goods, Japanese equipment)

Ralph market
(check your local store)

Sakae Oriental Grocery
4227 Convoy St.
San Diego 92111

Eiko Shoten
6082 University Ave.
San Diego 92115

Yanagi-ya Oriental Market
265 E. Pomona Blvd.
Monterey Park 91754

COLORADO

Granada Fish Market
1275 19th St.
Denver 80202

*Pacific Mercantile Co.
1925 Lawrence St.
Denver 80202
(303) 295-0293

CONNECTICUT

China Trading Co.
271 Crown St.
New Haven 06511

East/West Trading Co.
68 Howe St.
New Haven 06511

Kim's Oriental Foods & Gifts
202 Park Road
W. Hartford 06119

Young's Oriental Grocery
243 Farmington Ave.
Hartford 06105

DELAWARE

Oriental Grocery
1705 Concord Pike
Wilmington 19803

FLORIDA

Misako's Oriental Foods
129 N. Warrington Rd.
N. Pensacola 32506

Oriental Food Store
4559 Shirley Ave.
Jacksonville 32210

Oriental Market
1202 S. Dale Mabry Hwy.
Tampa 33629

Tomiko's Oriental
441 Bryn Athyn Blvd.
Mary Esther 32569

GEORGIA

Asian Trading Company
2581 Piedmont Rd. Birdview
Atlanta 30324

Makoto
1067 Oaktree Rd.
Decatur 30033

Oakland Park Oriental
2031 S. Lumpkin Rd.
Columbus 31903

Prince Oriental
960 Prince Ave.
Athens 30606

Satsuma-ya
5271-B Buford Hwy.
Doraville 30340

HAWAII

Daiei/Holiday Mart
801 Kaheka
Honolulu 96814

Safeway stores
(check your local store)

Star Supermarket
Kam Shopping Center
1620 N. School St.
Honolulu 96817

Tamura Supermarket
86032 Farrington Hwy.
Waianae 96792

IDAHO

Albertson's Inc.
Box 20
Boise 93707

Yuko's Gift
688 N. Holmes Ave.
Idaho Falls 83401

ILLINOIS

Diamond Trading Co.
913 W. Belmont Ave.
Chicago 60657

Far East Oriental Food
1524 Grand Ave.
Waukegan 60085

Furuya & Company
5358 N. Clark St.
Chicago 60640

Ginza & Co.
315 E. University
Champaign 61820

Kyotoya Corp. Food & Craft
1182 S. Elmhurst
Mt. Prospect 60056

Lucky Oriental Food
4550 North Clark St.
Chicago 60640

Star Market
3349 N. Clark St.
Chicago 60613

INDIANA

Asia Oriental Market
2400 Yeager Rd.
W. Lafayette 47906

IOWA

Jungs Oriental Food Store
913 E. University Ave.
Des Moines 50316

Tokyo Foods
1005 Pierce St.
Sioux City 51105

LOUISIANA

Korea House
Rt. 5 Box 268
Leesville 71496

Oriental Merchandise Co.
2636 Edenborn Ave.
Metairie 70002

MARYLAND

Asia House
1576 Annapolis Rd.
Odenton 21113

Far East House
33 W. North Ave.
Baltimore 21201

Fumi Oriental Mart
2102 Veirs Mill Rd.
Rockville 20851

MASSACHUSETTS

Mirim Trading Co. Inc.
152 Harvard Ave.
Allston 02134

*Yoshinoya
36 Prospect St.
Cambridge 02139
(617) 491-8221

MICHIGAN

Mt. Fuji Oriental Foods
22040 West 10 Mile Rd.
Southfield 48034

The Orient
P.O. Box 24
Portage 49081

MINNESOTA

International House
75 W. Island Ave.
Minneapolis 55401

*Oriental Plaza
25 Glenwood Ave.
Minneapolis 55403
(612) 338-2064

MISSOURI

King's Trading Inc.
3736 Broadway St.
Kansas City 64111

Maruyama, Inc.
100 N. 18th St.
St. Louis 63103

NEBRASKA

Oriental Market
611 N. 27th St.
Lincoln 68503

Oriental Trading Co.
10525 J St.
Omaha 68127

NEVADA

Asian Market
953 E. Sahara
Las Vegas 89104

Cal-Neva Produce
3554 South Procyon St.
Las Vegas 89103

NEW JERSEY

Aki Oriental Food Co.
1635 Lemoine Ave.
Fort Lee 07024

First Oriental Company
284–286 Fairmont Ave.
Jersey City 07306

Miyako Oriental Foods
490 Main St.
Fort Lee 07024

NEW MEXICO

Yonemoto Brothers Grocery
8725 4th St. N.W.
Albuquerque 87114

NEW YORK

Harumi
318–320 W. 231 St.
Bronx 10463

*Katagiri Company
224 East 59th St.
New York 10022
(212) 755-3566

Main Street Foods
137–80 Northern Blvd.
Flushing 11354

Meidiya
18 N. Central Park Ave.
Hartsdale 10530

Meiji-ya Trading Co.
2642 Central Ave.
Yonkers

Nippon Do
82-69 Parsons Blvd.
Jamaica 11432

Shinsen-Do Grocery
1285 Boston Post Rd.
Mamaroneck 10543

NORTH CAROLINA

Asia Market
1325 Buck Jones Rd.
Raleigh 27606

Oriental Food Mart
803 N. Main St.
Spring Lake 28390

OHIO

Dayton Oriental Foods
812 Xenia Ave.
Dayton 45410

Oriental Food & Gifts
500 W. Main St.
Fairborn 45324

Soya Food Products Inc.
2356 Wyoming Ave.
Cincinnati 45215
(513) 661-2250

OKLAHOMA

Dong-Ah Oriental
1103 N.W. 10
Oklahoma City 73170

Japan Imported Foods
808 N.W. 6th St.
Oklahoma City 73160

Ono's Oriental Food
4535 S.E. 29
Del City 73115

OREGON

Albertsons
(check your local store)

Fred Meyers
(check your local store)

PENNSYLVANIA

Asia Products Corp.
226 N. 10th St.
Philadelphia 19107

Euro-Asia Imports
5221 E. Simpson Ferry Rd.
Mechanicsburg 17055

Imported Food Bazaar
2000 Market St.
Camp Hill 17011

Oriental Food Mart
909 Race St.
Philadelphia 19107

RHODE ISLAND

East Sea Oriental Market
90–92 Warren Ave.
E. Providence 02914

SOUTH CAROLINA

Chieko Hardy
226 Jamaica Terrace
Columbia 29206

Oriental Food and Gift
4252 Rivers Ave.
N. Charleston 29418

SOUTH DAKOTA

Kitty's Oriental Food
P.O. Box 347
Box Elder 57719

TENNESSEE

Import Shop
1775 Fort Henry Dr.
Kingsport 37664

Park and Shop Oriental
3664 Summer Ave.
Memphis 38122

TEXAS

Asiatic Imports
821 Chartres
Houston 77003

Edoya Oriental
223 Farmer Branch
Dallas 75234

International Grocery
3103 Fondren
Houston 77063

Japanese Grocery
14366-B Memorial Dr.
Houston 77079

Nippon Daido International
1138 Westheimer
Houston 77042

Tachibana
4886 Hercules Ave.
El Paso 79904

*Tokyo Food & Gift
1214 FM 1960 W.
Houston 77090

UTAH

Oriental Mini-Mart
1786 West 5300 South
Roy 84067

Sage Farm Market
1515 South Main
Salt Lake City 84115

VIRGINIA

Oriental House
7816 Richmond Hwy.
Alexandria 22306

Tokyo Market
5312 Va. Beach Blvd.
Virginia Beach 23462

WASHINGTON

Albertson's
(check your local store)

First Hill Food Center
908 8th St.
Seattle 98002

House of Rice
4112 University Way N.E.
Seattle 98105

Ikeda & Co.
912 Maynard So.
Seattle 98134

Lucky store
(check your local store)

Mint Beverage
1207 S. Jackson
Seattle 98144

Northcoast Seafoods
1962 1st Ave So.
Seattle 98134

Safeway store
(check your local store)

Sakura Oriental Food & Gift
1554 Market
Tacoma

Seasia
651 S. Industrial Way
Seattle 98108

Star Tofu Co.
608 S. Weller
Seattle 98104

Tobo Co.
504 12th So.
Seattle 98144

Umajimaya
519 6th Ave. So.
Seattle 98104

Villa Thriftco
10110 Gravelly Lake Dr. S.W.
Tacoma 98499

WASHINGTON, D.C.

House of Hanna
7838 Eastern Ave. N.W.
20012

Mikado
4709 Wisconsin Ave. N.W.
20016

WISCONSIN

International House of Foods
440 W. Gorham St.
Madison 53703

Oriental Shop
618 South Park St.
Madison 53715

Index